Innovative Capabilities and the Globalization of Chinese Firms

Innovative Capabilities and the Globalization of Chinese Firms

Becoming Leaders in Knowledge-intensive Innovation Ecosystems

Edited by

Maureen McKelvey

Professor, School of Business, Economics and Law, University of Gothenburg, Sweden

Jun Jin

Associate Professor, School of Management, Zhejiang University, China

EE Edward Elgar PUBLISHING

Cheltenham, UK • Northampton, MA, USA

Published by
Edward Elgar Publishing Limited
The Lypiatts
15 Lansdown Road
Cheltenham
Glos GL50 2JA
UK

Edward Elgar Publishing, Inc.
William Pratt House
9 Dewey Court
Northampton
Massachusetts 01060
USA

A catalogue record for this book
is available from the British Library

Library of Congress Control Number: 2020948494

This book is available electronically in the **Elgar**online
Economics subject collection
http://dx.doi.org/10.4337/9781786434487

MIX
Paper from responsible sources
FSC® C013604

ISBN 978 1 78643 447 0 (cased)
ISBN 978 1 78643 448 7 (eBook)

Printed and bound by CPI Group (UK) Ltd, Croydon, CR0 4YY

Contents

Contributors

Claes G. Alvstam, University of Gothenburg, Sweden.

Vito Amendolagine, Università di Foggia, Italy.

Xiangdong Chen, Beihang University, China.

Elisa Giuliani, Università di Pisa, Italy.

Min Guo, Zhejiang University, China.

Valerie Marleen Hunstock, University of International Business & Economics, China.

Inge Ivarsson, University of Gothenburg, Sweden.

Jun Jin, Zhejiang University, China.

Astrid Heidemann Lassen, University of Gothenburg, Sweden, and Aalborg University, Denmark.

Xingkun Liang, Peking University, China.

Ju Liu, Malmö University, Sweden.

Zhichun Liu, Beihang University, China.

Arianna Martinelli, Scuola Superiore Sant'Anna, Italy.

Maureen McKelvey, University of Gothenburg, Sweden.

Roberta Rabellotti, Università di Pavia, Italy, and University of Aalborg, Denmark.

Xianwei Shi, Cambridge University, United Kingdom.

Yongjiang Shi, Cambridge University, United Kingdom.

Peder Veng Søberg, University of Southern Denmark.

Xi Sun, Capital University of Economics and Business, China.

Jiamin Wang, Zhejiang University of Technology, China.

Liying Wang, Zhejiang University of Technology, China.

Weijia Yu, Zhejiang University of Technology, China.

Zhengyi Zhang, Zhejiang University, China.

Preface

This book is particularly focused upon analyzing key issues about structural transformation of industries in China in terms of technology, innovation and internationalization, using the perspective of knowledge-intensive innovation ecosystems. The earlier Edward Elgar book *Innovation Spaces in Asia* (2015) also addresses related questions about the complex structural transformation undergoing in Asia more broadly. We would like to thank the many scholars and practitioners who have contributed to stimulating discussions with us about how they view such changes in China during recent decades. We would especially like to thank the authors, as well as the reviewers of chapters.

Indeed, the issues we study represent a moving target, because the phrase "becoming leaders" suggests that time and trajectories matter to how businesses act, and this will change in different periods. Moreover, the global economic and social conditions and relationships more broadly continue to change, including during the years we have been writing this book. Debates about globalization and international disputes have been on the rise, and at the same time digitalization has changed many social and economic patterns and business models. As we complete the manuscript in Spring 2020, COVID-19 has again changed the meaning of globalization, leading to re-examining visions for future social and economic patterns.

International collaboration also requires long-term interactions between individuals. Professors Jin and McKelvey have collaborated for many years, through the scientific organization Globelics and the related Cicalics PhD Academy. Both focus upon innovation and competence building for economic development. Most importantly for this book, Professor Jun Jin spent a year as visiting scholar at the Institute of Innovation and Entrepreneurship, Department of Economy and Society, University of Gothenburg. This facilitated our more regular collaboration – such as holding public lectures events and interviewing companies in both Sweden and China – as well as our work to edit this book and write related articles.

Jun Jin acknowledges financial support by the National Natural Science Foundation of China (CNSF: 71672172, U1509221, and 71232013) and the Zhejiang Natural Science Foundation (ZJNSF: LY16G020010). The project "Influence Mechanism to Create Leading Edge Innovation Capabilities in Knowledge-intensive Enterprises in the Global Innovation Network", financed by National Nature Science Foundation of China, also enabled collaboration between Professors Jin and McKelvey.

Maureen McKelvey acknowledges financial support from her Swedish Research Council Distinguished Professors' Research Program: "Knowledge-intensive Entrepreneurial Ecosystems: Transforming society through knowledge, innovation and entrepreneurship" (VR DNR 2017-03360). Moreover, we acknowledge the small grant "Creating leading edge technical competencies in Chinese companies", from External Relationships and partner companies, at the School of Business, Economics and Law, University of Gothenburg.

1. Introduction to *Innovative Capabilities and the Globalization of Chinese Firms*

Maureen McKelvey and Jun Jin

1. INTRODUCTION

How do Chinese companies learn to innovate and compete on global markets? This book explores how Chinese firms are developing capabilities for innovation and globalization, in relation to their economic environment. Firms studied here are active in a variety of different industries, ranging from pharmaceuticals and artificial intelligence to transportation, telecommunication, and mechanical manufacturing.

Taken together, the chapters in this book provide a conceptualization of one restricted part of the vast transformation ongoing in China. This book does not aim to cover all types of Chinese firms, nor all the transformations ongoing within China per se. Instead, our focus is upon the three intertwined processes involving innovation, technological capabilities, and globalization. Western countries have long taken the lead in developing knowledge and transforming it into business and social innovation, but in recent decades the Chinese economy has been rapidly advancing. Chinese firms are developing innovative capabilities and engaging in globalization, which affects not only China but also the world.

Hence, this book only focuses upon a selected few Chinese firms and industries which already have shown to be – or are actively striving to become – world-leading in their technologies and markets. We are interested in why and how they use and develop advanced technology as well as how they can obtain economic returns on the market, often global markets. More generally, we have chosen to study firms and industries which are attempting to move the basis of their competitiveness from imitation to innovation; from being a player on a home market to a global market; and from being a follower to being an innovative leader. Our analysis places these firms in relation to the macro processes in the ecosystem, such as economic growth, public policy for science and technology, and collaborative network relationships.

China is already aiming for – and in some cases taking – a leading position in developing important new technologies such as AI, e-mobility and nanotechnologies. In these emerging tech industries, China has become one of the three strongest countries in the field of artificial intelligence (AI), with more than 4000 high-tech firms in the AI field (Deloitte 2019). In addition, China has become a leading market and main competitors in the new energy vehicle industries (Jin and McKelvey 2019) and improved its competitiveness in the nano-tech industry (Zhang et al. 2017). Some of these shifts are leading to topics outside this book. For example, China is rapidly introducing disruptive technology into the global economy, which may help explain the changing global institutions and regimes for international trade and collaboration. Our aim is not to analyze these broad institutional changes, but instead to focus upon the underlying causes of how Chinese firms are becoming leaders within what we call a global knowledge-intensive innovative ecosystem. We do, however, include empirical indications of a paradigm shift in technology activities in China, as indicated by figures such as the long-term increase of foreign R&D investment in China, which is also accompanied by domestic investments in R&D. Our interpretation of the trends underlying such figures, as argued in Chapter 2, is that China has both increased internal technology and innovative capabilities, and also actors have increased their embeddness in collaborative networks.

Successful Chinese emerging market multinational enterprises can be found in several industries (see Chapters 5, 7, 8, 12, and 13). Two relevant examples are Alibaba and Huawei. Alibaba is a leading internet (e-commerce) firm, and Huawei has become the largest telecommunications equipment manufacturer in the world. Arguably, the technological proficiency of Huawei and ZTE underlie some of the recent trade disputes, which is interesting for other research. Moreover, knowledge-intensive innovative entrepreneurial (KIE) firms (Malerba and McKelvey 2018) are, we argue, also present in China, and rapidly developing their innovative capabilities based on advanced technology (see Chapters 4, 10 and 11). Knowledge-intensive industries where Chinese firms have been successful include a range from pharmaceuticals, windmills to AI and data analytics. So how did these various firms develop their technologies, along with their capabilities to innovate and globalize, in relation to the wider ecosystem?

Subsequent chapters help explain how interlinked micro and macro processes unfold over time, and do so by relating the strategic decisions of companies and entrepreneurs to trends in the Chinese knowledge-intensive innovative ecosystem. Thereby, each chapter will provide slightly different answers about how and why the three processes of innovation, technological capabilities, and globalization are driving this transformation in China. In doing so, subsequent chapters draw upon theoretical perspectives spanning innovation management, entrepreneurship, international business, economics of technology, and business strategy.

2. THE BROADER ANALYTICAL FRAMEWORK AND THREE THEMES

Lee and Malerba (2017) argue that nations can catch-up to leaders if latecomer firms and countries react appropriately, in relation to three windows of opportunity. The first dimension is changes in knowledge and technology; the second changes in demand; and the third is changes in institutions and public policy. Their perspective on catch-up includes the micro level of firms, as well as the macro level of sectoral innovation systems. This book is aligned with arguments in these related, broader streams of theoretical literature on catch-up from a Schumpeterian perspective (Malerba and Nelson 2012; Lee 2013; Lee and Malerba 2017; Zhang et al. 2017).

Figure 1.1 represents our broader analytical framework for conceptualizing a knowledge-intensive innovative ecosystem. We propose to conceptualize a knowledge-intensive innovative ecosystem as three-way interactions between firms, industrial dynamics and innovation systems. This broader theoretical framework builds explicitly upon McKelvey and Bagchi-Sen (2015) and McKelvey (2016). The purpose of this framework for this book is to help us identify a range of relevant factors which explain how Chinese companies can learn to innovate and compete on the global market. Taken together, these processes constitute the key interactions between the firm and knowledge-intensive innovative ecosystems.

Figure 1.1 visualizes that the micro level of the firms – set at the center – is highly affected by the macro level in terms of industrial dynamics and innovation systems.

Three core concepts in our analytical framework are: firm search and capabilities for technology and innovation, industrial dynamics, and innovation systems. Each concept is introduced below in relation to this overall process, and later chapters address an aspect of each, in relation to explaining how Chinese companies can learn to innovate and compete on the global market.

The box found at the center in Figure 1.1 represents the processes of firm search and capabilities for technology and innovation. According to literature in innovation management, we should focus upon firm-level processes whereby "an innovative outcome involves the successful application of new ideas, which results from organizational processes that combine various resources to that end" (Dodgson et al. 2014:5). The key notion is that the firm does not just passively acquire new knowledge, but must instead actively search, thereby

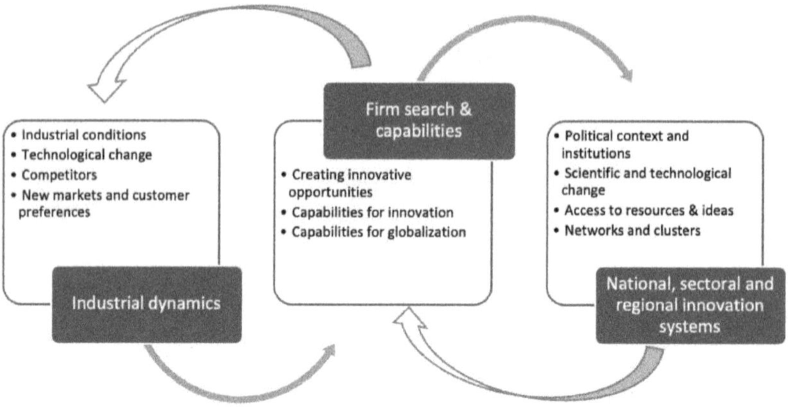

Source: Revised analytical framework, based upon prior work (McKelvey 2016; McKelvey and Bagchi-Sen 2015).

Figure 1.1 Firms within knowledge-intensive innovative ecosystems

devoting resources to both creating new knowledge and using it in innovation sold on the market. A key insight is that a combination of public and private knowledge is needed to create innovations (McKelvey 2014), and the firm searches and combines technology with other capabilities in order to innovate. Thus, firm search and strategy are interesting to analyze, because firms are heterogeneous in a way that impacts the outcomes – for example, there is no representative firm. This stream of literature is closely related to the theory of the firm by Edith Penrose, and later developments, especially dynamic capabilities (Teece et al. 1997; Teece 2007). A business model affects the firm's dynamic capabilities, which in turn impacts the viability of strategies within the firm (Teece 2018). Research on innovation management explicates how the internal capabilities of the firm also rely upon external sources of knowledge, and specifically that the firm must also rely on relationships and networks in order to search, identify and seize relevant business opportunities (Dodgson et al. 2014). Firms search for new knowledge, which solves internal problems, and must also balance routines for continuation and exploration of new ideas (Nelson and Winter 1982; Laursen 2012).

Another key concept is processes related to industrial dynamics, represented in Figure 1.1 in the left-hand box. We conceptualize industrial dynamics as factors, which sets the conditions and helps define the opportunity set within which any given firm can act upon within their sector (Carlsson 2016). We include industrial conditions, technological change, competitors, and new markets and customer preferences under industrial dynamics. Our interpretation of industrial dynamics is that they help to generate new technological opportunities, as well as market opportunities.

Industrial dynamics change the conditions for the economy, through new technologies and through business innovation in large companies and through entrepreneurship through new companies (Schumpeter 1934, 1942). In evolutionary and Schumpeterian economics, capitalism is conceptualized as restless, described as emergent properties of change which are endogenously created in the economy (Nelson 1996; Metcalfe 2002, 2008; Horst and Pyka 2004). In this literature, industrial dynamics are explicitly linked to the key role of knowledge and innovation in the economy in stimulating transformation. Metcalfe (2002, 2008) argues that the restless nature of capitalism has to do with knowledge, as the pre-eminent source which creates variation in the economy, and where markets are the primary arena for selection of firms. Thus, it is interesting to study the acquisition of new capabilities because the firm's internal combination of routines, resources, capabilities, and learning will change over time, in response to internal and external conditions (Nelson 1996).

Finally, in Figure 1.1, the right-hand box represents national, sectoral, and regional innovation systems. By using this concept of innovation systems, we focus upon the linkages between firms and other actors, and specifically those which promote knowledge generation and innovation. Institutional and evolutionary economics and related innovation systems perspective has long highlighted the key importance of knowledge, networks, learning and institutions in economic growth (Nelson 1993; Cooke et al. 1997; Edquist and McKelvey 2000; Lundvall et al. 2002; Malerba 2002, 2009; Edquist 2006). Innovation systems are useful in this conceptual framework, because they help to define a set of interactions, agents and processes within regions, sectors and nations. Moreover, the innovation system approach associated with learning and development of firm capabilities has also been applied to understanding emerging markets in terms of catch-up processes (Malerba and Nelson 2012).

There has been much discussion of the relationship between innovation systems and ecosystems, in different streams of literature. Initial strategy literature on ecosystems stressed the importance of firm strategy in relation to their supply chains (Jacobides et al. 2018), whereas other streams stress a variety of entrepreneurial and innovation ecosystems impacting regions (Stam 2015; Spigel 2017; Stam and Spigel 2017; Autio et al. 2018). Relating closely to an innovation system definition, an innovation ecosystem can be defined as the evolving set of actors, activities, and artifacts, and the institutions and relations, including complementary and substitute relations, that are important for the innovative performance of an actor or a population of actors (Granstrand and Holgersson 2019). Therefore, by placing innovation systems in relation to firms' search and capabilities as well as industrial dynamics, we highlight the transformation of the Chinese knowledge-intensive innovative ecosystem, as well as how Chinese firms may interact with other ecosystems.

Taken together as interlinked processes, Figure 1.1 leads to three main implications for this book: 1) new technological and market opportunities are generated by institutions and forces within the national and global economies; 2) firms must act upon opportunities, and create new technological and market capabilities in order to become leaders on the global market; and 3) by reacting to such opportunities, some firms will be successful, and others fail, but by increasing productivity, these economic processes will in turn positively impact economic growth and societal well-being.

Our theoretical view from Schumpeterian and evolutionary economics is that in the modern economy, the competitiveness of firms depends upon their use of advanced knowledge for innovation as well as their ability to act globally. The firms not only make their own decisions, but they are also affected by, and are working within, a context involving also public policy and innovation ecosystems. In our conceptualization, these firms are searching for market, technological and productive opportunities and accessing multiple resources through networks within a global knowledge-intensive innovation ecosystem. Therefore, many factors affecting the firms will include macro-level factors that affect knowledge creation and diffusions, such as collaborative networks and reverse engineering.

Chapters in this book are organized around these themes:

- Theme: Specifying where innovation systems can affect the ability of Chinese firms to identify and act upon innovative opportunities.
- Theme: Analyzing why Chinese firms' acquisitions and collaboration can affect their capabilities for technology, innovation and globalization.
- Theme: Exploring how Chinese firms develop new capabilities.

The concluding chapter provides an overview of the research results for each theme, as well as our propositions and topics for future research.

3. SUMMARY OF EACH CHAPTER

Chapter 2 explains how seven empirical phenomena about the development of China and Chinese firms is impacting technology, innovation and globalization. In doing so, the chapter conceptualizes innovative opportunities as consisting of technological, entrepreneurial, and productive opportunities, and categorizes the trends accordingly. These seven empirical phenomena are described through the data: 1) national innovation system, public policy and university–industry collaboration; 2) sheer size and growth of economies; 3) increasing competitiveness of Chinese business; 4) strengthening global ties –

flows inward and outward foreign direct investment (FDI); 5) increasing R&D investment; 6) increasing human capital on science and technology (S&T), including education on STEM; and 7) increasing S&T outputs. Based on the data, we argue that the rising market, technological, and productive opportunities contribute to Chinese firms capturing and upgrading their technological capabilities. These empirical trends matter for the future. This chapter thus analyzes the Chinese innovation system as part of a global innovation space, in order to help explain how China is affecting both Chinese and foreign firms.

Chapter 3 evaluates the National High- and New-Tech Industrial Development Zones in China, by applying the concepts of ecological theories and innovation ecosystem. Such zones are similar to science and technology parks and are one of the important policy instruments of the Chinese national innovation system for this purpose. The National High-Tech Industrial Development Zones have developed rapidly in China, from 53 in mainland China in the early 1990s to 188 in 2016. The chapter primarily evaluates the structure, function, and information flows of the innovation activities inside the zones – instead of only evaluating the usual measures of innovative capacity and output performances. The empirical examination is applied to 53 National High-Tech Industrial Development Zones in China between 1990 and 2014, and the cases of Zhongguancun (Beijing) and Zhangjiang (Shanghai). The results indicate that these zones play vital roles in stimulating a faster development of high-tech industries in China, but they do so in diversified ways because of the diversified regional innovation ecosystems.

Chapter 4 analyzes how patent cooperation networks influence the innovation performance of enterprises, applied to the case of technology-based SMEs in the pharmaceutical industry in China. The patent cooperation networks provide an opportunity for this type of knowledge-intensive enterprise to access innovation resources and to improve their innovative capabilities. Based on the specification of the breadth and depth of patent cooperation, this chapter analyzes and classifies the structure of patent collaborative networks. By analyzing this type of firms in the Chinese pharmaceutical industry, this chapter suggests that patent collaboration networks can be divided into two main types, namely exploration and exploitation. The patent cooperation network for exploration has a more significant positive impact on the innovation performance of these firms than the patent cooperation network for exploitation. The chapter proposes that the exploration patent cooperation network provides more breakthrough paths and also opportunities for this type of firms to acquire innovation resources and elevate their innovative capabilities.

Chapter 5 addresses what enables technological self-reliance for indigenous innovation, as well as empirical studies within three complex product industries in China. This empirical analysis of telecom equipment, concrete machinery and diesel engines helps explore technological self-reliance at the sectoral level. The chapter argues that the evolution of embedded demand and the accumulation of national technological capability in a sector help determine the relative reliance upon imported technology and indigenous innovation. Thus, this chapter proposes that technological self-reliance, as an independent concept which depicts the middle stage between technological dependence and innovating, is a useful tool to understand the logic and paths of capability building in catching-up countries such as China.

Chapter 6 explores Chinese KIE firms, specifically small and medium enterprises (SMEs) in high-tech industries, which undertake cross-border acquisitions in the EU, USA, and Japan, and focuses upon the technological characteristics. The chapter highlights the roles of these firms as connecting nodes between the home and host regions, where regions are characterized by different degrees of technological distance. The chapter uses a Technology Proximity Index in order to analyze how homogeneous the patents are in terms of technological classes in the home and host regions. The descriptive analysis is based on a sample of 95 acquisitions occurring between 2003 and 2011, and on the investors' patent portfolio characteristics, such as technology specialization, experience, size and number of collaborative patents. The chapter reveals that investors with stronger knowledge bases and with more diversified and larger patent portfolios are more likely to invest in more technologically distant regions. In addition, although they are more involved in collaborative patents at home and abroad, these investors are not more likely than other Chinese multinational firms to establish international collaborations for patents.

Chapter 7 investigates how firms build technological capability during internationalization, by examining one in-depth case study in the energy sector, namely wind energy. The case study outlines a 20-year-long process of internationalization in relation to technological capability building. The chapter examines the firm's strategic intention as well as strategic process in order to understand how the firm has built up its technological capability and transited from production to innovation. The chapter finds that the transition of the firm from production to innovation is facilitated by cross-border technological learning through human mobility between the headquarters and its foreign counterpart. In addition, the cross-border technological learning is enabled by cross-border relationships and trust developed through a long-term personal relationship building among the key managers.

Chapter 8 addresses the process of knowledge and technology transfer within an acquired firm, after acquisition by a Chinese multinational firm. The empirical case study is taken from the acquisition in 2010 of Volvo Car Corporation by Zhejiang Geely Holding Group. The process of knowledge transfer between Volvo Car and Geely Group includes many different aspects.

The chapter provides details of this knowledge transfer, through integrated greenfield plants, collaboration in a new engine plant, coordination and cooperation at supply systems, integration of management and engineering resources, joint R&D ventures, as well as development based on a joint platform Compact Module Architecture (CMA). It argues these are the aspects that are used by the Geely Group, in order to gradually upgrade their process, product, functional, and production capacity, and thereby achieve an upgrading in the global value chain.

Chapter 9 identifies and analyzes a new phenomenon of globalization, namely the reverse innovation, the processes whereby technology, innovation, and new products are developed or marketed in developing countries and are then transferred from developing countries to advanced countries. The chapter identifies three ideal types of reverse innovation, which are also empirically illustrated, based on a matrix framework based on type of innovation strategy and the location of commercialization. They are Ideal Type I: reverse innovation based on transferred technology; Ideal Type II: original reverse innovation; and Ideal Type III: original reverse innovation (front-end technology). The firm's innovation capabilities play a critical role in reverse innovation. The chapter indicates that Ideal Type I is a good strategy for firms in developing countries to achieve reverse innovation in mature technology, whereas the Ideal Types II and III are suitable for firms in developing countries to achieve reverse innovation in emerging technologies and markets.

Chapter 10 discusses Chinese indigenous innovation and the influence of global markets, within Chinese KIE ventures. This chapter questions whether Asian innovation efforts are primarily associated with imitation and efficient market exploitation, which has been found in previous theoretical and empirical research. In contrast to previous research, the findings demonstrate that these ten Chinese KIE ventures accord a low degree of importance to global knowledge, whereas their own internal skills and knowledge are the source of their innovations. Thus, these results capture novel empirical developments, and raise interesting questions about how this type of Chinese firm engages in domestic and international technological development, now and in the future.

Chapter 11 explores the development of advanced technical capabilities, in one Chinese knowledge-intensive venture in the emerging industry of artificial intelligence, applied to visual recognition and surveillance systems. Using theories from knowledge management, the analysis reveals the essential engagement of customers in new product development, and why their knowledge is needed due to the unclear description of market needs. Hence, this chapter suggests that a pre-linguistic embodiment of tacit knowledge can be found in field tests and prototypes, during knowledge creation. Moreover, that they can be useful tools for externalization of knowledge for the further development of advanced technical knowledge.

Chapter 12 explores the specific strategic roles that a Chinese overseas research and development (R&D) center can play in a Chinese multinational firm, and they do so by analyzing CEVT as an organization positioned between Geely and Volvo. The development of China Euro Vehicle Technology AB (CEVT), a wholly subsidiary of Geely Auto, shows a specific strategic role and management system of a Chinese overseas R&D center. Taking the fast growth of CEVT as a case, we explore the distinguished role of CEVT in Geely after its M&A of Volvo Cars and the co-development of Geely Auto, Volvo Cars, and CEVT. The analysis suggests that the independent technology firm can work as a broker between bilateral parties in an M&A event from the aspect of new product and technology development as well as the global market strategy. This chapter highlights the important role of an independent technology firm to promote the co-development of bilateral parties of an M&A with a hidden internal technology trade. The analysis has important implications for the global R&D strategy and technological M&A, especially for firms in mature industries from emerging countries.

Chapter 13 applies a conceptual perspective from the management of an innovation ecosystem perspective, in order to understand the strategies and development of Chinese multinational firms, which are latecomers. Two case studies explore two of the most innovative firms in the Chinese smartphone industry, Huawei and Xiaomi. The chapter identifies two complementary approaches to implementing latecomer strategies. Complementary to previous studies on technological catch-up in developing countries, the analysis of these two case studies reveals that a latecomer firm should interact and co-create value with many other players in its innovation ecosystem in order to catch-up to leading country firms through innovation.

Chapter 14 is organized according to our three themes of: 1) specifying where innovation systems can affect the ability of Chinese firms to identify and act upon innovative opportunities; 2) analyzing why Chinese firms' acquisitions and collaboration can affect their capabilities for technology, innovation, and globalization; and 3) exploring how Chinese firms develop new capabilities. The chapter then provides three propositions and outlines a future research agenda, and ends with some words about innovation and development facing the challenges of digitalization and globalization in the decades ahead.

REFERENCES

Autio, E., Nambisan, S., Thomas, L.D.W. and Wright, M. (2018). "Digital affordances, spatial affordances, and the genesis of entrepreneurial ecosystems", *Strategic Entrepreneurship Journal*, 12: 72–95.

Carlsson, B. (2016). "Industrial dynamics: A review of the literature 1990–2009", *Industry and Innovation*, 23(1): 1–61.

Cooke, P., Gomez Uranga, M. and Etzeberria, G. (1997). "Regional innovation systems: Institutional and organisational dimensions", *Research Policy*, 26(4–5): 475–491.

Deloitte China (2019). *Global Artificial Intelligence Industry Whitepaper*, accessed on 28 October 2019 at https://www2.deloitte.com/cn/en/pages/technology-media-and-telecommunications/articles/global-ai-development-white-paper.html#

Dodgson, M., Gann, D. and Phelps, N. (2014). *The Handbook of Innovation Management*. Oxford, UK: Oxford University Press.

Edquist, C. (2006). "Systems of Innovation. Perspectives and Challenges", in Fagerberg, J., Mowery, D.C. and Nelson, R.R. (eds.), *The Oxford Handbook of Innovation*. Oxford, UK: Oxford University Press.

Edquist, C. and McKelvey, M. (eds.) (2000). *Systems of Innovation. Growth, Competitiveness and Employment*. Vol 1, Vol 2. Cheltenham, UK and Northampton, MA, USA: Edward Elgar Publishing.

Granstrand, O. and Holgersson, M. (2019). "Innovation ecosystems: A conceptual review and a new definition", *Technovation*, 90(Feb–March). Available online doi: 10.1016/j.technovation.2019.102098

Horst, H. and Pyka, A. (eds.) (2004). *Companion on Neo-Schumpeterian Economics*. Cheltenham, UK and Northampton, MA, USA: Edward Elgar Publishing.

Jacobides, M.G., Cennamo, C. and Gawer, A. (2018). "Towards a theory of ecosystems", *Strategic Management Journal*, 39(8): 2255–2276.

Jin, J. and McKelvey, M. (2019). "Building a sectoral innovation system for new energy vehicles in Hangzhou, China: Insights from evolutionary economics and strategic niche management", *Journal of Cleaner Production*, 224(July): 1–9.

Laursen, K. (2012). "Keep searching and you'll find: What do we know about variety creation through firms' search activities for innovation?", *Industrial and Corporate Change*, 21(5): 1181–1220.

Lee, K. (2013). *Schumpeterian Analysis of Economic Catch-up*. Cambridge, UK: Cambridge University Press.

Lee, K. and Malerba, F. (2017). "Catch-up cycles and changes in industrial leadership: Windows of opportunity and responses of firms and countries in the evolution of sectoral systems", *Research Policy*, 46(2): 338–351.

Lundvall, B.Å., Johnson, B., Andersen, E.S. and Dalum, B. (2002). "National systems of production, innovation and competence building", *Research Policy*, 31(2): 213–231.

Malerba, F. (2002). "Sectoral systems of innovation and production", *Research Policy*, 31(2): 247–264.

Malerba, F. (2009). *Sectoral Systems of Innovation: Concepts, Issues and Analyses of Six Major Sectors*. Cambridge, UK: Cambridge University Press.

Malerba, F. and McKelvey, M. (2018). "Knowledge-intensive innovative entrepreneurship: Integrating Schumpeter, evolutionary economics and innovation systems", *Small Business Economics*, 54: 503–522.

Malerba, F. and Nelson, R. (2012). *Economic Development as a Learning Process: Variation across Sectoral Systems*. Cheltenham, UK and Northampton, MA, USA: Edward Elgar Publishing.

McKelvey, M. (2014). "Science, technology and business innovation", in Dodgson, M., Gann, D. and Phelps, N. (eds.), *The Handbook of Innovation Management*. Oxford, UK: Oxford University Press.

McKelvey, M. (2016). "Firms navigating through innovation spaces: A conceptualization of how firms search and perceive technological, market and productive opportunities globally", *Journal of Evolutionary Economics*, 26(4): 785–802.
McKelvey, M. and Bagchi-Sen, S. (2015). *Innovation Spaces in Asia: Entrepreneurs, Multinational Enterprises and Policy.* Cheltenham, UK and Northampton, MA, USA: Edward Elgar Publishing.
Metcalfe, S. (2002). "Knowledge of growth and growth of knowledge", *Journal of Evolutionary Economics*, 12(1): 3–13.
Metcalfe, S. (2008). *Restless Capitalism: The Evolutionary Nature of Capitalism.* Princeton, NJ: Princeton University Press.
Nelson, R.R. (1993). *National Systems of Innovation: A Comparative Analysis*. Oxford, UK: Oxford University Press.
Nelson. R.R. (1996). *The Sources of Economic Growth.* Cambridge, MA: Harvard University Press.
Nelson, R. and Winter, S. (1982). *An Evolutionary Theory of Economic Change.* Cambridge, MA: Belknap Press of Harvard University Press.
Schumpeter, J. (1934). *The Theory of Economic Development.* Cambridge, MA: Harvard University Press.
Schumpeter, J. (1942). *Capitalism, Socialism and Democracy*. New York: Harper and Brothers. Reprint by George Allen & Unwin (Publishers Ltd).
Spigel, B. (2017). "The relational organization of entrepreneurial ecosystems", *Entrepreneurship Theory and Practice*, 41(1): 49–72.
Stam, E. (2015). "Entrepreneurial ecosystems and regional policy: A sympathetic critique", *European Planning Studies*, 23(9): 1759–1769.
Stam, E. and Spigel, B. (2017). "Entrepreneurial ecosystems", In Blackburn, R., De Clercq, D., Heinonen, J. and Wang, Z. (eds.), *Handbook for Entrepreneurship and Small Business*. London: Sage.
Teece, D. (2007). "Explicating dynamic capabilities: The nature of (sustainable) enterprise performance", *Strategic Management Journal*, 28(13): 1319–1350.
Teece, D. (2018). "Business models and dynamic capabilities", *Long Range Planning*, 51(1): 40–49.
Teece, D.J., Pisano, G. and Shuen, A. (1997). "Dynamic capabilities and strategic management", *Strategic Management Journal*, 18(7): 509–533.
Zhang, Z., Jin, J. and Guo, M. (2017). "Catch-up in nanotechnology industry in China from the aspect of process-based innovation", *Asian Journal of Technology and Innovation*, 25(1): 5–22.

2. Becoming leaders: how the Chinese knowledge-intensive innovation ecosystem affects the firms' search for innovation

Jun Jin and Maureen McKelvey

1. INTRODUCTION

This chapter analyzes empirical material that helps provide an explanation for how and why some Chinese firms are becoming leaders. It does so by investigating seven empirical trends, within the Chinese knowledge-intensive innovative ecosystems, which are opening up new opportunities for technology, innovation and globalization. This chapter also provides details of the empirical context for later chapters by providing evidence on how the set of opportunities is rapidly expanding, through the development of new markets, new technologies and new business knowledge.

In doing so, we suggest that the seven empirical trends offer evidence of transformation. We argue they demonstrate a vast increase in three types of opportunities – namely market, technological and productive opportunities. Taken together, the detailed data include the science and technology (S&T) human resources, the research and development (R&D) investment and the globalization of S&T. They illustrate the performance of the Chinese ecosystem in recent decades, and suggest how it may affect firm search, and thereby the development of Chinese firms' capabilities in technology, innovation and globalization. As outlined in Chapter 1, this book is part of a long tradition of literature which analyzes how the firms are acting within a broader context, from Schumpeter, evolutionary economics, innovation systems, economic geography, international business literature and entrepreneurship. From these theoretical perspectives, we are interested in how and why firms are acting and learning within a broader context, or what we here call a knowledge-intensive innovative ecosystem.

This chapter builds upon the conceptual model presented in Chapter 1, as well as McKelvey and Bagchi-Sen (2015) and McKelvey (2016). Here, we focus upon how the knowledge-intensive innovative ecosystem can lead to three types of innovative opportunities – technological, market and productive ones. These are broad opportunities, which the changes in industrial dynamics and innovation systems help to generate and which the firm can act upon. These impact both search strategies and selection regimes (McKelvey 2004). Firms must navigate through an innovation space, in an evolutionary process, as they search and develop different types of business innovations. Changes may occur rapidly or slowly, depending upon the level of analysis (McKelvey and Holmén 2006). According to McKelvey and Bagchi-Sen (2015), innovation space constitutes a geographical and virtual context, which affects innovation through a process of the interaction of firms spanning industrial dynamics as well as the regional/national institutional setting.

In this chapter, we thus propose that the firms are searching in a broader innovation space, which can be analyzed along three axes. The first axis is the creation of technological opportunities through scientific and technological knowledge. The second axis is the creation of market opportunities related to new market and customer knowledge. The third axis is the creation of productive opportunities, dependent upon using business knowledge of how to operate innovation in the firm locally and globally, and leading to a reconfiguration of capabilities.

Empirically in this chapter, we define the innovative opportunities as consisting of three types as follows:

Technological opportunities, driven by new scientific and technological knowledge. A good illustration of this is the Chinese firms in the nano-tech industry, who are using and developing leading scientific and technological knowledge in their businesses (e.g. Zhang et al. 2017). These technological opportunities are discussed in Section 2, and they are created primarily through technological opportunities via scientific and technological knowledge. Here, we are primarily concerned with the enhancement and accumulation of scientific and technological resources within China. Therefore, this section addresses the increase in R&D investment; the increase in human resources in S&T; and the increase in S&T outputs.

Market opportunities, driven by expanding markets and also new types of customers. Illustrations include e-mobility, where previous research shows how the development of new energy vehicles (NEVs) industry in Hangzhou depends upon rapid market growth, among other things (Jin and McKelvey 2019), and the internationalization of a Chinese Photovoltaic firm (Jin et al. 2019). These market opportunities are discussed in Section 3, and are related to new market and customer knowledge as also used within the firm. Hence, this section addresses the growth and size of the Chinese economy, as well as the increasing competitiveness of Chinese firms.

Productive opportunities, where resources within the firm are moved to diversity into new businesses, as well as the overall impact of public policy and national innovation systems in creating support to move resources into emerging businesses. This is created through the reallocation of resources, for example the opening and movement of Chinese apparel factories into and across Southeast Asia, or large investments into science and technology (S&T). The creation of productive opportunities is discussed in Section 4. They are dependent upon using business knowledge of how to operate innovation in the firm locally and globally and leading to a reconfiguration of capabilities also through public policy. This section provides facts and figures about the increasing inward flows from global ties, as well as providing an overview of the increasing resources from public policy.

Section 5 provides a summary of the arguments, including a visualization of our conceptualization of how the Chinese knowledge-intensive innovation ecosystem can affect firms' search for innovation.

2. TECHNOLOGICAL OPPORTUNITIES

2.1 Increasing R&D Investment

Driven by the policy development target to be an innovative country, research institutes, companies, as well as government agencies invest heavily in R&D. China's R&D expenditure (percentage of GDP) enjoyed a stable increase from 0.563 in 1996 to 2.129 in year 2017 (Figure 2.1). As shown in Figures 2.2–2.4, the gap in the R&D intensity, the gross domestic expenditure on R&D (GERD), and GERD per researcher between China and advanced countries (the USA, Japan, Germany, and so on) is closing. China's average annual growth in R&D expenditure from 2000–2014 was 16.4 percent, ranking it in first place, and was significantly ahead of other countries. In 2015, China's gross domestic expenditure on R&D was just less than the USA, as shown in Figure 2.3.

Thus, China's ability to innovate has risen steadily, and it ranked 14th in the global innovation index (GII) in 2019 (Table 2.1).

Taken together, Figures 2.1–2.4 and Table 2.1 indicate that China is rapidly increasing investment into R&D as well as improving innovativeness in terms of the amount of R&D capabilities in the country as a whole and in businesses in particular.

Our interpretation is that this rapid increase and continuing growth in both domestic and foreign investment in R&D implies that China will also improve its position in global economic and technological competition in the future. China is already, and will continue to be, a locality where there is a high concentration of technological opportunities, as seen through the increase in R&D expenditure, and especially in the business sector.

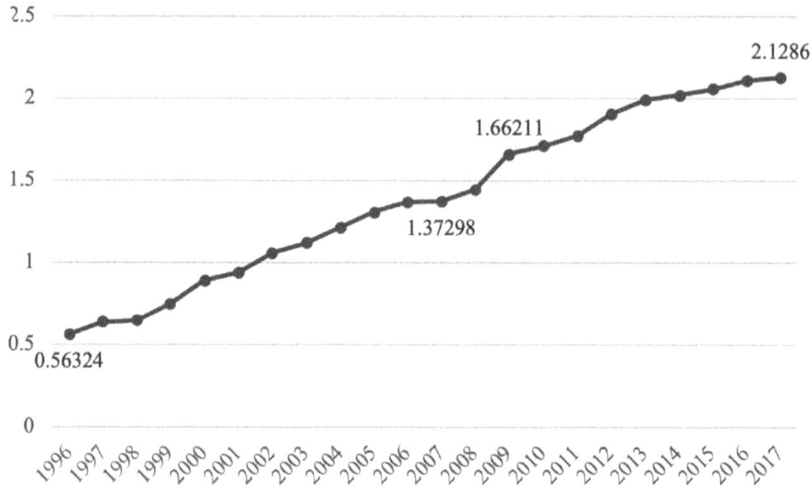

Source: Data bank of the World Bank, accessed on 23 October 2019 at https://data.worldbank.org/indicator/GB.XPD.RSDV.GD.ZS?locations=CN&view=chart

Figure 2.1 *R&D intensity of China, as expenditure percentage of GDP (1996–2017)*

2.2 Increasing Human Resources in Science and Technology

Following the reinstatement of the national college entrance examination in 1977, great changes have happened in Chinese higher education. For instance, the number of China's tertiary institutes reached 4358 in 2018, the enrollment ratio of the National College Entrance Examination in China was 48.1 percent in 2018, and the number of graduates was 8.14 million (including 7.53 undergraduates) in 2018, according to the statistics data from the Ministry of Education.[1]

The comparison of PhD (doctoral) degree holders in the fields of science and engineering in selected countries in Table 2.2 reveals that China has produced the greatest number of natural science and engineering PhD degrees per year in the world since 2007. These constitute the human resources pool of R&D in China.

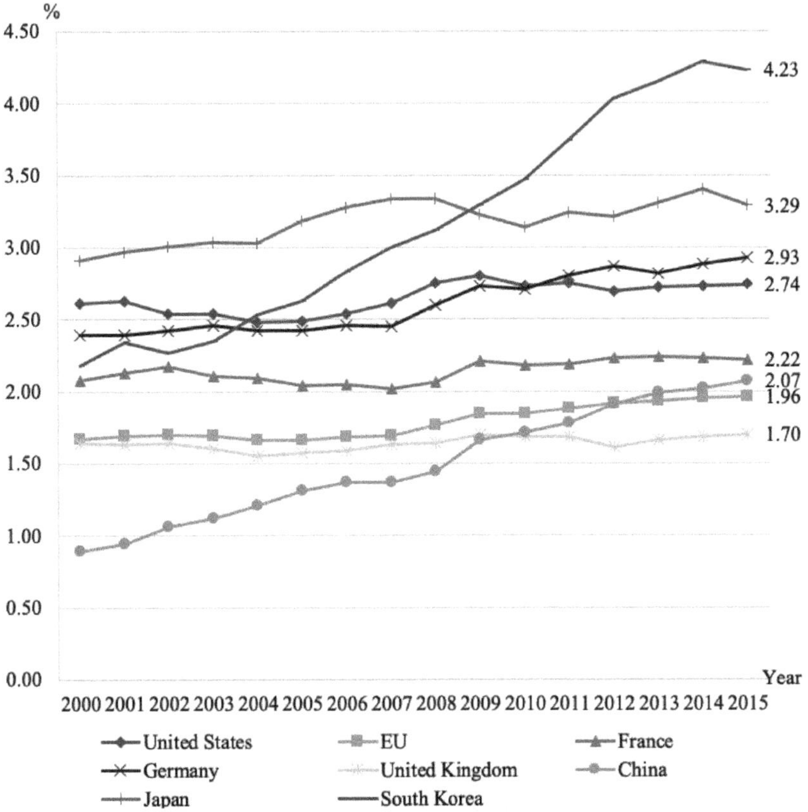

Source: Science and Engineering Indicators 2018, accessed on 23 October 2019 at https://www.nsf.gov/statistics/2018/nsb20181/assets/1038/figures/fig04-07.xlsx

Figure 2.2 *Intensity of R&D of selected regions or countries (2000–2015)*

The total full-time equivalent R&D personnel in China in 2014 was 4.034 million (Table 2.3), which means that for a consecutive eight years China was ranked first in the world, accounting for 31.3 percent of the world's total. The development of S&T personnel from 2008 to 2015 presents a stable increasing trend, and the R&D personnel number per 1000 population in 2015 was twice that of 2008. However, compared to the USA and other countries, researchers as a share of total employment in China was still quite low, as shown in Figure 2.5.

Thus, Tables 2.2 and 2.3 as well as Figure 2.5 indicate the rising level of Chinese human capital, especially in science, technology, engineering and math.

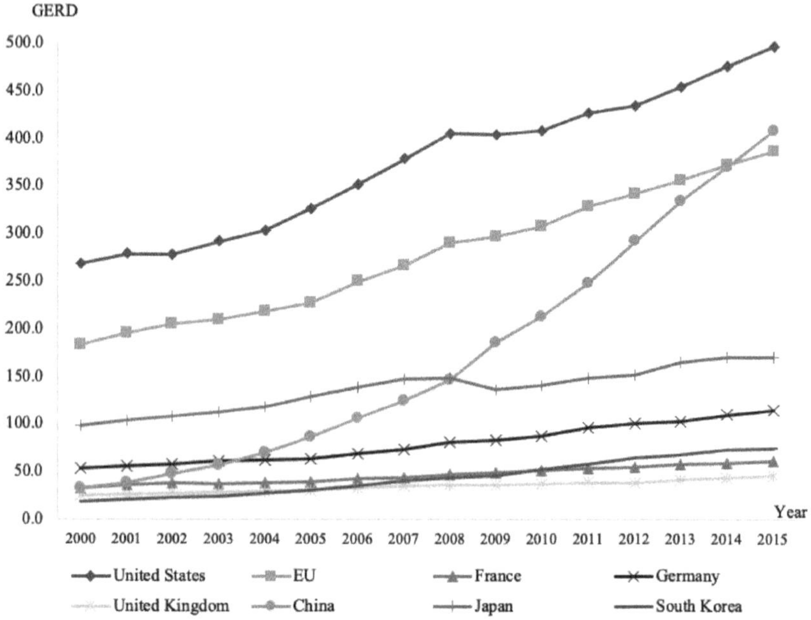

Source: Science and Engineering Indicators 2018, accessed on 23 October 2019 at https://www.nsf.gov/statistics/2018/nsb20181/assets/1038/figures/fig04-06.xlsx

Figure 2.3 *GERD of selected regions or countries (2000–2015) in billions of current PPP dollars*

Table 2.1 *Rank of China in the Global Innovation Index (2009–2019)*

Year	2009	2010	2011	2012	2013	2014	2015	2016	2017	2018	2019
Rank	37	43	29	34	35	29	29	25	22	17	14

Source: Data has been collected from the Global Innovation Index (2009–2019).

This increase can be seen internally as well as an increase as compared to other countries.

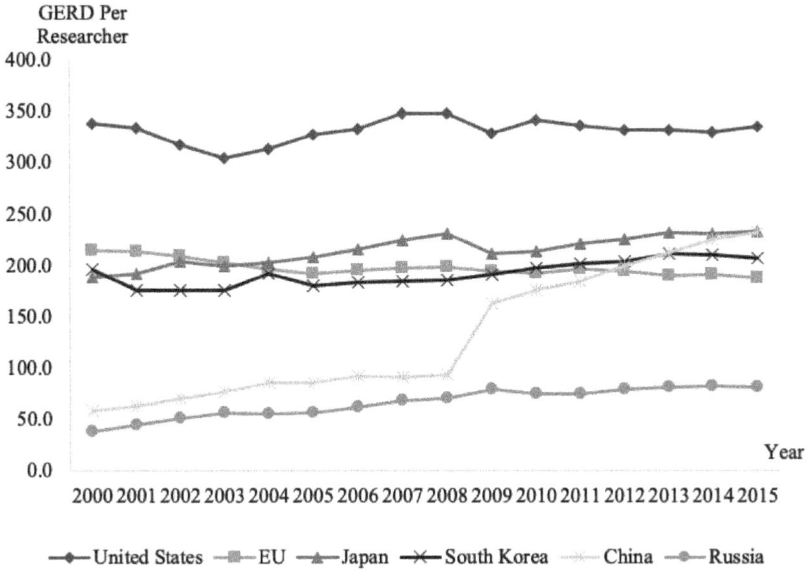

Source: Science and Engineering Indicators 2018, accessed on 23 October 2019 at https://www.nsf.gov/statistics/2018/nsb20181/assets/901/figures/fig03-40.xlsx

Figure 2.4 *GERD per researcher of selected regions or countries (2000–2015) in thousands of PPP constant 2010 dollars per researcher*

2.3 Increasing Science and Technology Outputs

This chapter has shown that the amount of R&D investment, R&D personnel, science and engineering PhD degree holders, and so on, all are increasing gradually. All of these in turn support the improvement of science and technology performance in China.

As shown in Table 2.4, in 2017, the number of Science Citation Index (SCI) papers from China reached 361 000, ranking second in the world for nine years, and the number of SCI papers in China accounted for about 18.6 percent of the global total.[2]

In 2017, the cases of the invention patent applications at the China National Intellectual Property Administration (CNIPA) filed by the Chinese domestic applicants reached 1 246 000 (Figure 2.6). In addition, in 2017, the CNIPA domestic invention patents grants filed by the Chinese domestic applicants reached 327 000 (Figure 2.7). As shown in Table 2.6, the total number of patent applications filed by domestic and foreign applicants in China was up to 3 698 000 cases in 2017 from 828 000 cases in 2008, while the granted patent number was up to 1 836 000 in 2016 from 412 000 cases in 2008. The number of PCT (Patent Cooperation Treaty) patent applications by China increased from 30 000 in 2015 to 49 000 in 2017, keeping the second position in the world, while the volume of triad patents in 2016 achieved 3890 issues.

Table 2.2 Natural sciences and engineering doctoral degrees, in thousands, by selected country (2001–2014)

Year	United States	EU-Top 8	China	Japan
2000	17.5	30.4	7.3	6.5
2001	17.3	31.6	7.5	6.8
2002	16.6	32.2	8.7	6.8
2003	17.7	32.5	11.0	6.8
2004	18.8	34.1	13.5	7.1
2005	20.4	35.0	16.0	6.7
2006	22.3	38.1	20.9	7.2
2007	24.2	38.5	24.4	7.0
2008	25.0	39.0	26.2	6.7
2009	25.3	40.6	29.0	6.4
2010	25.1	41.5	29.0	6.5
2011	26.1	44.3	29.8	6.1
2012	27.2	44.1	30.0	6.1
2013	28.3	50.0	31.2	5.9
2014	29.8	49.2	31.8	5.9

Notes: EU = European Union. Natural sciences and engineering include biological, physical, earth, atmospheric, ocean, and agricultural sciences; computer sciences; mathematics; and engineering. The Top 8 EU total includes aggregated data for the eight EU countries with the highest number of S&E doctoral degree awards in 2014: UK, Germany, France, Spain, Italy, Portugal, Sweden, and Romania.
Source: Science and Engineering Indicators 2018, accessed on 25 October 2019 at https://www.nsf.gov/statistics/2018/nsb20181/assets/561/figures/fig02-25.xlsx

However, the data in Table 2.5 reveals that the USPTO granted patents by China contributed 3.8 percent to the total USPTO patents granted in 2016, which was a significant lag behind the USA, Japan and even South Korea. It hints there is still a long way to go for Chinese firms to compete in innovation with firms from the USA, Japan, the EU, and other regions in the world market.[3]

Table 2.3 *R&D Personnel in China (2008–2017)*

	2008	2009	2010	2011	2012	2013	2014	2015	2016	2017
Full-time equivalent R&D personnel (1000/ year)	1970	2290	2550	2880	3250	3530	3710	3759	3878	4034
R&D personnel in 1000 population	260	300	340	380	420	460	480	485	500	520

Source: Data analyzed from The Development of Human Resources in Science and Technology in China 2015, 2016, 2017, available from http://www.most.gov.cn/mostinfo/xinxifenlei/kjtjyfzbg/kjtjbg/kjtj2018/201807/P020180713403082652715.pdf; http://www.most.gov.cn/mostinfo/xinxifenlei/kjtjyfzbg/kjtjbg/kjtj2017/201807/P020180713503992035393.pdf; http://www.most.gov.cn/mostinfo/xinxifenlei/kjtjyfzbg/kjtjbg/kjtj2019/201904/P020190409331955003970.pdf, and National Statistics of China http://www.stats.gov.cn/tjsj/ndsj/2018/indexch.htm

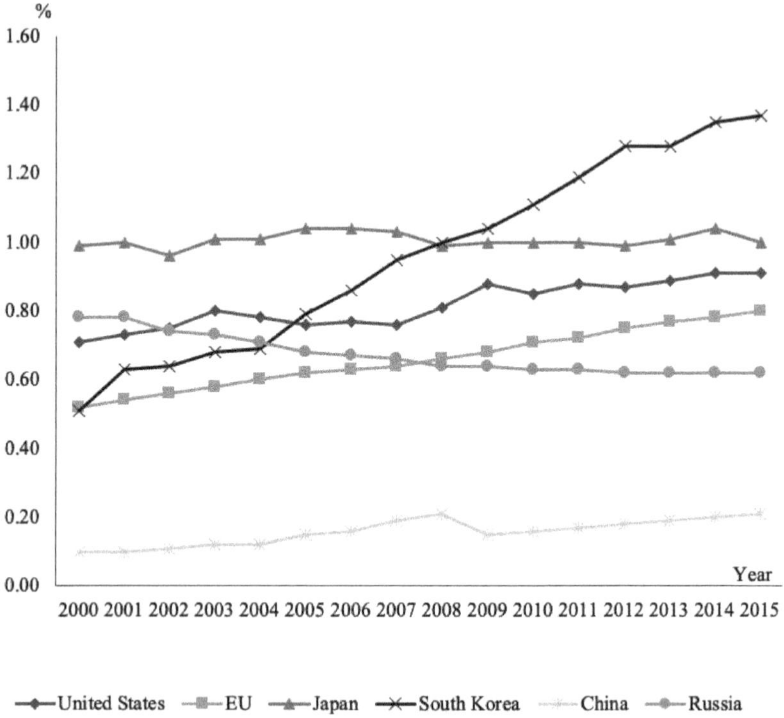

Source: Science and Engineering Indicators 2018, accessed on 23 October 2019 at https://www.nsf.gov/statistics/2018/nsb20181/assets/901/figures/fig03-39.xlsx

Figure 2.5 Researchers as a share of total employment in selected regions or countries (2000–2015)

3. MARKET OPPORTUNITIES

3.1 Growth and Size of the Chinese Economy

From 1990 to 2010, the gross domestic product (GDP) in China grew at an average growth rate of double digits. Since 2012, the GDP growth rate was down to less than 8 percent and decreased to 6.6 percent in 2018, as shown in Figure 2.8. It was recognized by the Chinese government that one of the characteristics of China's "new normal"[4] economy was that the GDP growth rate would not be as high as before. Since 2008 China has had the second largest GDP in the world (Figure 2.8), while since 2014 China has become one of the two countries in the world with more than one trillion USD of GDP, as shown in Figure 2.9. In addition, GDP per capita in China has increased from less

Table 2.4 *Science and technology outputs in China in thousands (2007–2017)*

Number	2007	2008	2009	2010	2011	2012	2013	2014	2015	2016	2017
Patent application	694	828	977	1222	1633	2051	2377	2361	2799	3465	3698
Application of invention patent	245	290	315	391	526	653	825	928	1102	1339	1382
Patent grants	352	412	528	815	961	1255	1313	1303	1718	1754	1836
Patent grants of invention	68	94	128	135	172	217	208	233	359	404	420
SCI papers	89	117	128	144	166	193	232	250	297	304	361

Source: Statistical Data from National Bureau of Statistic of China and Statistical Bulletin on National Economic and Social Development of China in 2016, China S&E Publication Analyses 2007, available from http://www.most.gov.cn/kjtj/201506/P020150630575138902414.pdf, and China S&E Publication Analyses 2017, accessed on 26 October 2019, available from http://www.sts.org.cn/Page/Content/Content?ktype=4&ksubtype=1&pid=24&tid=89&kid=2071&pagetype=1&istop=[IsShow]

than 320 USD in 1990 to 9770 USD in 2018.[5] However, because China has the largest population, at more than 1.38 billion, the GDP per capita in China was recorded at only 9770 USD in 2018, which was nearly 15.60 percent of GDP per capita in the USA (62 641 USD) and 15.13 percent of GDP per capita in Singapore (64 581.54 USD) in 2018, as shown in Figure 2.10.

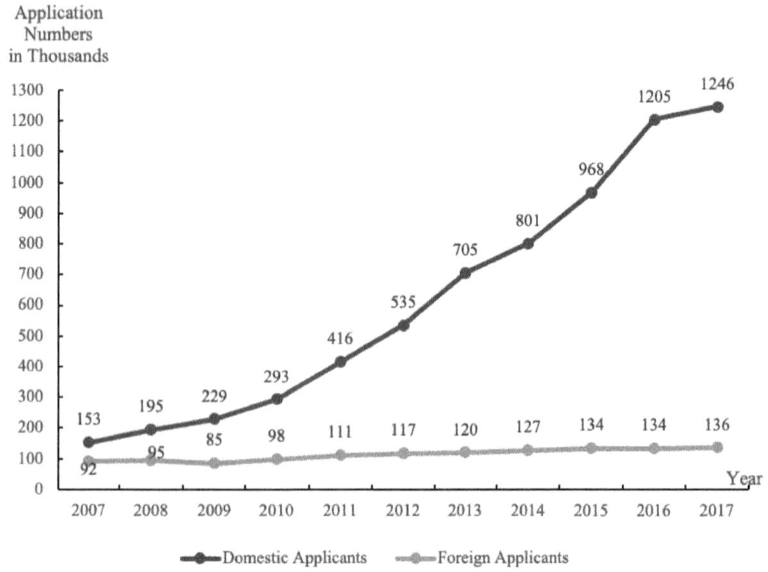

Note: CNIPA: China National Intellectual Property Administration.
Source: Ministry of Science and Technology of China, China Patent Statistics Analyses 2017, http://www.sts.org.cn/Page/Content/Content?ktype=4&ksubtype=1&pid=24&tid=89&kid=2073&pagetype=1&istop=[IsShow]

Figure 2.6 CNIPA invention patent applications filed, by Chinese domestic applicants and foreign applicants (2007–2017)

With the development of China, the tertiary industry (service industry) in China has gradually become the leading industry since 2013. In addition, the service industry has contributed to more than 50 percent of the GDP since 2015 and up to 52.2 percent in 2018, as shown in Figure 2.11. It indicates that the economic growth in China relies more on services than on the manufacturing and agriculture businesses.

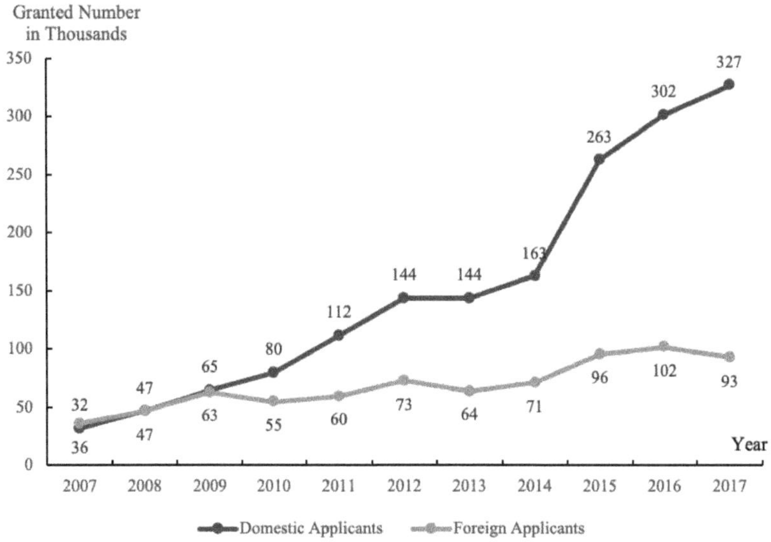

Note: CNIPA: China National Intellectual Property Administration.
Source: Ministry of Science and Technology of China, China Patent Statistics Analyses 2017, http://www.sts.org.cn/Page/Content/Content?ktype=4&ksubtype=1&pid=24&tid=89&kid=2073&pagetype=1&istop=[IsShow]

Figure 2.7 *CNIPA invention patents granted, by Chinese domestic applicants and foreign applicants (2007–2017)*

Thus, Figures 2.8–2.11 show the dramatic increase in GDP and GDP per capita as well as relative increases to other countries and a shift in the industrial base.

3.2 Increasing Competitiveness of Chinese Firms

Chinese firms have increased their competitiveness at the same time as the implementation of open and reform policies and the rapid development of the Chinese economy, as introduced above. As discussed in many chapters in this book, some Chinese firms have become the leading firms in the world, such as Huawei in the telecommunications industry and Alibaba in the internet (e-commerce) industry. China has become the largest market and vehicle producer in automobiles, new energy vehicles, high-speed trains, wind power, solar energy, and so on. For instance, the successful first maiden flight of the C919 aircraft at the Shanghai Pudong International Airport on 5 May 2017 means that China has made clustered breakthroughs in civil aircraft technology

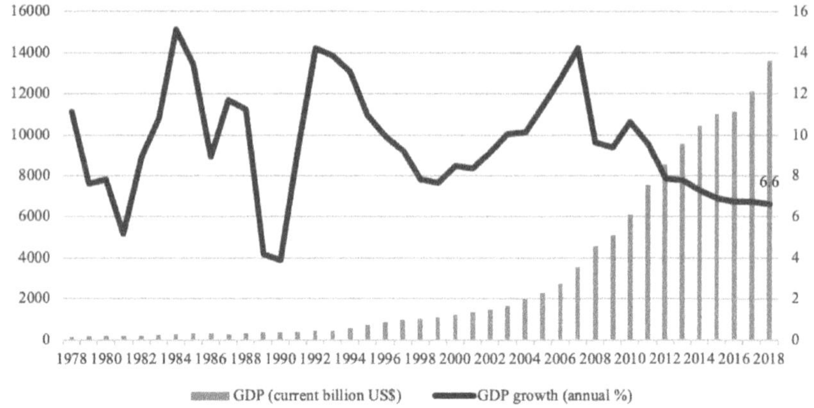

Source: Data were collected from the database of World Bank, accessed on 17 October 2018 at https://data.worldbank.org/indicator/NY.GDP.MKTP.KD.ZG?end=2018&locations=CN&start=1960&view=chart

Figure 2.8 *GDP and GDP growth rate in China (1978–2018)*

Table 2.5 *USPTO patents granted, by selected region or country of inventor (2006–2016), percentage share*

Year	United States	EU	Japan	South Korea	China	India
2006	51	14	21	3.4	0.6	0.3
2007	50	14	21	4.0	0.8	0.4
2008	49	14	21	4.8	1.0	0.4
2009	49	13	21	5.2	1.2	0.4
2010	49	14	20	5.3	1.5	0.5
2011	48	14	21	5.4	1.7	0.6
2012	47	14	20	5.2	2.1	0.7
2013	48	15	19	5.2	2.4	0.9
2014	48	15	18	5.5	2.7	1.0
2015	47	15	18	6.0	3.0	1.2
2016	47	15	16	6.4	3.8	1.2

Notes: USPTO = US Patent and Trademark Office. China includes Hong Kong. Patent grants are fractionally allocated among regions, countries, or economies based on the proportion of the residences of all named inventors.
Source: Science and Engineering Indicators 2018, accessed on 25 October 2019 at https://www.nsf.gov/statistics/2018/nsb20181/assets/1178/figures/fig08-05.xlsx, https://www.nsf.gov/statistics/2018/nsb20181/assets/1178/figures/fig08-07.xlsx

and gained the core competences of developing trunk liners under the collaboration of the Commercial Aircraft Corporation of China, Ltd. (COMAC) and its partners.[6] In addition, with the development of the high-speed train market in China, the technological capabilities of Chinese companies in that market are growing. The technologies underpinning the development of high-speed trains have been exported to other countries, as shown and discussed as reverse innovation in Chapter 9.

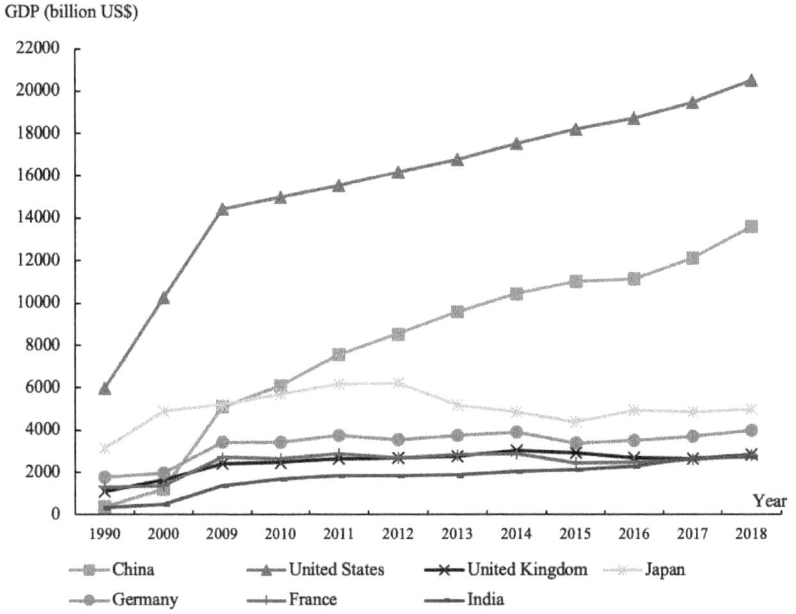

Source: Data were collected from the database of World Bank, accessed on 17 October 2018 at https://data.worldbank.org/indicator/NY.GDP.MKTP.KD.ZG?end=2018&locations=CN&start=1960&view=chart

Figure 2.9 *GDP of selected countries in billion USD (2000–2018)*

More and more Chinese firms have been listed on the Fortune Global 500.[7] In 2019, 129 Chinese firms (110 Chinese firms on the 2016 list) were ranked on the list of Fortune Global 500, including case firms in this book: Geely Holding (No. 220 in 2019, increasing from 343 in 2017 and 267 in 2018) in Chapters 8 and 12, Huawei (No. 61 in 2019 increasing from 83 in 2017 and 72 in 2018) and Xiaomi (No. 468 in 2019) in Chapter 13. Geely has been on the List of Global 500 for eight years,[8] Huawei has been on the List of Global 500 for ten years,[9] while Xiaomi is on the list for the first time.[10] In addition, the Sinopec Group, China National Petroleum and the State Grid were ranked Nos 2, 4 and 5 respectively in the 2019 Global 500 list. Moreover, Huawei in Chapter 13 was recognized as one of the top 50 most innovative firms in the BCG Report on Most Innovative Companies 2019.[11] Since 2014, Huawei has been stable in this list of 50 Most Innovative Companies issued by BCG. Meituan Dianping was No. 1 in the Most Innovative Companies 2019 by the Fast Company.[12] Alibaba was recognized as one of the most innovative companies in the world in 2019 by BCG and Fast Company.[13] All of these statements indicate the increasing competitiveness of Chinese firms, especially in e-commerce.

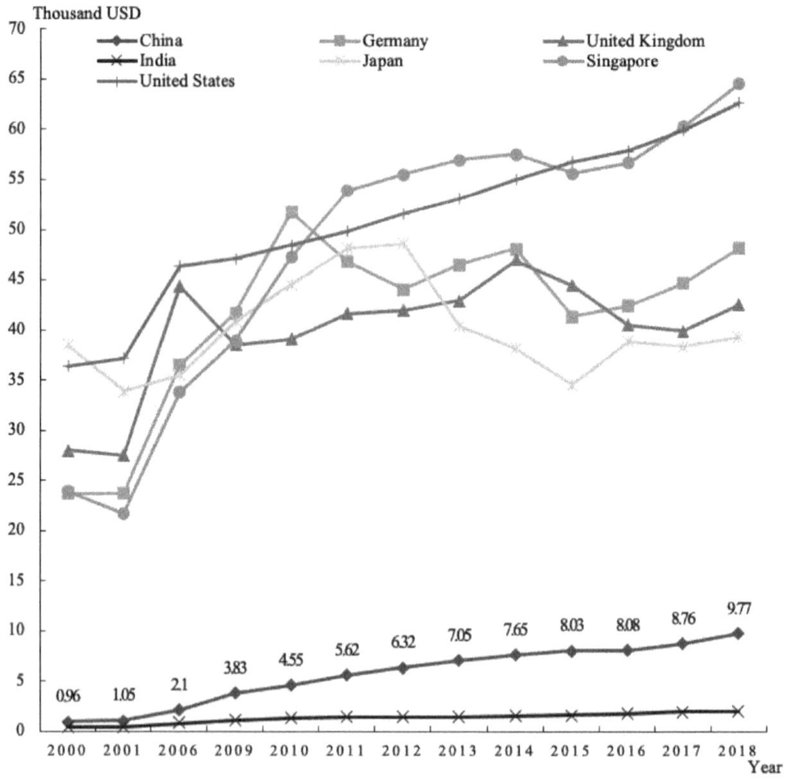

Source: Data were collected from the database of World Bank.

Figure 2.10 *GDP per capita of selected countries (2000–2018) in USD*

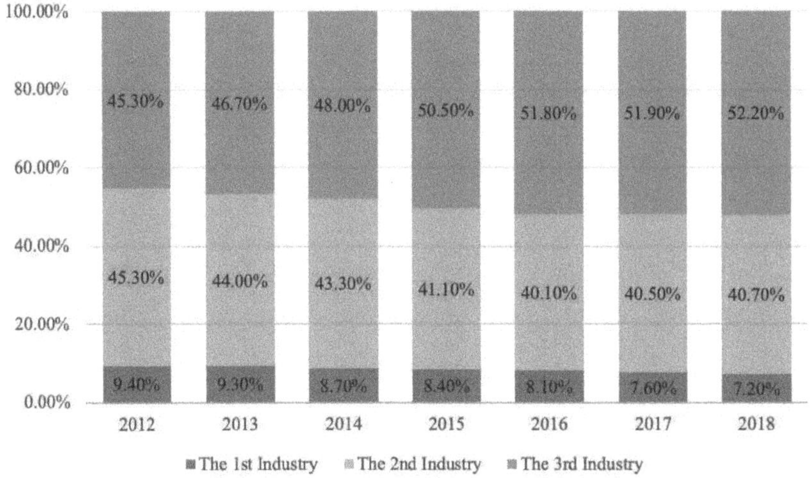

Source: The Annual Statistics Communiqué of China in 2016 and 2018, by the Statistics Bureau of China, accessed on 26 June 2017 and 23 October 2019, at http://www.stats.gov.cn/tjsj/zxfb/201702/t20170228_1467424.html, and http://www.stats.gov.cn/tjsj/zxfb/201902/t20190228_1651265.html

Figure 2.11 Contributions of industries to GDP in China (2012–2018)

4. PRODUCTIVE OPPORTUNITIES

4.1 Increasing Inward and Outward Flow from Global Ties

With the enforcement of open policy, inward foreign direct investment (IFDI) and outward foreign direct investment (OFDI) in China have been increasing. In particular, with China's increasing competitiveness and innovative capabilities, high-tech products and commercial knowledge-intensive services are being exported from China to other countries (Tables 2.6 and 2.7). With the exception of one slight decrease in 2009, the exports of high-tech products have gradually increased up to 615 billion USD in 2016 (Table 2.6), while the exports of commercial knowledge-intensive services reached 91 billion USD in 2016 (Table 2.7). The international trade of high-tech products of China accounted for more than 30 percent of Chinese international trade in 2016, as shown in Figure 2.12. Since 2010, the percentage of exports of high-tech products in the world has remained stable around 24 percent, as shown in Table 2.6. With an explosion in the economic growth rates, a burgeoning pool of well-educated, low-cost labor in China has increasingly attracted new R&D sites of multinational firms from developed economies (UNCTAD 2005;

Table 2.6 *Exports of high-technology products, by selected region or country (2005–2016)*

Year	United States	EU	Japan	China	Other selected Asia	ROW
2005	213	287	157	286	466	134
2006	249	314	161	347	533	153
2007	261	336	152	366	538	181
2008	255	364	154	404	533	210
2009	236	325	124	364	472	197
2010	252	361	153	489	605	229
2011	261	406	156	540	623	263
2012	280	411	151	545	647	274
2013	287	430	134	564	706	284
2014	298	438	129	601	734	281
2015	302	420	119	597	756	272
2016	303	424	122	615	795	296

Notes: EU = European Union; HT = high technology; ROW = rest of world.
In billions of USD. HT products include aerospace, communications and semiconductors, computers and office machinery, pharmaceuticals, and scientific instruments and measuring equipment. China includes Hong Kong. The EU excludes Cyprus, Estonia, Latvia, Lithuania, Luxembourg, Malta, and Slovenia. Exports of the United States exclude exports to Canada and Mexico. Exports of the EU exclude intra-EU exports. Exports of China exclude exports between China and Hong Kong. Other selected Asia consists of Malaysia, Philippines, Singapore, South Korea, Taiwan, and Thailand.
Source: Data was collected from Science and Engineering Indicators 2018, accessed on 25 October 2019, available at https://www.nsf.gov/statistics/2018/nsb20181/assets/1235/figures/fig06-26.xlsx

Barnard and Cantwell 2007; Karabag et al. 2011). By 2018, more than 2000 multinational corporations had set their R&D centers in China.[14] In addition, Chinese firms are quickly expanding their innovation activities into developed countries by means of technology-oriented mergers and acquisitions (M&As), greenfield R&D investments and cross-border innovation collaborations (Chaminade 2011; Chen & Li-Hua 2011; Jin et al. 2014; von Zedtwitz et al. 2015).

With the growth of Huawei, Alibaba, Tencent and Haier, research on globalization and the global R&D of Chinese multinational enterprises is focusing on information and communication technology (ICT) industries and electronic industries (Duysters et al. 2009). The internationalization of Chinese firms has the characteristic that it can be directed towards other emerging economies and towards advanced economies, and that they consider both lower end industries, and higher value adding activities (Parmentola 2011).

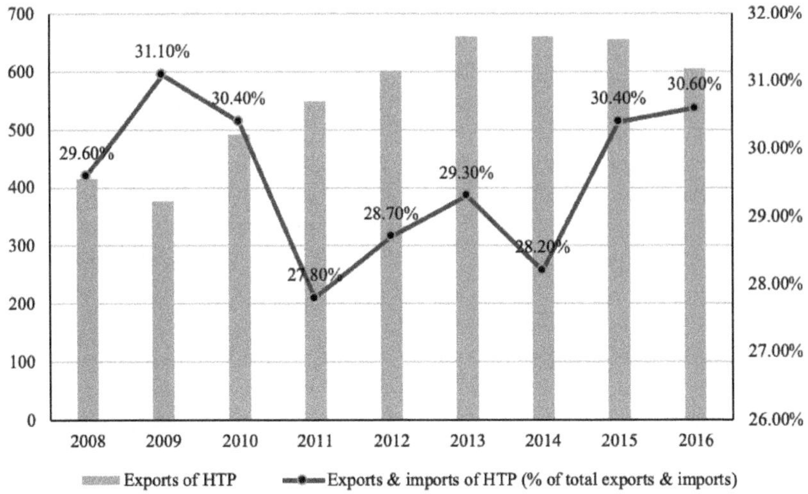

Source: High-tech Products Trade in China in 2016, accessed on 25 October 2019, available at http://www.most.gov.cn/kjtj/201804/P020180402662167189051.pdf

Figure 2.12 *Exports and imports of high-tech products in China in billion USD (2008–2016)*

Table 2.7 *Commercial knowledge-intensive service exports, by selected region or country in billions of USD (2008–2016)*

Year	EU	United States	China	India	Singapore	Switzerland	Japan
2008	378	186	31	79	34	53	41
2009	351	192	27	67	34	48	42
2010	382	207	14	83	39	49	38
2011	432	229	74	94	47	55	44
2012	453	240	72	104	52	55	32
2013	499	263	82	109	60	57	36
2014	549	284	98	111	68	62	49
2015	503	285	90	112	71	61	49
2016	520	288	91	116	69	61	56

Notes: EU = European Union; KI = knowledge intensive. Commercial KI service exports consist of communications, business services, financial services, telecommunications, and computer and information services. Financial services include finance, pension, and insurance services. EU exports do not include intra-EU exports.
Source: Science and Engineering Indicators 2018, accessed on 25 October 2019 at https://www.nsf.gov/statistics/2018/nsb20181/assets/1235/figures/fig06-22.xlsx

In addition to the ICT and electronic industries, 60 merger and acquisition (M&A) deals have been completed by Chinese auto firms from 2013 to 2015, according to the Report on Outward Foreign Investment of Chinese Auto Firms issued by Deloitte China in 2016 (Deloitte China 2016). However, with the number of 210.4 billion USD of deal value, the international M&A deals initiated by Chinese firms in 2016 reached their peak and then slumped 50 percent to 94.1 billion USD, according to the PWC reports (2019).

We believe that along with the implementation of the Belt and Road Initiative,[15] the global ties of Chinese firms and S&T will continue to strengthen, but progress will be slow because of the influence of the trade and technology conflicts between China and the USA since 2018. Nevertheless, because of their knowledge of foreign markets and accumulated prior experience with foreign business operations in the process of internationalization, individuals with international experience who are involved on more strategic levels will influence the internationalization practices of Chinese firms (Fu et al. 2017), and we assume the increasing overseas returnees will contribute to the internationalization of Chinese firms.

4.2 Increasing Resources from Public Policy

After the open and reform policy in 1978, there has been a strong sense that public policy has been able to promote change. The public policy for the Chinese national innovation system has been seen to increasingly provide a more solid foundation to improve the innovation and globalization of Chinese firms. From a policy perspective, the Chinese national government as well as regional and municipal governments have invested intensively into policies with the aim of promoting science, technology and innovation. Sun (2002) traces the development of Chinese policy from a centrally controlled segregated system, towards one focused upon civilian goods and more cooperation and more participation by enterprises in technology and development. Gu and Lundvall (2006) analyze the move towards "harmonious growth and endogenous innovation" and pose a series of policy challenges. In a follow-up article, Gu et al. (2016:443) argue that "we observe the emergence of learning regions signaled by ambitious investments in knowledge resources and supportive institutions". Public policy is active in many areas – S&T policy, innovation policy and industrial policy continue to be important, although now more attempts are made at interagency cooperation. Ling and Naughton (2016) argue that after 2003, Chinese policy moved back to supporting specific technologies and industries, and in so doing has "direct government interventions to shape specific industrial sectors".

The Chinese government has launched a national strategy to build an innovation-driven economy and society by 2020 following a serious of innovation policies, such as the Chinese Medium- and Long-term Science and Technology Development Plan (2006–2020). Under the support of innovation policies, China's national innovation system (NIS) is improving, as shown in the above sections, which provide facts and figures about Chinese science and economic development. However, China's NIS is not fully developed and many linkages between key actors and sub-systems (for example regional innovation systems) remain weak and inefficient (OECD 2008). The regional innovation systems (RIS) in different provinces and cities have played and will continue to play a key role in the advancement of S&T in China (OECD 2008). These are topics covered in the chapters of this book. For example, Chapter 3 discusses the high-tech zones in China. The industrial network and its contribution to the growth of firms is reviewed in Chapter 4. In addition, Chapter 5 proposes the role of RIS in the development of emerging industry.

In order to promote the role of firms in the NIS and reduce the inefficiency of key actors, university–industry cooperation is encouraged (Motohashi and Yun 2007) since universities are important technology and innovation sources in developing countries (Lee and Lim 2001; Chen and Qu 2003; Metcalfe and Ramlogan 2008; Jin et al. 2011), especially for the development of emerging knowledge-based industries, as found in the discussion in Chapter 5. The interaction between firms, universities and research institutes was becoming increasingly frequent and complicated in China. The research institutes, universities and firms cooperate continuously and intensively not only for the firm-funded projects but also for the national-funded large S&T projects, such as the National High Technology Research and Development Program (863 programs in short) and others. The Chinese firms have improved their innovative capabilities and gradually become the key actors of NIS. For instance, the R&D expenditure from firms contributed more than 77 percent of R&D expenditure in 2018 in China.[16]

5. SUMMARY

This chapter has organized the discussion of three types of opportunities that are transforming China, in relation to technological, market and productive opportunities.

Figure 2.13 represents our analysis of the main indicators which suggests many new opportunities are opening up within the Chinese knowledge-intensive innovative ecosystem in recent years. Our view is that these empirical trends are rapidly opening up new innovative opportunities, which Chinese firms take advantage of to develop their capabilities for innovation and globalization. Thereby, we feel that these seven trends are having a positive impact on innovation in Chinese firms. This in turn enables them to compete on the global market.

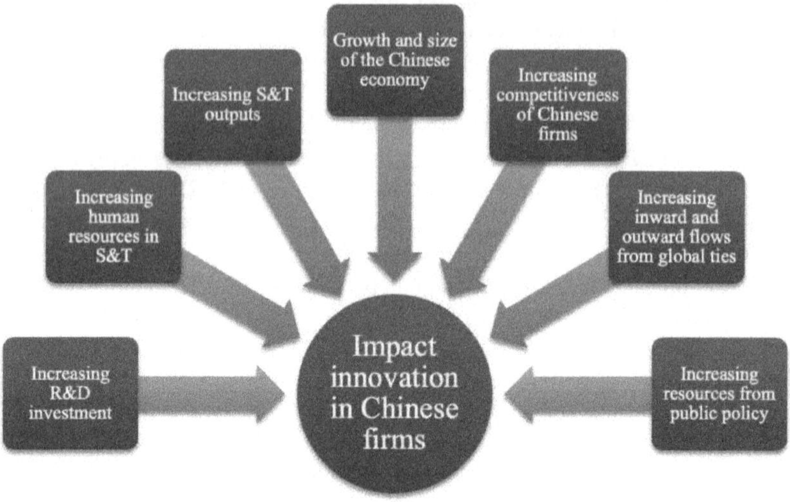

Figure 2.13 *Seven trends which create new opportunities and therefore impact the Chinese firms' search for innovation*

The first dimension is of the creation of technological opportunities through scientific and technological knowledge. Here, we are primarily concerned with the enhancement and accumulation of scientific and technological resources within China, which we have shown as rapidly examined in recent years. Section 2 demonstrates the increase in R&D investment, in human resources in S&T and in S&T outputs. On the one hand, the increasing R&D investment in China hints at the innovation activities of organizations which leads to their S&T performance under the support of increasing innovative human resources. On the other hand, the increasing S&T outputs indicate the development of innovation capabilities and will encourage the investment in R&D and R&D personnel in different organizations. Thus, the increasing R&D expenditure, HR in S&T and the S&T performance will gradually generate a self-enhancement system on R&D in China.

The second dimension is that of the creation of market opportunities related to new market and customer knowledge, which the firm can use to expand. We have shown the massive increase in scale in Section 3 on the growth and size of the Chinese economy. Moreover, we demonstrate that Chinese firms are rapidly developing market and business knowledge, impacting their increasing competitiveness. The increasing Chinese economy reveals the existence of the internal consumption market which will be the base to sustain and attract the inward FDI of foreign firms and outward FDI of Chinese firms. Naturally, we assume that all of these are influenced by the increasing S&T capabilities as shown in the first dimension, namely the increasing economics solidly bolsters the investment in S&T.

The third dimension is the creation of productive opportunities, which is dependent upon using business knowledge of how innovative the firm is locally and globally, and leading to a reconfiguration of capabilities also through public policy. Section 4 provides facts and figures about the increasing inward and outward flows from global ties, and provides an overview of the increasing resources from public policy. In short, the globalization provides opportunities to Chinese firms to improve their productive capabilities and innovation capabilities. In addition, the regional and national levels of innovation systems in China play roles in the development of Chinese firms and the emerging industries.

NOTES

1. Data is from the Statistical Communiqué of National Education in 2018 issued by the Ministry of Education of China on 24 July 2019, accessed on 26 October 2019. Its Chinese version is available at http://www.moe.gov.cn/jyb_sjzl/sjzl_fztjgb/201907/t20190724_392041.html
2. Data was from the China S&E Publication Analyses 2017, accessed on 26 October 2019, available at http://www.sts.org.cn/Page/Content/Content?ktype=4&ksubtype=1&pid=24&tid=89&kid=2071&pagetype=1&istop=[IsShow]
3. Data was from Ministry of Science and Technology of China, China Patent Statistics Analyses 2017, accessed on 26 October 2019, available at http://www.sts.org.cn/Page/Content/Content?ktype=4&ksubtype=1&pid=24&tid=89&kid=2073&pagetype=1&istop=[IsShow]
4. New Normal is a term referring to China's current economy. It was mentioned by President Xi Jinping when he visited Henan in May 2014. The explanation of new normal can be found at the website: https://www.chinadaily.com.cn/opinion/2014-10/10/content_18716671.htm, accessed on 26 October 2019.
5. Data is from the database of the World Bank, https://data.worldbank.org/indicator/NY.GDP.PCAP.CD, accessed on 26 October 2019.
6. News title as 'C919, the first aircraft independently developed by China, commences its maiden flight in Shanghai', which is available at http://english.comac.cc/news/latest/201705/16/t20170516_5220397.shtml, accessed on 26 October 2019.
7. The information is available at http://fortune.com/global500/2019, accessed on 28 October 2019.
8. The information is available at https://fortune.com/global500/2019/zhejiang-geely-holding-group, accessed on 28 October 2019.
9. The information is available at https://fortune.com/global500/2019/huawei-investment-holding, accessed on 28 October 2019.
10. The information is available at https://fortune.com/global500/2019/xiaomi, accessed on 28 October 2019.
11. Most Innovative Companies 2019: The Rise of AI, Platforms, and Ecosystems, BCG, https://www.bcg.com/en-us/publications/collections/most-innovative

-companies-2019-artificial-intelligence-platforms-ecosystems.aspx, accessed on 28 October 2019.
12. Information can be available from https://www.fastcompany.com/most-innovative-companies/2019, accessed on 28 October 2019.
13. Information is available from https://www.bcg.com/en-us/publications/collections/most-innovative-companies-2019-artificial-intelligence-platforms-ecosystems.aspx and https://www.fastcompany.com/most-innovative-companies/2019, accessed on 28 October 2019.
14. Information can be found from the website: https://www.iyiou.com/intelligence/insight113683.html, accessed on 26 October 2019.
15. The Belt and Road Initiative is a strategy in terms of the Silk Road Economic Belt and 21st-Century Maritime Silk Road was raised by President Xi Jinping and issued by the Chinese government in 2013. The initiative focuses on connectivity and cooperation of Asian, European and African continents and their adjacent seas. Its official website is: https://eng.yidaiyilu.gov.cn/index.htm, accessed on 15 February 2018.
16. Data is from the Statistics Communiqué of China's S&T Expenditure 2018, which was accessed on 24 October 2019, available at the website: http://www.sts.org.cn/Page/Content/Content?ktype=7&ksubtype=1&pid=46&tid=113&kid=2611&pagetype=1&istop=[IsShow].

REFERENCES

Barnard, H., and J. Cantwell (2007), 'The internationalization of R&D and the internationalization of innovation', *Research Policy*, 36(8), 1289–1291.

Chaminade, C. (2011), 'Are knowledge bases enough? A comparative study of the geography of knowledge sources in China (Great Beijing) and India (Pune)', *European Planning Studies*, 19(7), 1357–1373.

Chen, D., and R. Li-Hua (2011), 'Modes of technological leapfrogging: Five case studies from China', *Journal of Engineering & Technology Management*, 28(1/2), 93–108.

Chen, J., and W. Qu (2003), 'A new technological learning in China', *Technovation*, 23(11), 861–867.

Deloitte China (2016), *The Report on Outward Foreign Investment of Chinese Auto Firms in 2016* (in Chinese), accessed on 10 August 2016 at https://www2.deloitte.com/content/dam/Deloitte/cn/Documents/manufacturing/deloitte-cn-mfg-china-automotive-industry-outbound-investment-report-2016-zh-160606.pdf.

Duysters, G., J. Jacob, C. Lemmens, and J. Yu (2009), 'Internationalization and technological catching up of emerging multinationals: A comparative case study of China's Haier group', *Industrial and Corporate Change*, 18(2), 325–349.

Fu, X., J. Hou, and M. Sanfilippo (2017), 'Highly skilled returnees and the internationalization of EMNEs: Firm level evidence from China', *International Business Review*, 26(3), 579–591.

Gu, S., and B.-Å. Lundvall (2006), 'Introduction: China's innovation system: and the move towards harmonious growth and endogenous innovation.' *Innovation: Management, Policy & Practice*, 8, 1–26.

Gu, S., S. Schwaag Serger, and B.-Å. Lundvall (2016), 'China's innovation system: Ten years on', *Innovation: Organization and Management*, 18(4), 441–448.

Jin, J., and M. McKelvey (2019), 'Building a sectoral innovation system for new energy vehicles in Hangzhou, China: Insights from evolutionary economics and strategic niche management', *Journal of Cleaner Production*, 224(July), 1–9.

Jin, J., Z. Zhang, and L. Wang (2019), 'From the host to the home country, the international upgradation of EMNEs in sustainability industries: The case of a Chinese PV company', *Sustainability*, 11(19), 5269.

Jin, J., S. Wu, and J. Chen (2011), 'International university–industry collaboration to bridge R&D globalization and national innovation system in China', *Journal of Knowledge-based Innovation in China*, 3(1), 5–14.

Jin, J., Y. Wang, and W. Vanhaverbeke (2014), 'Patterns of R&D internationalisation in developing countries: China as a case', *International Journal of Technology Management*, 64(2–4), 276–302.

Karabag, S.F., A. Tuncay-Celikel, and C. Berggren (2011), 'The limits of R&D internationalization and the importance of local initiatives: Turkey as a critical case', *World Development*, 39(8), 1347–1357.

Lee, K., and C. Lim (2001), 'Technological regimes, catching-up and leapfrogging: Findings from the Korean industries', *Research Policy*, 30(3), 459–483.

Ling, C., and B. Naughton (2016), 'An institutionalized policy-making mechanism: China's return to techno-industrial policy', *Research Policy*, 45(21), 2138–2152.

McKelvey, M. (2004), 'How and why dynamic selection regimes affect the firm's innovative search activities', *Innovation: Organization and Management* (previously journal called *Innovation: Management, Policy and Practice*), 6(1), 3–24.

McKelvey, M. (2016), 'Firms navigating through innovation spaces: A conceptualization of how firms search and perceive technological, market and productive opportunities globally', *Journal of Evolutionary Economics*, 26(4), 785–802.

McKelvey, M., and S. Bagchi-Sen (2015), *Innovation Spaces in Asia: Entrepreneurs, Multinational Enterprises and Policy*. Cheltenham, UK and Northampton, MA, USA: Edward Elgar Publishing.

McKelvey, M., and M. Holmén (2006), *Flexibility and Stability in the Innovating Economy*, Oxford: Oxford University Press.

Metcalfe, S., and R. Ramlogan (2008), 'Innovation systems and the competitive process in developing economies', *The Quarterly Review of Economics and Finance*, 48(2), 433–446.

Motohashi, K., and X. Yun (2007), 'China's innovation system reform and growing industry and science linkages', *Research Policy*, 36(8), 1251–1260.

OECD (2008), *OECD Reviews of Innovation Policy: China*, Paris: OECD.

Parmentola, A. (2011), 'The internationalization strategy of new Chinese multinationals: Determinants and evolution', *International Journal of Management*, 28(1), 369–386.

PWC (2019), *Review of the M&A by Chinese Firms in 2018 and Outlook in 2019* (in Chinese), accessed on 28 October 2019 at https://www.pwccn.com/zh/deals/publications/ma-2018-review-and-2019-outlook.pdf.

Sun, Y. (2002), 'China's national innovation system in transition', *Eurasian Geography and Economics*, 43(6), 476–492.

UNCTAD (2005), *Globalization of R&D and Developing Countries*, Geneva and New York: United Nations.

von Zedtwitz, M., S. Corsi, P. Soberg, and R. Frega (2015), 'A typology of reverse innovation', *The Journal of Product Development and Management*, 32(1), 12–28.

Zhang, Z., J. Jin, and M. Guo (2017), 'Catch-up in nanotechnology industry in China from the aspect of process-based innovation', *Asian Journal of Technology and Innovation*, 25(1), 5–22.

3. Evaluation of science parks in China from an innovation ecosystem perspective

Xiangdong Chen, Zhichun Liu and Valerie Marleen Hunstock

1. INTRODUCTION

This chapter evaluates science parks in China using an innovation ecosystem perspective, which is linked to various ecological theories. Science parks in the Chinese context may include a variety of things, and are often known as National High- and New-Technology Industrial Development Zones (NHNTIDZs or NHTZs).[1] They are usually characterized by highly clustered knowledge bases in open facilities, and are aimed at integrating advanced domestic and international technological resources, necessary venture funds, and managerial experiences. Various government policy instruments are also increasingly implementing beneficial policies for those firms and individuals that are operating high-tech firms, incubators, and start-ups in these science parks and related zones. NHNTIDZ, or development zones, were one of the important parts of this program (Chen and Ouyang, 1996). This chapter focuses upon analyzing the science parks through a combination of factors, whereas Chapters 4 and 14 address dimensions of how an innovation ecosystem affects companies, using methodologies of quantitative network analysis and case studies.

These government policy instruments for science parks started in August 1988, via the so-called National Torch Program – an important government plan for speeding up high-tech industries from fundamental research, conducted via the Ministry of Science and Technology of China.[2] Since 53 national science parks were first approved by the State Council of China in 1992, the number of these science parks has been continually increasing under the National Torch Program. As of December 2015, there were 149 national-level science parks all over China. Once a science park has been approved as a national-level science park, the firms within that science park receive many economic benefits, such as low import and export tariffs (in particular, they obtain zero import tariff for materials or components if these are to be used for product exporting). They also receive better opportunities and positions for financing by means of company bonds via special banks, for example. Furthermore, they obtain support through other relevant policies such as the rapid depreciation that is adopted for instruments developed in companies for high-tech products.

In 2013, when 114 national science parks were operating with around 71180 firms (more than 30 percent of which were high-tech firms), their total revenue reached 20.3 trillion RMB. In addition, out of a total of 14 million employees in these science parks, almost half were working in high-tech firms. Most of the high-tech sectors in China are strategic "pillar" industries in emerging technology fields.

Evaluating them is of great interest. As such science parks are located in different cities and regions in China, with varied knowledge and technology bases due to differences in universities, research institutes, and many other relevant resources, they can be developed quite differently in terms of innovative quality and productive quantity. Chen's (2014) study of 88 high-tech science parks identified five different dominating operating patterns: (1) zones characterized by backing from local universities and research institutes, along with vertical technology transfer, such as Zhongguancun Science Park (ZGC-SP) in Beijing and Donghu Science Park in Wuhan; (2) zones backed by international advanced production resources (especially R&D-centered clusters from large foreign multinational enterprises (MNEs)), such as Zhangjiang Science Park in Shanghai; (3) zones backed by regional entrepreneurial clustered start-ups, such as the high-tech zone in Shenzhen; (4) industry-transfer zones based on strong Southeast Asian businesses, such as the Korean, Taiwanese, and Hong Kong-based investment clustered science parks in Suzhou and Wuxi; and (5) industrial-transfer zones backed by local government policy and supported from different sources, such as the science parks in medium-sized cities in Central and Western China. Yan et al. (2018) used systems analysis to evaluate collaborative ecosystems in relation to science parks.

This chapter provides an overview on science parks from the perspective of the innovation ecosystem, in order to evaluate their functions under various driving forces – especially under stronger government innovation policies – since most promising firms developing and manufacturing high-tech products require immediate market responses. However, there are generally shortages of necessary resources such as financial and marketing resources, making policy support strongly required. Moreover, to conduct our analysis, we view innovation processes in certain regions as involving a non-linear movement that is influenced by regional markets and policies, companies and universities, business routines and entrepreneurial cultures, and so on, similar to the development of a biological system embedded in a diversified nutritious environment. With this theoretical framing, we conduct this study on Chinese science parks, specifically the policy for the National High-Tech Industrial Development Zones. Thus, we place the science park within the innovation ecosystem, which combines factors from regional innovation including government policy factors, and market-demand factors. Our analyses are related to innovation in terms of flows of knowledge, current input status, and output position.

2. LITERATURE REVIEW FOR OUR THEORETICAL FRAMEWORK

Although many concepts of innovation ecosystems exist in the literature, we view that the concept of the innovation ecosystem as used herein originates from a paper titled "Sustaining the Nation's Innovation Ecosystems: Report on Information Technology Manufacturing and Competitiveness" by PCAST (2003). According to that paper, the leading position of a country's technology and innovation depends on a vital and dynamic "innovation ecosystem," rather than on a linear terminal-to-terminal process.

Existing research publications and reports have attempted to use ecosystem concepts by adapting concepts and theoretical explanations in order to evaluate high-tech zones – particularly Chinese science parks – as well as economic and technological development zones (under different government plans with similar motivations for regional and national economic output). For example, Rishikesha (2011) studied high- and new-tech industry parks in the USA's Silicon Valley and India by applying an innovation ecosystem framework. In terms of studies about China, Wu and Wei (2005) and Miao and Huang (2007) applied a multilevel fuzzy synthetic evaluation method to the case of the Suzhou International Science Park. Sun (2007) analyzed company-level innovation within high-tech development zones, by integrating an ecological niche analysis method with qualitative and quantitative measures in order to evaluate technological development zones.

Of relevance to this chapter, one of the key issues is identifying appropriate indicators for evaluating scientific parks. Chen and Ouyang (1996) chose structural and functional dimensions for their evaluation, such as the nature of the area, number of enterprises under incubation, and number of incubated enterprises, in order to propose function indexes. Other scholars focus more on the performance side of science parks; for example, Pang et al. (2009) emphasized three kinds of cluster – formation, production process, and industrial innovation – based on data from 53 science parks in China. Wang and Liu (2009) applied the entropy evaluation method to 15 science parks in China, and suggested an innovation capability evaluation index system for high-tech zones, with five capacity dimensions: indigenous innovation, resource allocation, management, facility supporting, and productive competence. By adopting a method that combined data envelopment analysis (DEA), principal divisor analysis, and clustering analysis techniques, Liu (2010) provided an efficiency rating system for 13 pilot science parks in China. In contrast, Du (2012) focused on the relationships between three subsystems of innovation capability measures: technical innovation, institutional innovation, and facility supporting innovation.

All of the above studies attempt to establish a ranking system for facilities and performance (including technology and institutions), or a relationship between them. What is missing in the existing literature are attempts to perform evaluation via an integrated framework from the innovation ecosystem perspective. We are also interested in whether innovation policy may initially facilitate innovation, but later be more related to market forces, whereby the science park becomes more sustainable over time. We are therefore interested in the dynamic nature of and interactions among the necessary factors, and so this chapter provides an evaluation framework based upon "flow"-based evaluations of Chinese science parks.

2.1 Concepts and Structure of the Innovation Ecosystem of a Science Park

We propose a three-dimensional model.

The first part of the evaluation from our innovation ecosystem perspective is how to capture innovation in terms of the sustainable dynamic nature of the system – especially the activeness of relevant factors that transfer input resources into effective output. Our evaluation of innovation focuses upon knowledge and information flows between input resources and output performance. Our framework includes Flows of Knowledge, Current Input Status, and Output Position, relying upon factors typically used to evaluate innovation. We therefore include: high-tech product output; capital, material, and talents as input resources; and flows between them. The overall performance of an innovation ecosystem within a certain time range can be investigated through these three dimensions, with a particular focus on the tangible and intangible flows in the science park.

The second part of our analysis is that the innovation ecosystem of a science park also comprises innovative elements, similar to organisms in biology. We therefore include enabling factors (e.g., human capital), environmental factors (e.g., policies and market demand), and ecological factors that include major enabling factors (e.g., human capital factors, facilitating capital factors, etc.) and element flow factors.

In regard to innovation-enabling factors, we consider innovative organisms to include knowledge owners and technical producers from the supply side, comprising mostly human capital plus the necessary facilitating and financial capital. In a given time–space, the population and service organization of an industry constitute the innovative community, which includes universities, scientific research institutes, and high-tech firms. The innovative service organization includes public service organizations and public technical platforms. Public service organizations usually provide appropriate ecological niches for the initial growth of innovative incubation; they may also provide special services, such as intellectual property guidance, technical transfer, talent training, financial aid, and other consulting services. This framework focuses more on factors and "flows" than on the factors themselves. Government policies and market responses are used as necessary environmental factors for the whole organism.

The following two charts are provided to summarize the key functions of science parks through the perspective of the innovation ecosystem. Figure 3.1 illustrates the three dimensions of science parks, while Figure 3.2 emphasizes the tangible and intangible flows in science parks, within an operating background of joint interactions between government policies and market demand.

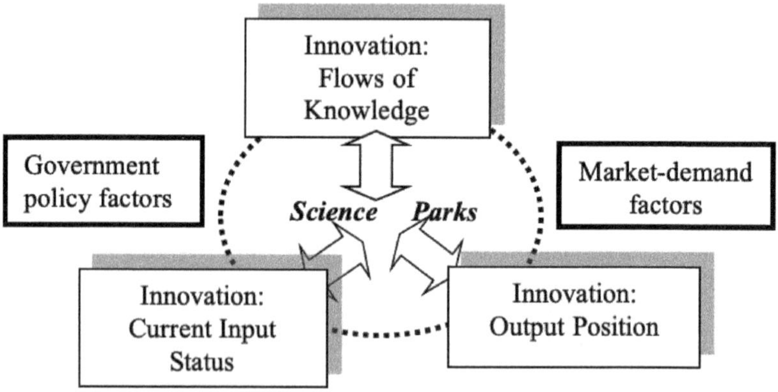

Figure 3.1 *Research framework for an investigation of Chinese science parks using the innovation ecosystem perspective*

When examining the nature of flows in science parks from the innovation ecosystem perspective – that is, looking at the potential power to influence different flows of elements or factors toward more innovative regions – we have found that two kinds of driving force or flow are particularly important: tangible flows (i.e., material- and facilitation-based flows) and intangible flows (i.e., knowledge- and information-based flows).

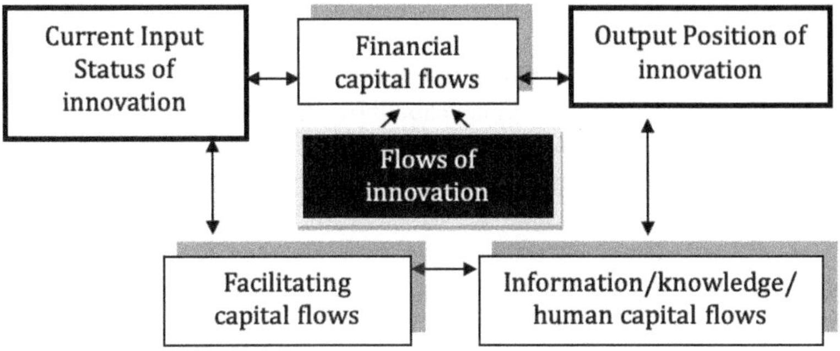

Figure 3.2 *Framework for analyzing flows to science parks*

In this chapter, we consider the attributes of talent flow to be especially crucial, as human capital not only carries existing knowledge and related information from research and communities, but also introduces creative thinking for the future. In addition, the talent flow itself will bring knowledge and dynamic information from one position to another, and from one location to another. At the same time, we recognize that the facilitation of capital flows – including facilities or devices for R&D and production, and facilities acting as policy-backed collaboration platforms – is usually connected to human capital flows.

2.2 An Evaluation Framework for Science Parks from the Innovation Ecosystem Perspective

This chapter will now develop and use the three-dimensional evaluation framework, divided into the three dimensions of Current Input Status, Flows of Knowledge, and Output Position. Among these dimensions, the Current Input Status dimension is mainly used to evaluate the various innovative resource inputs of the science park, the Flows of Knowledge may reflect the active level of the innovative ecosystem, and the Output Position evaluates innovative output (and later potential developments). These three dimensions can also be considered as an ecological niche, to reflect natural biological communities, here applied to evaluate innovation in science parks.

2.2.1 Current Input Status: evaluation index

Tables 3.1, 3.2, and 3.3 provide the detailed structure of the corresponding indicators that can usually be found in the innovation-related statistical yearbook on science and technologies in a country or region. Table 3.1 provides three levels of measures on "status" dimensions, while Table 3.2 provides measures on "position" dimensions, and Table 3.3 provides measures on "flow" dimensions.

The ecological niche within the Current Input Status dimension of a science park can be financial capital, human capital (talent), and/or facilitating capital (material/asset based), in addition to a policy ecological niche. Certainly, an excellent innovative system can obtain a larger and more superior ecological niche; similarly, when the innovation system of a science park is operating well on its own, that science park can continue to obtain a larger and more superior ecological niche and to develop in a rapid and sustainable way.

2.2.2 Output Position: evaluation index

As shown in Table 3.2, Output Position stands for innovative output, which covers three aspects: science and technology (S&T) output with significant actual market value; the subsequent economic output; and, finally, the social benefit output. Social output represents the positive impact the innovation brings in every social aspect, including personal employment, fiscal income, institutional innovation radiation, development mode output, and so forth.

2.2.3 Flows of Knowledge: evaluation index

The innovation activities in an innovative ecosystem can be reflected by the active flows of elements, talents, information, and cash stream created by the innovation, as shown in Table 3.3. The value flow can be primarily high-tech revenues created during the innovative production process, while the value increase and the transfer process can also be important components of the flow system. The information flow refers to communication and exchanges in various R&D and productions in or between high-tech firms. Talent flow is even more important for innovation activities, as advanced knowledge and related product and process innovation can be generated through active talent flows within and between organizations. Furthermore, information flows that go beyond the overall science park, or that come from external resources, are heavily dependent upon talent flows. This is especially true in the Chinese case, as scholars returning from overseas play crucial roles in radical innovation in various high-tech industries and in science parks.

Table 3.1 "Status" dimensions of evaluation on science parks

Level 1 index	Level 2 measures	Level 3 measurements
Dominated ecological niche	Capital measures	Percentage of the R&D expenditure against local production value Technology transfer expenditure Realized accumulative investment of foreign companies at year end Expenditure of entrusted domestic research institutions for conducting scientific and technological activities Share capital financed by listed enterprise on a stock market
	Talent measures	No. of people with degree of bachelor or above per 10,000 persons Percentage of people engaged in S&T activities over total employees
	Policy measures	Percentage of financial and technical expenditure to the financial expenditure in the current year Total number of scientific and technological projects Percentage of exempted amount of R&D expenditure after deducting income tax in the total R&D expenditure Number of national-level S&T enterprise incubators
	Tangible measures (fixed asset etc.)	Percentage of high-tech firms S&T instruments to total enterprise number Total investment in fixed assets finished in the current year for the actual management area per square kilometer

Table 3.2 Output position evaluation index

Level 1 index	Level 2 measures	Level 3 measurements
Output Position innovation achievement	Knowledge/ technological output	Number of newly increased invention patents per 10,000 persons Number of articles in science and technology published Number of national or industrial standards
	Economic output	Percentage of total income of high-tech industry to the operating revenue
	Social output	Profit rate of enterprise sales revenue Taxes paid per capita Average salary of employed persons Number of R&D and manufacture institutions established abroad

3. DATA SOURCE AND EVALUATION SAMPLE SELECTION

The data for this innovative ecosystem evaluation study were collected from the *Chinese Torch Statistical Yearbook*, the *Statistical Statement of Enterprises in National High- and New-Tech Development Zones* compiled by the Torch High Technology Industry Development Center, Ministry of Science & Technology of China, and the *Comprehensive Statistical Statement of High-Tech Zones* compiled by the Ministry of Technology of China. Since the number of science parks in China is being adjusted continuously, the authors of this chapter chose to examine the science parks with more complete statistical information in order to ensure the effectiveness and authenticity of the research results. Eventually, 53 science parks as the first group of national-level parks, approved between 1988 and 1997, were selected as the research sample in this chapter.

Various quantitative methods can be used to evaluate science parks and similar innovative institutions through the innovative ecosystem perspective, and to apply an evaluation index to innovation ecosystems. Examples of methods include principal component analysis (PCA), the analytic hierarchy process (AHP), energy analysis, ecological analysis, the fuzzy evaluation method, and neural networks. Each evaluation method has its own respective advantages and scope of application. We consider PCA to be the best way

Table 3.3 *Flow evaluation index system*

Level 1 index	Level 2 measures	Level 3 measurements
System flow	High-tech Revenue flow	Volume of business/technical contract per capita Percentage of new product value to the increased value (RMB10,000) Percentage of technical revenue to the total revenue of scientific park Percentage of technical service export to the total export Total guarantee capital
	High-tech Information flow	Number of high-tech enterprises recognized in the current year Number of national science and technology awards Percentage of total number of enterprises newly registered in the current year to the total enterprise number
	High-tech Talent flow	Percentage of returned overseas students increased newly in the current year to the newly increased employees Number of people newly selected and in national "1,000 Talent" program Percentage of current year graduates from universities to total newly hired employees
	Energy flow	Comprehensive energy consumption to increased value (RMB10,000) of industrial enterprises

to retain the original information while reducing the number of indicators or measurements, especially when there are a great many measures (see Ma and Huang, 2009). In a comprehensive evaluation, the weight of each principal component depends on the level of its contribution to the original set of measurement information. This can help to determine an objective and reasonable weight while overcoming the subjective bias on weight found in some other evaluation methods (see Yu et al., 2009). The PCA method was therefore applied in this research in order to obtain enough information for the "position," "status," and "flow" indexes of an innovative ecosystem over 53 science park cases in China.

Table 3.4 Ranking on innovation ecosystem measures (top 10 NHTZs)

NHTZ	Current input status	System flows	Output position	Summary	Rank
Beijing	11.34	15.21	26.79	53.33	1
Shanghai	11.37	10.2	15.73	37.3	2
Shenzhen	10.44	10.22	14.62	35.28	3
Chengdu	10.58	11.24	12.15	33.96	4
Wuhan	10.29	10.63	12.63	33.55	5
Guangzhou	9.99	10.22	12.81	33.02	6
Jinan	10.06	12.14	10.34	32.53	7
Xi'an	10.59	10.28	11.47	32.34	8
Hangzhou	10.64	10.63	10.34	31.6	9
Hefei	10.35	10.21	10.85	31.4	10
STD	*0.469*	*1.573*	*4.902*	*6.535*	
STD (NT)	*0.318*	*0.260*	*0.661*	*0.825*	
STD (total)	*0.436*	*0.868*	*2.738*	*3.775*	

Note: STD is the standard deviation for the top 10 science parks only, while STD (NT) is the standard deviation for the remaining 43 science parks, and STD (total) is the standard deviation for all the sample 53 science parks.

4. RESULTS AND ANALYSIS

Based on the PCA method, the total score (i.e., a summary of the corresponding value in three dimensions) of each of the 53 sample science parks was calculated in order to reflect the overall level of the innovative ecosystem. The top 10 science parks are shown in Table 3.4.

Table 3.4 shows only the top 10 science parks because the remaining samples are rather similar in terms of their scoring level in the three dimensions.

From Table 3.4, four significant findings can be derived:

All 53 sample science parks have a similar level of Current Input Status; however, there are larger differences in terms of Output Positions, meaning that innovation efficiency is highly diverse among these science parks.

All of the performance parameters used here are unevenly distributed among the sample, especially within the top 10; this finding implies that a limited number of these science parks are playing significantly more outstanding roles under the innovation ecosystem framework than others, especially in terms of Output Position measures.

Table 3.5 *Results on ranking of science park cities under innovation ecosystem evaluation – Output Position*

Windows		Northern China	Southern China
Output Position +	Input status +A	Beijing, Xi'an, Jinan	Shanghai, Nanjing, Hangzhou, Chengdu, Shenzhen, Hefei, Wuhan
	Input status –A	Tianjin, Changchun	Guangzhou, Changsha, Foshan

Note: The benchmark line is defined as the average value of all samples on that dimension, and +A and –A indicates respectively the positions of the related samples above or under the average lines.

The Flows of Knowledge measure is considered to be especially important in this study, and the empirical results show that this measure matters in most of the sample science parks. This importance is especially reflected in the top 10 group, as the flow dimension indicates the second most significant variant measure. It is interesting that, for the 43 science parks with a less significant Output Position, the measures in the Flows of Knowledge dimension seem to be less relevant. It should be noted here that the flow-related parameter can fluctuate during different time zones.

Interestingly, science parks in Southern China outperform those in Northern China; therefore, Southern versus Northern locations are divided into two groups for more detailed investigation in the following discussion.

In order to determine the general pattern of these 53 sample science parks in the three dimensions, two tables are provided that chart their positions in the relevant directions. As shown in Table 3.4, the Current Input Status values of the sample science parks converge more significantly than the values in the other two dimensions. This input-related measure is used in the vertical direction, while other two directions can be contrasted in the horizontal directions.

These findings indicate that Zhongguancun Science Park in Beijing stands at the top of the ecological niche, while Zhangjiang (Shanghai), Chengdu, Shenzhen, Hangzhou, Xi'an, Wuhan Donghu, Hefei, Tianjin, Guangzhou, Changsha, and others[3] make up the top 14 science parks (refer to some of these sample science parks in Figures 3.3 and 3.4, located in the upper right range, above the average in both dimensions). However, there are variances and differences among these sample parks along the three-dimensional measures. Tables 3.5 and 3.6 provide more detailed information on the typical city-based science parks in terms of the three-dimensional evaluated position. In order to contrast the differences and similarities, only those cities with a positive

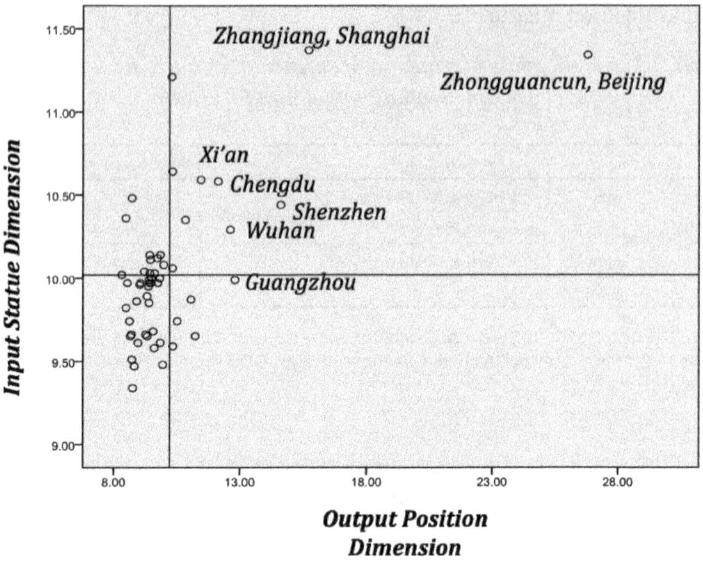

Note: The benchmark line is defined as the average value of all samples on that dimension.

Figure 3.3 *Evaluation results for the innovation ecosystem of science parks (NHTZs) in China: input vs. output dimension*

position in Output Position (Table 3.5) and Flows of Knowledge (Table 3.6) are listed in these two tables.

Table 3.6 *Results on ranking of science park cities under innovation ecosystem evaluation – Flows of Knowledge*

Windows		Northern China	Southern China
Flow Dimension +	Input status +A	Beijing, Xi'an, Zhengzhou, Jinan.	Shanghai, Hangzhou, Chengdu, Wuhan, Shenzhen, Hefei
	Input status –A	Shijiazhuang, Dalian, Tianjin, Lanzhou	Guangzhou, Chongqing

Note: The benchmark line is defined as the average value of all samples on that dimension, and +A and –A indicates respectively the positions of the related samples above or under the average lines.

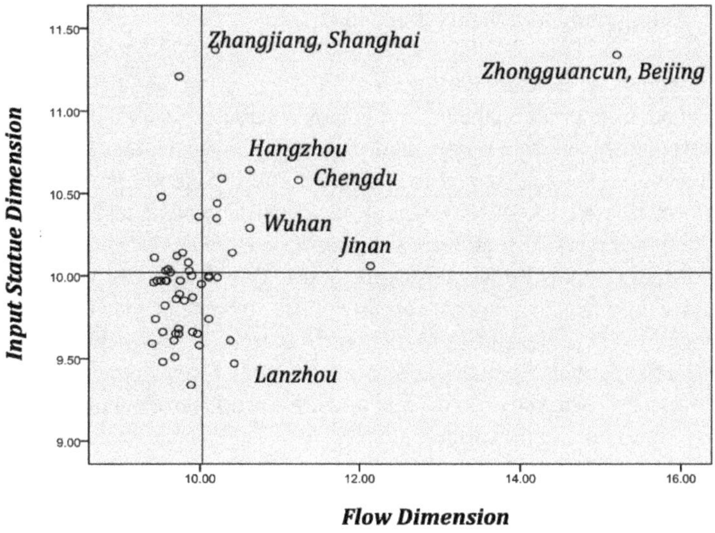

Note: The benchmark line is defined as the average value of all samples on that dimension.

Figure 3.4 *Evaluation results for the innovation ecosystem of science parks (NHTZs) in China: Input vs. flow dimension*

Based on the results of the empirical analysis, we can see that the comprehensive level of the innovative ecosystem of each scientific park is different in terms of Flows of Knowledge dimensions. However, we also note that such differences vary from year to year, indicating that such measures are significantly dynamic. Basically, the top 12–16 city-based science parks are essential locations that host important innovation in China. This evaluation also shows fewer differences between coastal and inland cities, but greater differences among northern and southern cities; these findings may indicate the influences of cultural and market environmental conditions, together with local economic development, on those science parks. The main stimulus of local economy development, along with important social and community factors, may play a crucial role in regional innovation, which will also be reflected in local science parks.

5. TYPICAL CASES OF SCIENCE PARKS IN CHINA

5.1 Zhongguancun Science Park in Beijing

The Zhongguancun Science Park (ZGC-SP) is located in Beijing, the capital of China and an international city, and is thus located close to high-end innovation resources, with high numbers of pioneering high-tech talents available from universities and advanced research institutes. Science parks such as this one, which are backed by resources, have six main advantages. (1) They have greater numbers of high-tech and start-up companies, such as Lenovo, Baidu, Eastern Capital, Yonyou Software, and so on, which usually have their own unique intellectual property resources. (2) They have greater numbers of advanced R&D centers from MNEs, such as from Intel, Microsoft, IBM, AMD, Oracle, Nokia, Siemens, Ericsson, Fujitsu, ABB, French Telecom, NEC, and so on. Naturally, Beijing is already a world-level innovation hub receiving resources from various sources. (3) They have access to more universities and national labs – in this case, to 32 prestigious universities, including Tsinghua University and Peking University, 206 key S&T institutes, 112 national key labs, 95 national engineering (technology) research institutes, and 38 national engineering labs. (4) They have access to greater numbers of advanced talents in the academic and high-tech business fields – in this case, to 591 national academicians from the Chinese Academy of Sciences and the Chinese Academy of Engineering, which represent about 40 percent of the total number across China; 1.59 million high-tech firm employees, including 172,000 PhDs and master degree graduates; and 16,000 overseas returned scholars with some 6000 start-ups (accumulated numbers). (5) They have access to more S&T-oriented venture capitals and financing funds, such as various S&T banks, angel funds, venture funds, start-up foundations, credit financing brokers, intellectual property brokers, industrial property transfer brokers, and so on. (6) Finally, they have a strong culture for entrepreneurial motivations. These advantages provide ZGC-SP with a unique position in terms of input, output, and flows of innovation within an innovation ecosystem framework.

In 2009, ZGC-SP became the first national innovation model zone (also known as an innovation demonstration zone), with a great deal of policy novelties, including equity (stock) incentives and S&T financing reforms. In the following year, 2010, the "1+6" policy series was approved in order to transition ZGC-SP into an innovative platform, especially in terms of attracting talents, technology transfer, resource restructuring, and industry development. From the innovation ecosystem perspective, the dynamic flows of talents, information, and value creation were highly encouraged and greatly speeded up, turning ZGC-SP into a shining model for other science parks that were established afterwards.

Tracing back along the development route of ZGC-SP reveals that this active transformation story can be divided into four periods.

The start period: "Electronic Street" (January 1983–April 1988)

Zhongguancun was originally a street in the north of Beijing that was full of electronic shops, mostly privately or collectively owned. It was exactly this type of ownership within an active electronic market that resulted in a large number of businesspeople or entrepreneurs with a technology background from originally publicly owned research institutes nearby (primarily from the institutes of the Chinese Academy of Sciences) establishing themselves through so-called "Xia Hai" – which literally means "going to the sea" and refers to "engaging in free yet risky start-up business" – and thus temporarily or permanently leaving state-owned entities.

The developmental and experimental period (May 1988–May 1999)

In 1988, based on these smaller companies with electronic shops, the Beijing New Technology Industrial Development and Experiment Zone was approved and established, and the "Five Parks in One Zone" initiative was formed in the following year.

The growing period: the Zhongguancun Science & Technology Park (June 1999–February 2009)

In 1999, the Administration Committee of the Zhongguancun Science & Technology Park (ZSTP) was formed based on the original administrators for the Zhongguancun area. This newly formed governing body covered 10 parks, called the "10 Parks in One Zone" initiative.

The mature period: the National Endogenous Innovation Demonstration Zone (March 2009 to the present)

Since it was approved in 2009 and revised in 2012, the newly upgraded National Endogenous Innovation Demonstration Zone (which is also the first National High-Tech Industrial Development Zone) has been a space to host 16 parks.

With such a unique development route and unmatched position, the ZGC-SP has numerous achievements, and thus ranks as the top science park in China. The total revenue from this zone reached 3 trillion RMB in 2013, and showed an annual 20 percent growth rate on average for six years in a row. The income from advanced services accounts for one third of this revenue. The major high-tech industries in ZGC-SP include electronic and information, environmental protection, advanced manufacturing, new energy, biopharmaceuticals, and new materials. Among these, information and communication technology (ICT; both electronic and information) has traditionally been the leading sector in ZGC-SP. Another significant face of ZGC-SP is its active entrepreneurial firms and start-ups, which are backed by a tremendous volume of educational capacity and human resources. The usual ratio of newly established entrepreneurial firms to the total number of such firms in China is about 25 percent, with around 16 billion RMB (data from 2012) in entrepreneurship investment. There are also science parks based on top-ranked universities (14 in 2012, about 15 percent of total university-run science parks in the country) and national S&T incubators (28, accounting for 6.5 percent of the whole). With these tremendous innovation resources, ZGC-SP has developed at a marvelous speed and scope. In 2019, the total revenue of high-tech firms from ZGC-SP reached 6.6 trillion RMB, with more than 30 percent average annual growth continually for the past 32 years.

5.2 Zhangjiang Science Park in Shanghai

The Zhangjiang Science Park was established in Shanghai in 1992, and has a similar volume of resources as Zhongguancun in Beijing. This example is another moving story of Chinese science parks. Its knowledge and information support conditions are similar to those of the ZGC-SP, and include 43 prestigious universities, more than 50 national research institutes, 34 national key labs, and 31 national engineering research centers. Shanghai is also an innovation hub and attracts many technical talents. In 2012, the revenue from the high-tech firms in Zhangjiang reached 1.9 trillion RMB, with an export value of 57.5 billion USD.

The unique advantage of Zhangjiang is that it is easily accessible to the international market and possesses flexible financing facilities. There are diversified channels and tools to choose from for investment and financing, such as the Shanghai Equity Exchange Center and S&T banks, which include more than 10 financial guarantee organizations and 150 investment banks for start-ups. Due to flexible local policies, heavy investment from around 2000 domestic and overseas high-tech companies and MNEs was directed to Zhangjiang, including the Semiconductor Manufacturing International Corporation (SMIC), Roche Group, Pfizer, and AMD. This has provided Zhangjiang in Shanghai with a unique position for importing and transferring overseas technologies. In fact, one of the major differences between Zhangjiang in Shanghai and Zhongguancun in Beijing is that the former has closer ties with international high-tech multinational companies and fewer policy operations, while the latter has more linkages to domestic universities and national research institutes, and both show stronger policy innovations. Today, Zhangjiang has been transferring from "Parks" to "Cities", facilitating more dynamic innovation centers and advanced manufacturing based particularly on the three: integrated circuits (more than some 200 firms), biopharmaceuticals (more than 80 billion RMB revenues), and artificial intelligence (AI island being developed since 2018).

It should be noted that during 2006, the Torch Center from the Ministry of Science and Technology of China announced an action plan for six national science parks to be pilot world-level high-tech parks, including ZGC-SP, ZJ-SP (Zhangjiang), Shenzhen, Wuhan-Donghu, Xi'an, and Chengdu, and added another four (Hangzhou, Suzhou Industrial Park, Hefei, and Guangzhou) during 2015 and 2016. Altogether ten model world-level parks were to be further developed in China.

In 2019, as significant output, 169 national science parks in China operated with a revenue totaling 38.3 trillion RMB and production value of 12.2 trillion RMB, equivalent to 12.3 percent of total GDP nationwide. In the meantime, these parks produced 37.5 percent of granted patents, and 44.7 percent of Chinese PCT patenting files in China.

6. CONCLUSIONS AND IMPLICATIONS

After conducting a thorough analysis of 53 typical science parks in China from the perspective of the innovation ecosystem, we find that these science parks, which were set up relatively early, play vital roles in leading faster development of various high-tech industries in China. However, these science parks have developed in diversified ways. A strongly contrasting situation exists between market-driven and policy-driven cases in China, in terms of the efficiency and dynamic nature of the associated science parks in China. Typical science parks are primarily driven by resources backed by government policy; however, the nature of the development and the major players involved vary among different sample locations and in different time periods. The origins of science parks in several important cities in China were free-market oriented, represented by the Zhongguancun case in Beijing. Policy resources are then significant means of support. Interestingly, due to the different natures of the cities and regions these science parks are located in, the innovation output can be extremely diverse. This finding can be explained in part by the diversified geographic concentration of universities and research institutes (i.e., talent resources) and in part by local entrepreneurial willingness (i.e., a supportive environment, risk-taking business culture, and active market economies). Aside from those located in very special large cities such as Beijing and Shanghai, it seems that science parks in Southern China are more active than those in northern cities. In general, even when input resources are similar, the innovation output can be significantly diverse.

When considering our proposed perspectives of the innovation ecosystem, we believe that this diversity adds value to the analysis. Key aspects of our analysis include the perspectives that were used to examine the dynamic nature of the system (i.e., the movement of factors inside science parks and within the outside market), or the so-called resource flows, which are reflected by the three dimensions measured in this study. We find that the 53 science parks are rather similar in terms of Current Input Status, but differ significantly in their Output Position dimension, and less significantly in their Flow dimension. This finding indicates that innovation efficiency varies greatly among the studied science parks, and implies that the Flow dimension is an important measure for investigating the operation of science parks. However, in this chapter, the level of the Flow dimension was shown to fluctuate across different time spans. This is particularly true in well-running science parks, such as the top 10 parks examined in this study, making them important case studies for further research. More details in a mixed-method study would be helpful, in terms of both the influence of these initial science parks on the setting up of later science parks, and the function of innovation policies in stimulating science parks.

ACKNOWLEDGMENTS

The authors of this chapter would like to thank the anonymous reviewers' valuable comments and suggestions, and the NSFC for the relevant research grant (No. 71941027).

NOTES

1. National-level science parks in China are formally named National High- and New-Technology Industrial Development Zones (NHNTIDZs). Typically located in important cities and approved by the State Council of China, NHNTIDZs can be considered to be comparable to science parks in Europe and North America. However, for clarity and to improve readability, NHNTIDZs will be referred to as "science parks" throughout this chapter.
2. During that time, the "high-tech" policy concept was defined as technologies covering micro-electronics, electronic and information technologies, space science and aeronautic and astronautic technologies, material science and new material technologies, optical-electronics and optic-electronic-mechanical integrated technology, life science and biotechnologies, energy science and new energy resources, high-efficiency energy-saving technologies, ecological science and environmental-protection technologies, earth science and marine engineering technologies, fundamental material science and emission technologies, pharmaceutical science and biopharmaceutical technologies, and other new techniques and technologies for upgrading traditional industries.
3. It should be noted here that the names of science parks in China vary from city to city; some parks are directly named after the local city, such as Chengdu Science

Park, Xi'an Science Park, and so on, while others are named after a particular location in the city, and these names then become famous, such as Zhongguancun Science Park (Beijing), Zhangjiang Science Park (Shanghai), Donghu Science Park (Wuhan), and so on. The authors of this chapter use the names taken directly from the formal statistical yearbook.

REFERENCES

Chen, W. (2014), *The Five Typical Patterns of China's High Tech Development Zones*, accessed 03 February 2017 at http://chanye.focus.cn/news/2014-09-01/5472570.html.

Chen, Y., and Z. Ouyang (1996), 'Design for an appraisal and evaluation index system of national high-tech zones', *Scientific Research Management*, **6**, 31–35. (In Chinese)

Du, H. (2012), 'Analysis on the influence factors of the innovative capacity of scientific parks on the basis of a dynamical system model', *Scientific Management Research*, **2**, 9–12. (In Chinese)

Liu, Y. (2010), *Evaluation on the Development Status of Scientific Parks in China on the Basis of the Innovation Perspective*, PhD dissertation, Hunan University. (In Chinese)

Ma, T., and C. Huang (2009), 'Dimension reduction and evaluation of a regional planning index system with the principal component analysis method', *Sci-Tech Information Development and Economy*, **29**, 125–127. (In Chinese)

Miao, H., and L. Huang (2007), 'Primary study on the health of an innovative ecosystem of regional technology', *Technological Management Research*, **11**, 101–103. (In Chinese)

Pang, Y., Z. Liu, and S. Jiang (2009), 'Comparative study on high- and new-technology industrial development zones in China', *Scientific and Technological Progress and Countermeasures*, **3**, 68–71. (In Chinese)

PCAST (2003), *Sustaining the Nation's Innovation Ecosystems: Information Technology Manufacturing and Competitiveness*, accessed 03 February 2017 at https://www.medicalmodsim.com/file/pcast-04-itreport.pdf.

Rishikesha, K. (2011), 'Silicon Valley to India: Build an innovation ecosystem and good thinking will come', *Ivey Business Journal*, **10**, 55–60.

Sun, H. (2007), *Building, Evaluation, and Secondary Innovation Study of the Innovative Ecosystem of Development Zones*, PhD dissertation, Tianjin University. (In Chinese)

Wang, P., and S. Liu (2009), 'Study on comprehensive evaluation for the independent innovative capability of high-tech zones on the basis of the entropy evaluation method', *Scientific and Technological Management Research*, **7**, 161–163. (In Chinese)

Wu, C., and T. Wei (2005), 'Study on the health of the development zone ecosystem – by taking Suzhou International Science Park as an example', *Sichuan Environment*, **6**, 54–58. (In Chinese)

Yan, M., K. Chien, L. Hong, and T. Yang (2018), 'Evaluating the collaborative ecosystem for an innovation-driven economy: A systems analysis and case study of science parks', *Sustainability*, **10**(3), 887.

Yu, L., Y. Pan, and Y. Wu (2009), 'Comparative study of a different objective weighting evaluation method in the evaluation of science and technology', *Science and Technology Management Research*, **7**, 148–150. (In Chinese)

4. The influence of patent cooperation network on growth of technology-based SMEs: an example of the pharmaceutical industry in China

Liying Wang, Jiamin Wang and Weijia Yu

1. INTRODUCTION

This chapter aims to analyze and classify the structure of the patent collaborative network, focusing on the Chinese technology-based SMEs in the pharmaceutical industry. Technology-based small and mid-sized enterprises can be considered KIE Ventures, or here technology-based SMEs, as also analyzed in Chapters 10 and 11. KIE ventures are an important carrier to speed up cultivating and developing the strategic emerging industries such as biomedicine, which are also of extreme importance and profound significance to the national economic growth and social progress. But a lack of innovation resources and weak innovation capabilities has always been an impenetrable bottleneck to their growth.

In a world of open innovation and Internet survival today, a mass of technology-based SMEs, by means of collaborative patent application, purchase, transfer or licensing and alliance, are gradually establishing full-fledged patent cooperation networks to acquire innovation resources and improve innovation capabilities. Therefore, patent cooperation has become an important form of cooperative innovation, and is showing a steadily rising scale, strength, coverage and density. Against the background of booming patent cooperation, the management and development of patent cooperation network (PCN) resources have become one of the important ways to break through the growth bottleneck for technology-based SMEs. Patent cooperation between technology-based SMEs and multiple innovation subjects is gradually spreading to relation proximity with social networks as the carrier. The extent and closeness of cooperation among various innovation subjects will affect the enterprises in their innovation resources acquisition and innovation capabilities enhancement. In reality, there is no lack of hollowed-out enterprises due to excessive dependence on external technologies from extensive cooperation; there are also enterprises trapped in a dilemma of technological rigidity due to repeated cooperation (Nathan and Kovoor-Misra, 2002; Zhang and Dang, 2009). Obviously, only by choosing and embedding themselves in a PCN that suits their growth can these SMEs truly improve their innovation performance. However, existing research is not deep enough on the enterprises' active construction and selection of different models of PCN, as well as setting up a coordination mechanism based on collaborative partnership to upgrade their innovation performance (Chesbrough et al., 2006; Schilling and Phelps, 2007; Chen et al., 2011). This chapter focuses upon the pharmaceutical industry, which we have also contrasted with the information and communication technology industry (Yang et al., 2019). Therefore, this chapter is motivated by the need for more objective patent cooperation data to construct a visualized network structure and carry out longitudinal study on network dynamic evolution, which makes an important entry point to learn how to improve technology-based SMEs' innovation performance under a network context.

2. LITERATURE REVIEW ON PATENT COOPERATION NETWORKS

2.1 The Definition and Construction of Patent Cooperation Networks (PCN)

With a gradually improved patent database and the development of the related analysis software worldwide, an innovation model of patent cooperation networks has gradually become a domestic and international research highlight, which is based on a patentee's cooperation information, inventor cooperation information, patent citations and reference information, and relationship with patentee etc. From a network perspective, it adopts a complex network theory (Burt, 1995) and social network analysis tools (such as UCINET, NETDRAW, PAJEK) to study the patent cooperation network between enterprises and other organizations. From the Web of Science database, the researcher has carried out literature retrieval on "Patent Network" from January 1994 to January 2015, focusing on the field of social science and economic management, with a total of 273 articles available. Judging from the number of publications during the past two decades as well as the number of citations each year, we can see that the patent network research has been a hot subject in the last five years. Our study made a further retrieval on "Patent Cooperation Network", and found that related research has grouped closely in the last ten years, and has been a hot topic for the last three years. Our study also makes classification of and analysis on the literature retrieval of the "Patent Cooperation Network". Related literature mainly centers on research fields like innovation networks, R&D networks, patent cooperation, knowledge transfer, industry clustering, industry–university–research cooperation, technology forecasting, etc. Among them, those using patent data or social networks analysis account for 85 percent, in which the researchers not only paid attention to the relevant information analysis of patent cooperation applicants, but also used multidimensional data such as citations to analyze the PCN and its impact on innovation performance. The researchers follow related research on the self-centered networks based on the enterprises' perspective, including technology-based SMEs' networks role (Franco and Haase, 2011), the impact of the patent cooperation on enterprise competition relations (Peck-hool, 2010; Chen et al., 2011; Murphy et al., 2013), and R&D cooperation networks structure (Arza and Lopez, 2011; Eslami et al., 2013; Cassi and Plunket, 2014). The object of study is not confined to cooperation networks between enterprises and universities, but also involves those between enterprises, and between enterprises and public organizations. By means of multidimensional exploration of patent cooperation application and patent citation data, the researcher further studies the network's effects on knowledge spillover and knowledge interactions (Romero de Pablos, 2011; Miguelez and Moreno, 2013). It indicates that the study of PCN is moving towards a direction based on the enterprises' perspective and is exploring the inner mechanism and promotional factors of the multidimensional network structure's impact on innovation performance. To sum up, this chapter defines PCN as a multidimensional complex network formed in the process of a technology-based SME–R&D cooperation, industry–university–research cooperation or technology transfer, during which the technology-based SMEs, by means of cooperation and application, purchase and transfer or cross-license patents.

PCN is divided and constructed mainly based on geographical, technological or social proximity. The specific classifications are shown in Table 4.1. It is common for research to focus on patent cooperation networks between crossing-border, inter-regional and inter-enterprises, which tend to identify a network's overall layout on the basis of geographic space. Studies focusing on networks of industry–university–research cooperation as well as inventor cooperation are normally constructed in accordance with the dissimilarities in cooperation objects. Regardless of whether it is constructed by geographical distribution or the differences between the cooperation objects, the PCN builds a relationship mainly dependent on patent cooperation application or patent citations, thus falling into the realm of research of patent application networks. Only a small proportion of research is geared to patent technology transfer networks. A technology alliance or a patent pool is a kind of patent cooperation network that is established based on a contractual relationship, epitomizing

Table 4.1 *The construction classification of PCNs*

Index Classification	Index Difference	Construction Classification	Reference
Geographical proximity	Regional difference	Crossing-border PCN Inter-regional PCN Inter-enterprises PCN	Lei et al. (2013); Paier and Scherngell (2011); Xiang et al. (2010); Liu et al. (2013); Ye and Yu (2013)
Technological proximity	The difference of technical cooperation models	Patent Cooperation Application Networks Patent Technology Transfer Networks	Beaudry and Schiffauerova (2011); Murphy et al. (2013)
	The difference of technology application model	Patent Alliance Patent Pool	Phelps (2010); Peck-hool (2010)
Social proximity	Cooperative objects difference	Industry–University–Research Patent Cooperation Networks Scientific Research Cooperation Networks Inventor Cooperation Networks	Arza and Lopez (2011); Bertrand-Cloodt et al. (2011); Luan et al. (2008); Ma et al. (2011); Liu et al. (2013)

the type of complicated networks to be formed by a combined relationship of patent cooperation application and patent technology transfer. In fact, research on the PCN model can draw on related research on cooperative innovation and expand further. For instance, Rothaermel and Deeds (2004), based on the different objectives of the three parties, such as enterprise, supplier and customers in cooperative innovation, divided it into explorative cooperative innovation and applied cooperative innovation, with each exerting various influence on an enterprise's innovation performance. Lam (2003) adopted case study methodology to attribute the cooperation innovation network of American multinationals to the centralized network, but classified the Japanese multinational innovation network as the decentralized network. After interviewing 46 high-tech companies in the same entrepreneurship network, Corsaro (2012) found that three different network allocation models, namely, skeptical, explorative and trusting models, can coexist in the same innovation network, and exert influence upon each other through the cross-border activities. These studies all provide positive insight to explore the formation of enterprise-centered PCNs. Considering differentiating patent cooperation purposes, width and depth, and the location of network resources, we can make an in-depth analysis on the formation of a patent cooperation subnetwork in an effort to generate more scientific validation in studying the impacts of network self-correlation on enterprise growth, as well as the endogenous factors of common subject characteristics and networks.

Table 4.2 *Comparison of different views on the impact of PCNs on innovation performance*

Views	Main Idea	Reference
Resource-based view	Patent cooperation is beneficial to integrating heterogeneous resources, enhancing the ability of the partners and exerting a positive effect on innovation performance growth	Chen and Guan (2009); Ozbugday and Brouwer (2012)
Evolutionary view	The impact of patent cooperation on innovation performance appears in an inverted U. Networks with too close or lack of cooperation show lower innovation performance than those with average cooperation intensity, with repeat cooperation even exerting negative impact	Bertrand-Cloodt et al. (2011); Tom and Ron (2012); Liu et al. (2013)
Ability view	Only by an interactive integration of the enterprise's ability with the external network's resources, can the enterprise expect real innovation development	Dovin and Gooderham (2008); Graf (2011); Graf and Krüger (2011); Zhang and Lang (2013)

2.2 Influence of PCN on Enterprise Growth

Although scholars have explored enterprise growth mechanism from different perspectives, fundamental factors that affect an enterprise's growth lie in the quality of its own resources, the interactivity with its external environment, its customer market adaptability and technological innovation advancement. The dynamic evolution of the PCN brings changes to the growth of enterprises that are embedded. Therefore, how to dynamically and effectively build, optimize and adjust PCN to realize a sustained corporate growth has increasingly attracted intensive research attention. However, the impact on an enterprise's innovation performance from PCN remains controversial. The existing research focuses on the three major classifications, as shown in Table 4.2.

Scholars with a resource-based view believed that patent cooperation was beneficial to integrate heterogeneous resources, and exerted a positive effect on innovation performance growth. For instance, Chen and Guan (2009) analyzed nine innovative countries and regional R&D cooperation networks with small-world properties, and pointed out that their shorter average path length and stronger small-world properties tended to lead to more innovative outputs. Study on Dutch manufacturing factors affecting industrial innovation between 1993 and 2007 indicated the increase of patent applications among enterprises has a significant impact on industrial innovation performance growth (Ozbugday and Brouwer, 2012). Scholars with a resource-based view paid more attention to the impact on innovation performance by static PCNs, but neglected the impact of such a network's dynamic evolution features.

Scholars holding an evolutionary view pointed out that the impact of patent cooperation on innovation performance appeared in an inverted U-shape. Networks with too close or lack of cooperation showed lower innovation performance than those with average cooperation intensity, with repeated cooperation even exerting negative impacts. For instance, a study by Beaudry and Schiffauerova (2011) of Canada's invention cooperation in nanotechnology revealed that repeated cooperation exerted a negative impact on patent output. Tom and Ron (2012) used patent cooperation application data to analyze the 270 service areas in the German electrical and electronic industry. The result showed that the intensity of regional cooperation had an inverted U-shaped impact on regional innovation performance, with regions of average cooperation intensity scoring higher in innovation performance than those of too close or lack of cooperation. Research on the PCN's knowledge diffusion factor of the integrated circuit industry revealed that the enterprise's network density was in negative correlation with its knowledge diffusion (Liu et al., 2013). Although scholars with evolutionary views have paid close attention to the impact of the dynamic PCN on innovation performance, they have not, however, revealed the internal process mechanism through which the evolution of the PCN influenced innovation performance.

Scholars with an ability view stressed that only by interactive integration of the enterprise's ability with its external network resources can the enterprise expect real innovation development. Dovin and Gooderham (2008) pointed out that network capability was inseparable from the improvement of enterprise performance. Research on German and French regional organizational innovation networks indicates the networks' gatekeeper influence on the organizational absorptive capacity (Graf, 2011). The study on the inventor cooperation network points out that the difference resulted from different levels of self-monitoring in the construction of networks (Zhang and Lang, 2013). In addition, the utilization opportunity would lead to the development of different knowledge innovation (Bertrand-Cloodt et al., 2011). From the ability view, scholars highlight the indirect impact of PCNs on innovation performance in order to achieve a more comprehensive understanding of the PCN's impact on the growth of enterprise innovation. In addition, a dynamic monitoring of the interaction of embedded networks' diversity and their enterprise behavior is required.

The above-mentioned views fully demonstrate the limitation of the direct impact of PCN upon the enterprise growth. Those scholars holding the view of network resources have paid attention to the effect of the vital role of the network's capability and internal resources integration on the performance of enterprise innovation and the constant interaction among the enterprises (Hagedoorn et al., 2006; Fang, 2011; Zhang and Dang, 2011). The scholars with the network evolution view believe that factors like network selection mechanism and network proximity all affect network evolution and its breakthrough from network inertia (Glückler, 2007; Cai and Pan, 2008). The scholars of network capacity hold that a PCN's effect on enterprise innovation performance is subject to the influence and regulations of factors like the enterprise network capability and absorptive capacity. Precisely these differences generate different growths and innovation performances. Still there are other scholars who point out that if the enterprise possesses strong network capability, it can achieve rapid improvement in technological power through the external network. But in the existing studies, enterprise behavior, an important characteristic variable, has yet to be incorporated satisfactorily into the network study model. On one hand, enterprises of different categories, size and growth stage tend to have drastic different behaviors and are affected by a multitude of factors. There is a lack of a consistent and feasible analysis framework. On the other hand, the existing social and economic complex network models based on individual selection are mainly the WS model of Duncan J. Watts and Steven Strogatz, and the BA model of Albert-Lászlό, but these fail to explain well the corresponding relationship between network growth rules and individual behavior choices. However, the PCN does not restrain itself to a collection of enterprises and institutions that contact each other in specific areas and share geographical proximity. It is more of a cooperation relationship among enterprise-centered outward expanding multiple subjects affected by both technology and social proximity. Therefore, the enterprise's cognition and choice of network resources play a significant role in a PCN's influence upon innovation performance. Research on the enterprise's growth should pay particular attention to the indirect impact mechanism by diversified PCNs' co-evolution on innovation performance. Focusing on the differentiation and initiatives of enterprise behaviors will be the next research hot spot in the relationship between PCN and enterprise growth.

2.3 Construction of Patent Cooperation Network Model and Hypotheses

The essence of PCN lies in the interactive innovation process of social network-based knowledge flow and resources integration, and especially in the knowledge increase in the cooperation network, which in turn can result in management upgrading and can provide the opportunity to uncover untapped resources. Therefore, the research on PCNs' influences on enterprise development can lead to a deeper understanding of the enterprise growth mechanism under a social networks context. Breaking away from the paradigm of studying the networks as a whole, as was done in previous studies, this research proceeds with the self-centered PCN, examines the structural differences of the PCN affecting the width and depth of the enterprise's access to resources, analyzes the inherent driving factor of the key ability in the PCN's impact upon enterprise growth, and offers technology-based SMEs a breakthrough path and growth plan along "relying on PCN-cultivating enterprise ability-promoting enterprise growth".

2.3.1 Theoretical assumptions on construction of PCN model

Contrary to past research that mainly focuses on the entire networks and categorization from the perspectives of geographical, technological or social proximity, this research starts from the structure of self-centered enterprise PCNs, based on the width and depth of the patent cooperation, carries out dual structure classification and multi-model construction of the network, and explores and analyzes its characteristics (Figure 4.1). For PCN model construction, this research refers to the research by Corsaro (2012). Regarding the interaction between self-centered networks and an enterprise's behavior and ability, this chapter divides technology-based SMEs PCN into two models as "explorative" and "exploitative". It plans to use characterizations like network scale, density and diversity to represent patent cooperation width, and use network relation intensity, node distance and centricity to indicate patent cooperation depth. Attempts will be made to enhance the patent cooperation width to build network resources of high heterogeneity, with an aim to define the network that acquires broad new external knowledge sources as an "explorative PCN". Efforts will also be made to expand the patent cooperation depth to build network resources of low heterogeneity, with an aim to define the network that makes deeper use of existing new external knowledge resources as an "exploitative PCN". The PCN with different width and depth combinations exerts different effects on the growth of technology-based SMEs. Based on the above analysis, this study puts forward the following hypothesis:

Hypothesis 1: The PCN's Model be Divided into Explorative and Exploitative.

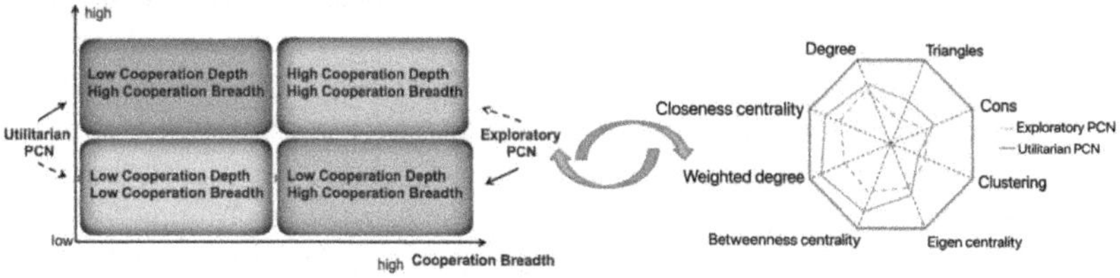

Figure 4.1 The model of PCN and its characteristics

3. METHODOLOGY: EXPLORATION AND VERIFICATION ANALYSIS OF PCN MODEL CONSTRUCTION

Taking the pharmaceutical industry as an example, this research selects the pharmaceutical technology-based SMEs to be listed respectively in Main Board, SME Board and GEM Board as the research target. The granted invention patent data are derived from China's State Intellectual Property Office (SIPO) patent database. In view of their highest technical content and creation level, this research is only limited to invention patents for this case study. The corresponding cooperative patent information of the listed pharmaceutical companies is available from the SIPO patent database, which contains two or more patent applicants, and with one from a listed pharmaceutical company. All the relevant information has been input into an Excel spreadsheet in a unified format, including the date of filing, classification number, inventors, patent holder and patent document data. The timespan of 2000–2014 was chosen for the research samples. After data filtering and purification, a total of 125 patent applicants, 817 granted cooperative patent applications and finally 389 indirect cooperation objectives were made available.

The research summarizes the 389 cooperative invention patents of technology-based SMEs, extracts the cooperative patent applicant/s, and uses Gephi software to map out the overall network topology, taking companies as nodes and inter-company patent cooperation as links (Figure 4.2). An analysis of the scale of the whole network yields 300 nodes and 389 links. Further analysis is carried out on its subnetwork and, as the research indicates, the largest among them has 97 nodes, accounting for 32 percent of the whole network; as well as 210 links, accounting for 53 percent of the whole network. It constitutes the largest subnetwork in the current entire patent network. Therefore, the subnetwork is selected as the sample for analysis, which includes a total of 97 cooperative patent applicant enterprises from the 210 links (patent cooperation objectives) as seen in Figure 4.3.

In order to study the patent cooperation network model of pharmaceutical enterprises, the research further constructs the egocentric network of each cooperative subject of the patent cooperation network, and has acquired an eight index vector data of the corresponding network, including node degree, center proximity, intermediate centricity, characteristic eigenvector centrality, weighted degree, clustering coefficient, triangle number and structure holes. Using SPSS16.0 statistical software, this research carries out explorative factor analysis on the sample's index vectors of each egocentric network, and shows that the KMO index is 0.674 and the Bartlett sphericity test registers as significant, indicating that the patent cooperation network featured a two-dimensional

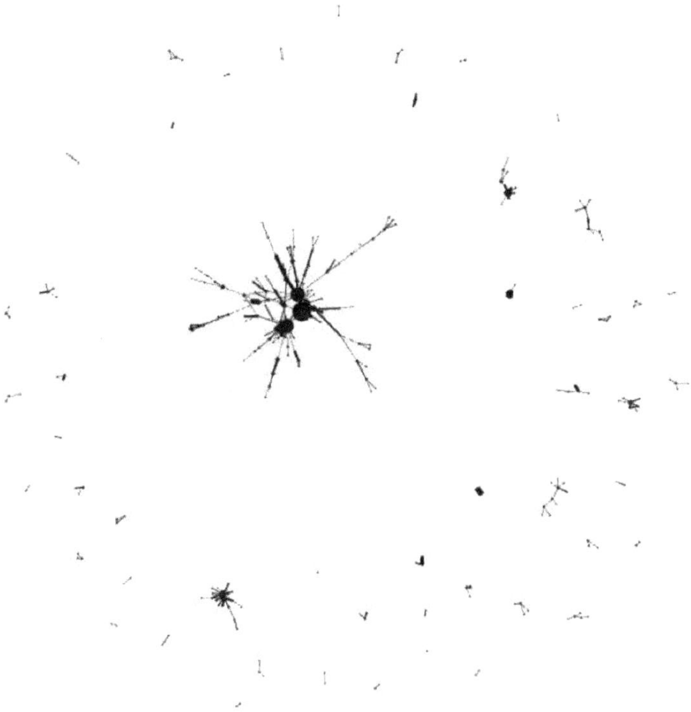

Figure 4.2 *Topology of the entire PCN*

structure. Among them, the explained variance is 70.403 percent and the reliability coefficient is 0.84, which shows that the patent cooperation network of pharmaceutical technology-based SMEs features a two-dimensional structure. Explorative factor analysis results show the existence of two types of factors. Factor 1 contains the four indicators of weighted degree, center proximity, intermediate centricity and characteristic eigenvector centrality, which mainly reflect the intensity of the link between nodes, emphasizing the frequency and depth in patent cooperation, and thus in line with the hypothesized definition of the exploitative patent cooperation network. Factor 2 contains the four indicators of node degree, clustering coefficient, triangle number and structure hole that reflect the number of connected nodes in the network and measure their importance, highlighting the width of the enterprise patent cooperation, and the number of cooperative projects between enterprises, in line with the hypothesized definition of the explorative patent cooperation network.

The research further takes the indicator of "weighted degree" to measure the depth of a patent cooperation network and of "nodding degree" to measure its

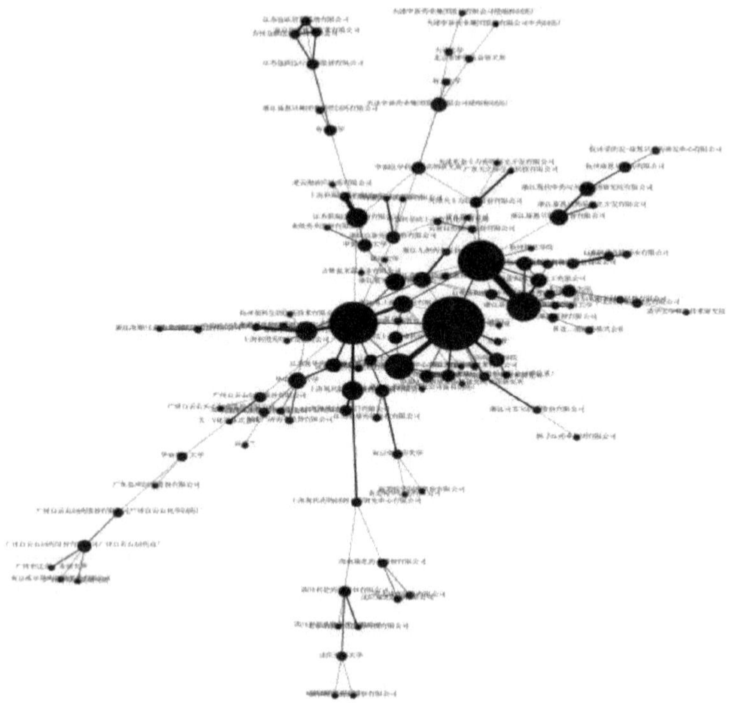

Figure 4.3 *Topology of the largest subnetwork of the PCN*

width. The relationship of the width and depth is mapped out on the coordinate axis, and a dividing line is established based on average width and depth value. So, technology-based SMEs are divided into four different areas (Figure 4.4). In the low cooperation width area, more enterprises are distributed in the low cooperation depth area, while some are in the high cooperation depth area. Based on the above observation, this type of patent cooperation network is defined as an "exploitative patent cooperation network". In the area of high cooperation width, most enterprises are in the high cooperation depth area, while some are in the low cooperation depth area. Based on the above observation, this type of patent cooperation network is defined as an "explorative patent cooperation network". The topological structure characteristics indicators of the explorative patent cooperation network are superior to those of the exploitative type, which shows the patent cooperation network of pharmaceutical technology-based SMEs tends to evolve towards an explorative network of high cooperation width and depth, revealing a wider range and more diversified partnership. But there still exist issues of low frequency and lack of depth. Thus, the technology-based SMEs' patent cooperation network displays the two features of explorative and exploitative and verifies the existence of Hypothesis 1.

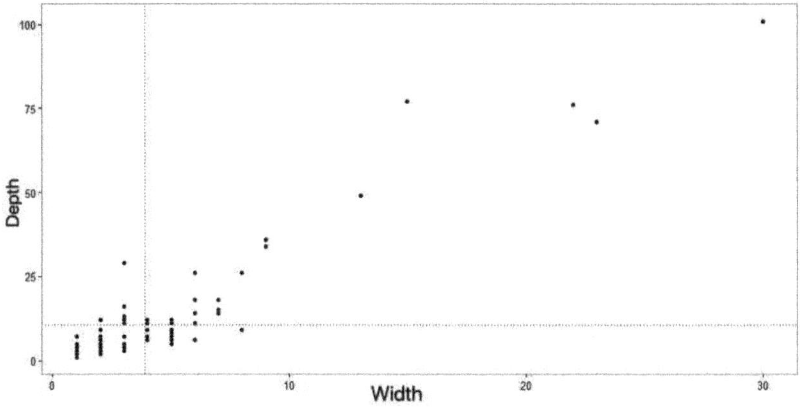

Figure 4.4 *PCN structure models based on patent cooperation width and depth*

4. ANALYSIS OF THE INFLUENCE MECHANISM OF PCN ON SMES

Enterprise growth theory is subject to the influences of classical economics, new classical economics, new institutional economics, Post-Keynesianism and Penrose's (1995) *Theory of the Growth of the Firm*. These researches cover wide areas, including basic connotations like enterprise behavior, growth, organizational structure and management, etc. As a result, what is known as the "Jungle Phenomenon" emerges in enterprise growth theory from which no unified theory system has been formed so far. This research attempts to look at the enterprise growth from the perspective of integration of internal ability and external network resources, and proposes that it is a process under constant influences and intervention from the enterprise's internal ability, one of constant exploring, integrating and utilizing external resources, improving internal capacity, and finally attaining sustainable growth. For the technology-based SMEs' growth mechanism there are numerous expositions, and scholars have tried to study the diversified factors of influence from different perspectives. To sum up, the following 11 factors are the most prominent ones: entrepreneurs (including management ability and entrepreneurship), governance structure, manpower, finance and accounting, production operations, product and market, R&D, corporate culture, internal and external information exchange, clustering and incubation, and external competitive environment.

In sum, the key factors influencing the growth of technology-based SMEs' growth are concentrated in the quality of resources, interaction with the external environment, customer market adaptability and the advancement of technology innovation. The performance of technological creation, invention and patent are closely drawn to the enterprise's technological innovation ability. The construction of a PCN is not only conducive to improving the quantity and quality of the enterprise's patent, but also offers the opportunities and pathways to find new resources. Therefore, facing an open network competition environment, dynamic and effective building, optimizing and adjusting the PCN to realize the sustained growth of technology-based SMEs is undoubtedly the research focus. Based on the above analysis, this research puts forward the following hypotheses:

Hypothesis 2: Explorative PCNs have a significant impact on technology-based SMEs' growth.

Hypothesis 3: Exploitative PCNs have a significant impact on technology-based SMEs' growth.

4.1 Analysis on the Influence Mechanism of PCNs and Exploration of their Development Path

Before making regression analysis of patent cooperation network and company innovation performance, this research first tests the reliability and validity of the two network models. Using SPSS software for a reliability of data test, it finds that the internal consistency coefficient (Cronbach-Alpha) is above 0.75, indicating the data is quite reliable. At the same time, with AMOS software, it carries out confirmatory factor analysis to test the structure validity. Through the test, the goodness of fit index is at: $\chi^2 = 140.94$, RMSEA = 0.08, RMR = 0.024, NFI = 0.94, NNFI = 0.93, CFI = 0.92. It hints that the patent cooperation network model data has good structural validity. Afterwards factors of the two models were given correlation analysis with a result showing a weak significantly positive correlation between the two network models and innovation performance, and the correlation coefficient below 0.7, within an acceptable range. Therefore, this research proceeds to make regression analysis on the patent cooperation network and enterprise innovation performance. In this analysis, the two factors from explorative factor analysis of network indicators are independent variables. The number of granted invention patents

Table 4.3 *Positive results of different network models of impact on technology-based SMEs innovation performance*

Variables	Coefficient	Exploitative type	Explorative type
	6.1344*	0.1966**	0.3156***

Note: Standard errors in parentheses: $*p < 0.05$, $**p < 0.01$, $***p < 0.001$

is a dependent variable. The three controllable variables are enterprise nature, scale and industry. The Poisson method is adopted to do a regression analysis. The outcome reveals that both types of network models exert significant positive effect on technology-based SMEs' innovation performance (Table 4.3), thus, Hypotheses 2 and 3 are proven. At the same time, the exploitative network model is more effective in intermediate centricity than that of the explorative type, which indicates that in the exploitative network model scenario, technology-based SMEs enjoy obvious advantages in their role of resources and information transfer and liaison, and the role functions more significantly in promoting company innovation performance than that of the explorative type. While the explorative model exhibits stronger influence in terms of weighted degree and structural holes on innovation performance, indicating that for enterprises in the exploring network model, a broad cooperation base and a key position in the network bring more advantages in promoting innovation performance. In general, the explorative network model produces a more significant impact on the enterprise innovation performance and the exploitative type is somewhat weaker in this regard.

5. DISCUSSION OF RESULTS

This chapter has argued that a key issue to be resolved is how to define and construct the different models of PCN. Based on the cooperative filing of patents by pharmaceutical technology-based SMEs, this chapter identifies the exploitative and explorative patent cooperation networks. In the latter mode, technology-based SMEs feature a high cooperation width, i.e. relatively more partners in invention patent filing. This kind of enterprise often has broad social relations, and is linked with multiple development partners. For instance, companies like Jiangsu Kanion Pharmaceutical Co., Ltd. and Zhejiang Zhenyuan Pharmaceutical Co., Ltd. have more than five R&D partners, but the number of patents resulting from cooperation with each partner is relatively small, only reaching 11 and 9 respectively; while technology-based SMEs in an exploitative patent cooperation network mode feature a low cooperation width, i.e. with fewer invention patent filing partners, and cooperation is carried out only between those with a foundation of cooperation. For instance, although companies like Shanghai Hengrui Pharmaceutical Co., Ltd. and Suzhou Yuyue Medical Technology Co., Ltd. have only three institutional partners, the number of their cooperations has reached 29 and 16 respectively.

This chapter has conducted quantitative research on the direct impact of multiple PCNs on technology-based SMEs' growth via patent measurement and social network analysis, exploring different types of PCN influence on firm growth. Considering technology-based SMEs' growth, an explorative patent cooperation network generates a bigger boost than that of the exploitative type, because the pharmaceutical industry has a wealth of patent output, and pharmaceutical R&D depends more heavily on technology. Hence open innovation is more suitable for technology-based SMEs engaged in pharmaceutical R&D. R&D collaboration with research institutions and personnel both at home and abroad provides rich development opportunities. For companies with high cooperation width but low depth in the explorative patent cooperation network, their management resources allocation is so dispersed that they tend to depend excessively on external technology. Such enterprises should, while keeping a high cooperation width, enhance the depth and make full use of the technological resource sharing between enterprises, strengthen the connection between the existing partners, and lay a good cooperative R&D foundation to promote their growth. At the same time, it is necessary to strengthen the enterprises' internal management of patent strategy. An exploitative patent cooperation network also, to some extent, boosts an enterprise's innovation performance, but with too low patent cooperation width and too high depth, enterprises are confined to innovation of the existing paradigm, and thus are unable to fundamentally tackle the full potential of the patent cooperation network. So those with low cooperation breadth but high depth in an exploitative patent cooperation network should, while maintaining high depth, engage in collaboration with research institutions, colleges and businesses to accumulate network resources for more valuable patent output. Enterprises with both low cooperation width and depth in the exploitative patent cooperation network should strengthen the extent of their involvement in both explorative and exploitative patent cooperation networks, expand cooperation with other enterprises and increase the frequency, and gradually transit themselves to patent cooperation network enterprises of high cooperation width and depth, so as to achieve the goal of accelerated development.

We acknowledge the limitation of this research, including the definition of PCNs and data. The definition of PCNs is currently only based on data from cooperative filing of invention patents. Patent cooperation can also be defined as technology transfer, licensing and patent index. Future research may further expand the screening scope of the PCN. In addition, studies based on the patent data may reflect the enterprise's innovation performance, but only in one dimension. In addition, future research could combine patent data with market value data, and investigate the impact on enterprise innovation performance from both explorative and exploitative PCNs and their evolutionary mechanism.

ACKNOWLEDGMENT

The chapter was written under the support of National Planning Office of Philosophy and Social Key Project (16AGL001), and Zhejiang Province Soft Science Key Project (2015C25040). Then the chapter had support from Zhejiang Province Natural Science Fund Project (LY16G020022) and Zhejiang Province Philosophy and Social Science Research Base "Technology Innovation and Internationalization of Enterprises", and from the Collaborative Innovation Center of Micro, Small and Medium Enterprises' Transformation and Upgrading, and the key innovation team of Zhejiang University of Technology.

REFERENCES

Arza, V. and A. Lopez (2011), 'Firms' linkages with public research organisations in Argentina: Drivers, perceptions and behaviours', *Technovation*, **31**(8), 384–400.

Beaudry, C. and A. Schiffauerova (2011), 'Impacts of collaboration and network indicators on patent quality: The case of Canadian nanotechnology innovation', *European Management Journal*, **29**(5), 362–76.

Bertrand-Cloodt, D., J. Hagedoorn and K. H. Van (2011), 'The strength of R&D network ties in high-tech sectors: A multi-dimensional analysis of the effects of tie strength on innovation performance', *Technology Analysis and Strategic Management*, **21**(10), 1015–30.

Burt, R. S. (1995), *Structural Holes: The Social Structure of Competition*, Cambridge, MA: Harvard University Press.

Cai, N. and S. Pan (2008), 'The coupling of network relationship strength and enterprise technology innovation model and its co evolution: In the technical innovation network Hisun as an example', *China Industrial Economics* (in Chinese), **4**, 137–44.

Cassi, J. and A. Plunket (2014), 'Proximity, network formation and inventive performance: In search of the proximity paradox', *Annals of Regional Science*, **53**(2), 395–422.

Chen, J., Z. Jiang and Y. Chen (2011), 'Research on the influencing factors of enterprise knowledge absorptive capacity from the perspective of open innovation', *Journal of Zhejiang University (Humanities and Social Sciences)* (in Chinese), **41**(5), 71–82.

Chen, Z. and J. Guan (2009), 'The influence of small world of cooperation network on innovation performance', *Chinese Journal of Management Science* (in Chinese), **17**(3), 115–20.

Chesbrough, H., W. Vanhaverbeke and J. West (2006), *Open Innovation: Researching a New Paradigm*, Oxford, UK: Oxford University Press.

Corsaro, D. (2012), 'The impact of network configurations on value constellations in business markets: The case of an innovation network', *Industrial Marketing Management*, **41**(1), 54–67.

Dovin, E. and P. N. Gooderham (2008), 'Dynamic capabilities as antecedents of the scope of related diversification: The case of small firm accountancy practices', *Strategic Management Journal*, **29**(8), 841–57.

Eslami, H., A. Ebadi and A. Schiffauerova (2013), 'Effect of collaboration network structure on knowledge creation and technological performance: The case of biotechnology in Canada', *Scientometrics*, **97**(1), 99–119.

Fang, G. (2011), 'Research on network capability structure and its effect on enterprise innovation performance', *Studies in Science of Science* (in Chinese), **29**(3), 461–70.

Franco, M. and H. Haase (2011), 'The role of networks for small technology-based firms', *Proceedings of the 6th European Conference on Innovation and Entrepreneurship, ECIE2011*, Academic Conferences Limited, 309.

Glückler, J. (2007), 'Economic geography and the evolution of networks', *Journal of Economic Geography*, **7**(5), 619–34.

Graf, H. (2011), 'Gatekeepers in regional networks of innovation', *Cambridge Journal of Economics*, **35**(1), 173–98.

Graf, H. and J. Krüger (2011), 'The performance of gatekeepers in innovator networks', *Industry and Innovation*, **18**(1), 69–88.

Hagedoorn J., N., Roijakkers and H. Kranenburg (2006), 'Interfirm R&D networks: The importance of strategic network capabilities for high-tech partnership formation', *British Journal of Management*, **17**(1), 39–53.

Lam, A. (2003), 'Organizational learning in multinationals: R&D networks of Japanese and US MNEs in the UK', *Journal of Management Studies*, **40**(3), 673–703.

Lei, X., Z. Zhao, X. Zhang, D. Chen, M. Huang, J. Zheng, R. Liu, J. Zhang and Y. Zhao (2013), 'Technological collaboration patterns in solar cell industry based on patent inventors and assignees analysis', *Scientometrics*, **96**(2), 427–41.

Liu, F., L. Liu and R. Ma (2013), 'Analysis of the evolution of scientific research cooperation network based on the 973 Projects', *Science of Science and Management of S.&T.* (in Chinese), **34**(6), 14–21.

Luan, C., X. Wang and H. Hou (2008), 'Evolution of inventor collaboration network and its impact on technology invention productivity', *Science of Science and Management of S.&T.* (in Chinese), **3**, 28–30.

Ma, Y., F. Liu and Y. Sun (2011), 'University enterprise cooperation network structure and its effect on enterprise innovation output', *R&D Management* (in Chinese), **23**(6), 1–7.

Miguelez, E. and R. Moreno (2013), 'Do labour mobility and technological collaborations foster geographical knowledge diffusion? The case of European regions', *Growth and Change*, **44**(2), 321–54.

Murphy, K. J., G. Elias and H. Jaffer (2013), 'A study of inventiveness among society of interventional radiology members and the impact of their social networks', *Journal of Vascular and Interventional Radiology*, **24**(7), 931–37.

Nathan, M. L. and S. Kovoor-Misra (2002), 'No pain, yet gains: Vicarious organizational learning from crises in an interorganizational field', *Journal of Applied Behavioral Science Arlington*, **38**(2), 245–66.

Ozbugday, F. C. and E. Brouwer (2012), 'Competition law, networks and innovation', *Applied Economics Letters*, **19**(8), 775–78.

Paier, M. and T. Scherngell (2011), 'Determinants of collaboration in European R&D networks: Empirical evidence from a discrete choice model', *Industry and Innovation*, **18**(1), 89–104.

Peck-hool, S. (2010), 'Network patterns and competitive advantage before the emergence of a dominant design', *Strategic Management Journal*, **31**(4), 438–61.

Penrose, Edith T. (1995), *The Theory of the Growth of the Firm*, New York: Oxford University Press.

Phelps, C. C. (2010), 'A longitudinal study of the influence of alliance network structure and composition on firm exploratory innovation', *Academy of Management Journal*, **53**(4), 890–913.

Romero de Pablos, A. (2011), 'Regulation and the circulation of knowledge: Penicillin patents in Spain', *Dynamis*, **31**(2), 363–83.

Rothaermel, F. T. and D. Deeds (2004), 'Exploration and exploitation alliances in biotechnology: A system of new product development', *Strategic Management Journal*, **25**(3), 201–21.

Schilling, M. and C. Phelps (2007), 'Interfirm collaboration networks: The impact of large-scale network structure on firm innovation', *Management Science*, **53**(7), 1113–26.

Tom, B. and B. Ron (2012), 'Knowledge networks in the Dutch aviation industry: The proximity paradox', *Journal of Economic Geography*, **12**(2), 409–33.

Xiang, X., H. Cai and Y. Pei (2010), 'The role of three approaches in transnational patent cooperation network', *Journal of Management Science in China* (in Chinese), **23**(5), 43–52.

Yang, L., Y. Yang, Y. Lou and J. Jin (2019), 'Impact of different patent cooperation network models on innovation performance of technology-based SMEs', *Technology Analysis & Strategic Management*. Published online 19 Dec 2019.

Ye, C. and X. Yu (2013), 'Research on multidisciplinary knowledge network patent cooperation between enterprises', *Journal of Intelligence* (in Chinese), **32**(4), 113–20.

Zhang, H. and C. Lang (2013), 'The impact of past performance and network heterogeneity on knowledge innovation: The centrality of network is not enough', *Studies in Science of Science* (in Chinese), **31**(10), 1582–88.

Zhang, S. and X. Dang (2009), 'Research on the network organization governance of technological innovation under the coupling relationship', *Science of Science and Management of S.&T.* (in Chinese), **30**(9), 58–62.

Zhang, W. and X. Dang (2011), 'Research on the relationship between enterprise network power and network capability: Based on the analysis of technology innovation network', *Studies in Science of Science* (in Chinese), **29**(7), 1094–101.

5. What enables technological self-reliance? Theoretical discussion and comparative case study

Xi Sun

1. INTRODUCTION

This chapter addresses how Chinese multinational firms in the telecommunication equipment, concrete machinery and vehicle diesel engine industries develop in-house capabilities in relation to the evolution of embedded demand and the accumulation of national technological capabilities. In the context of this book, this chapter offers important insights into catching-up through technological self-reliance, thus illustrating how these firms can benefit from the Chinese knowledge-intensive innovation ecosystem. The key point here is to define "self-reliance" and "dependence" clearly under a theoretical framework of technical change in an era of globalization, which changes the learning context of developing economies.

The decisive role of technological learning in catching-up has been the focus of much research in the past two decades (Amsden, 1989; Bell and Pavitt, 1993; Malerba and Nelson, 2012). A crucial topic is the divergence in latecomers' competitiveness and catching-up performance. Such divergence could be observed in firms (Gao, 2003; Xiao et al., 2013) at the sectoral (Malerba and Mani, 2009) and state levels (Nelson, 1993; Hikino and Amsden, 1994). Chinese transformation in relation to catch-up to developed countries is also discussed in Chapter 2.

Potential explanations for such divergence, particularly for the successful stories, include the openness and access to foreign technologies (Gu, 2000; Lee and Lim, 2001), the technological learning strategies (Gao, 2003; Xiao et al., 2013) and the intensity and continuity of latecomers' technological learning (Kim, 1997). It is widely accepted in this stream of literature that local capability-building can be facilitated greatly by absorbing foreign technologies and that a long-lasting enhanced learning is necessary for this absorption and capability-building progress. Openness, access and learning strategies shape latecomers' knowledge base, including the evolution and development of their absorptive capacities (Cohen and Levinthal, 1990).

Many interesting issues remain to be addressed. One is the historical transformation of the latecomers' access to foreign technologies and their protection of local markets. Japan and New Industrial Economies protected their local market heavily before economic liberalization, which created a favorable environment for technological learning (Odagiri and Goto, 1993; Kim, 1993; Mathews and Cho, 2000). Market liberalization since the 1980s has made protectionism complicated. At a time when Western technologies must continue to be adapted to a local context in India (Herstatt et al., 2008), the Chinese policy of "trading market for technology" made foreign direct investment (FDI) increasingly dominant in technology transfer and exposed the domestic market to multinational corporations (MNCs) (Lu and Yu, 2013).

This substantial change in the market environment led to greater uncertainty in technological learning (see Chapters 10, 12 and 14). Competition from foreign first-mover firms may result in both greater pressure for change and less revenue to dedicate to latecomers' capability-building. The increasing pressure needs more effective strategic control, whereas the lower levels of revenue threaten the financial commitment in learning and innovation. Both aspects make it more difficult for the emergence of local innovative enterprises and technological leaders. A decreasing marginal revenue in technological learning means the intensity and continuity in learning, which may have led to the successful transition (imitative to defensive) in the 1970s, may result in a "stumbling back" (imitative to dependent) in the 1990s and 2000s, as shown in the research by Xiao et al. (2013). Furthermore, technological dependence is much easier in the liberalization era; this can be the opposite of the latecomers' strategic intent.

This chapter thus addresses how firms search for opportunities and develop innovative capabilities and globalization. The external changes in the learning context have led to more ambiguous results from an imitative strategy based on enhanced learning, which in the past was used to push imitation into innovation (Kim, 1997), or original equipment manufacturing (OEM) into original design manufacturing (ODM) and original brand manufacturing (OBM) (Hobday, 1995). This chapter argues that such ambiguity calls for a more thorough discussion on imitative strategy: which kind of imitation may lead to innovation, as well as the transition to defensive strategy, while other kinds of imitation may lead to dependence? Additionally, what is the difference between these two types of imitations?

The chapter labels the first kind of imitative and the defensive (learning) strategy as "technological self-reliance" and the latter as "technological dependence." We identify these strategies as two kinds of learning strategies, which result in completely different catching-up performances in a modern context. On the one hand, technological self-reliance enables latecomers to adapt Western-originated technologies and can therefore be viewed as the middle stage in the transformation to technological leader, including successful catching-up. On the other hand, a dependence on foreign technology strategy may leave latecomers in an endless catching-up trap.

In the remainder of this chapter, we will further develop and discuss this classification. The theoretical component outlines a taxonomy including firm strategies of innovating, technological dependence and self-reliance, and is based on the framework of technical change. Section 2 also stresses the increasing importance of product development for technological catching-up. Section 3 provides empirical illustrations of this argument that are based on three sectors with complex products in China. Section 4 discusses the managerial and policy implications.

2. TECHNOLOGICAL CAPABILITIES: TECHNOLOGICAL SELF-RELIANCE AND PRODUCT DEVELOPMENT

In the early context of catching-up strategies, the literature has shown how a self-reliant strategy may lead to successful catching-up of the country. Therefore, many latecomers have emphasized the importance of technological self-reliance, also known as technological security, as a component of state autonomy prior to the 1980s (Samuels, 1994). For example, technological self-reliance was the core of Japanese techno-nationalism since Meiji (Samuels, 1994). This reliance was also expressed as independence in India (Dore, 1984; Chamarik and Goonatilake, 1994) and self-sufficiency in Latin America (Pack, 2000). Although all these countries protected their local market heavily during specific periods, there are also differences among these different kinds of self-reliance, as summarized below (see Table 5.1).

As Pack (2000) classified the processes, the elites in Latin America and India who suspected the benefits of foreign technologies did believe in self-sufficiency in technology generation/creation (Dore, 1984). In contrast, self-reliance in East Asia was viewed as the ability to absorb/learn needed technologies rather than autarky (Samuels, 1994; Kim, 1997). The latter uses foreign technologies as important references and benchmarks for local learning. In China after the 1980s, an export-oriented economy was combined with the retreat of industrial administration and, taken together, the Chinese context made FDI the growing mainstream of technology transfer. This finding means that Chinese technological self-reliance is unique and specific compared to the paths followed by countries previously. This statement calls for a thorough understanding of "technological self-reliance" from the perspective of technical change. For example, in both Asia and Latin America, their self-reliance or self-sufficiency focused on the latecomers' disadvantages in technical change and global competition.

Table 5.1 *Comparison among three kinds of technological self-reliance*

Kinds of technological self-reliance	Dominant access to foreign technologies	FDI's access to local market	Capability-building path
Technological independence/ self-sufficiency: India and Latin America before economic liberalization (Dore, 1984; Pack, 2000; Forbes and Wield, 2002; Krishman, 2003; Nassif, 2007) and China before 1978	Highly regulated technology imports	Controlled by protectionist instruments	IS-oriented indigenization, especially by local S&T infrastructure
Technological self-reliance: Japan and NIEs (Kim, 1993; Samuels, 1994; Hobday, 1995; Kim, 1997; Mathews and Cho, 2000)	Capital goods import (including turnkeys) in an organized approach	Controlled by protectionist instruments	Export-oriented reversed A-U model by local firms
China since 1978	FDI and capital goods import with decreasing regulations	Retreat of protectionist instruments	New approach to self-reliance?

2.1 Definitions Related to Technological Change

To further develop the argument, understanding the general framework of technical change is a fundamental criterion. Therefore, our theoretical definition of technological self-reliance begins from a theoretical framework of technical change. This definition also makes it possible to understand the dependent and innovative strategy through the same lens.

There is much research about technical change in the economy (Dosi, 1982, 1988; Pavitt, 2005; Dosi and Nelson, 2010). Here, we borrow several seminal works to build our framework, which focuses on the cyclicity and basic structure of the change process (Abernathy and Utterback, 1978; Dosi, 1982; Utterback, 1994). In these theories, technical evolution was analyzed as a cycle, which begins from the formation of a novel product concept. This concept is related to a new technological paradigm as well as a new principle that satisfies specific demand (Arthur, 2007).

Based on this principle, both innovators and followers contribute various product designs or technological trajectories. A dominant technological trajectory finally survives the competition (Utterback and Suarez, 1993; Suarez, 2004), which is affected by social, economic and institutional factors

(Dosi, 1982), and the contenders are forced to exit. The survivor moves into its specific phase until the next cycle, which is labeled by the emergence of a new paradigm or principle. Therefore, technical change can be analyzed as the whole cycle from the emergence of a new concept to the development of a dominant technological trajectory and the maturing of product technology. Obviously, all technology transfers and diffusions to latecomers occur in the mature phase. This finding should be understood as the context of technological learning.

Therefore, based on the framework discussed above, we can make a distinction among innovating, technological self-reliance and dependence under the same criterion (Figure 5.1).

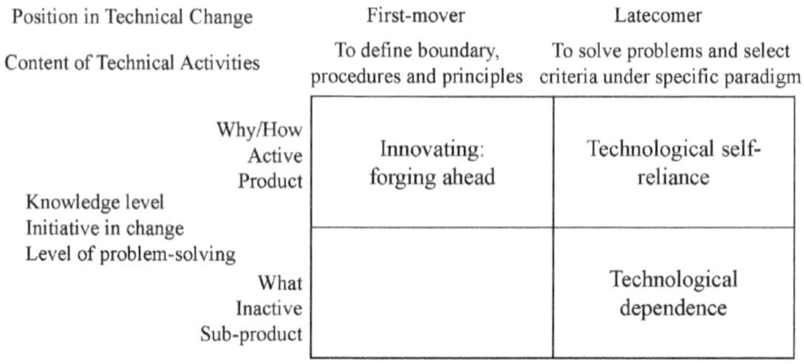
Position in Technical Change
First-mover
Latecomer
Content of Technical Activities
To define boundary, procedures and principles
To solve problems and select criteria under specific paradigm
Why/How
Active
Product
Innovating: forging ahead
Technological self-reliance
Knowledge level
Initiative in change
Level of problem-solving
What
Inactive
Sub-product
Technological dependence

Source: Adapted from Sun and Lu (2015).

Figure 5.1 Specifying innovating and technological learning

The dependent learning strategy leads to only operation knowledge and the sub-paradigm/principle solution under the imported paradigm. Therefore, latecomers are not able to understand product design and to integrate technologies into their product. The lack of know-why and know-how in product architecture makes their devotion to components and processes useless when a paradigm shifts. That statement means that any substantial turbulences in market or technology, such as a new import from abroad, would result in a catching-up trap.

Comparatively, technological self-reliance, including reverse engineering, is more active and initiative. This self-reliance targets a local accumulation on know-why and know-how at the product level, which enables latecomers to understand the imported trajectories and principles. Therefore, self-reliant latecomers are able to develop new products under imported architecture rather than to follow the Western criteria and key components passively. Adaptations driven by local demand and competences open the window to create indigenous technological trajectories and new technologies, which allows latecomers to understand imported product concepts and to accommodate such turbulence by indigenous adaptations.

Finally, innovating means more autonomy in technical change. Latecomers innovate by the following: 1) generating new product concepts independently under new paradigms and basic principles; 2) cooperating with others to develop novel concepts and technologies; and 3) contributing new trajectories based on Western concepts to compete for market dominance. Both the substantial understanding on existing technologies and the rich experience in product development are necessary in this period, which call for industrial and scientific accumulation at the state level. Although latecomers in this period must continue to learn foreign technologies, their knowledge base and initiative in technical change make such technical transfer more equal and reciprocal.

2.2 Product Development as the Micro-foundation of Technological Self-reliance

A theoretical perspective on the technological self-reliance above shows us the importance of technological learning at the product level. In this section, we will provide further analysis on product development in technological self-reliance.

2.2.1 Deviation from East Asian Model: possibility and necessity

In the East Asian Model, successful latecomers, such as Japan and South Korea, did not develop products from the very beginning. Theoretical summaries on the capability-building path (Hobday, 1995; Kim, 1997) describe a step-by-step sequence of technological learning, which begins from engineering and production capability, particularly the local capability development of key components. Such an incremental path is practical in and shaped by a specific context, one facet of which is the heritage of vertical integration in the West; the other is the poor industrial foundation in the Far East. Such context forced the latecomers to begin their learning from assembling and copying, such as learning by doing. Additionally, trade protection made it possible for these countries to build the necessary knowledge base before international competition.

However, such an incremental path has been challenged by the trend and regime of globalization, including restrictions on both learning approaches (such as reverse engineering and a pro-IPR regime under TRIPS) and market liberalization. Globalization also provides Western MNCs access to emerging markets and made the cross-border expansion of their first-mover advantage (Lieberman and Montgomery, 1998) possible. This change may greatly set back or wipe out the local firms in developing countries before they could build their capabilities to match the first-mover advantage. Such latecomers' disadvantage (Gao, 2005) harms local firms' intent for and benefit from technological learning. At the same time, vertical disintegration has become possible in Western industries since the 1970s, which makes the globalization of the supply chain easier and weakens the necessity of localization. Therefore, a deviation from the East Asian Model, technological learning that began with assembling, becomes an urgent issue.

Obviously one possible deviation here is product development at the very beginning of technological learning, such as learning by innovating (Lu and Mu, 2011). It starts from the development of indigenous product concepts, follows with understanding and utilization of Western-originated technologies and finally integrates technologies into working products. Here, the indigenous product concepts must consider both the local endowment and the domestic market. Therefore, a local product concept is necessary for latecomers in technological assimilation and local capability-building, which enables them to generate and manage technical change (Bell and Pavitt, 1993) and leads to autonomy in international technological competition.

Hence, product development, which derives from and creates architectural knowledge, is not only the most important approach in technological competition (Christensen and Lundvall, 2004) but also the micro-foundation in technological self-reliance.

2.2.2 Why is technological self-reliance the necessary middle stage for innovating?

In terms of technological capabilities, we discuss why technological self-reliance, such as learning by innovating, is the middle stage for latecomers' innovating.

First and foremost, as the micro-foundation of self-reliance, product development calls for a substantial understanding of existing technologies. That statement means learning by innovating would result in the enhanced accumulation of technological knowledge. This accumulation in existing technologies can also be used in innovating.

Second, latecomers could build their development processes by trial-and-error in lower cost and uncertainties. The "why" knowledge in product design and architecture is not embodied in imported products (Nelson and Winter, 1982); therefore, reverse engineering imported architectures also involves "purposive search of relevant information, effective interactions … within the firm …

(and) with other organizations" (Kim, 1993, p. 369). Additionally, all these organizational process-building devotions in self-reliance are "in fact the same in innovation process in R&D" (ibid.).

Finally, latecomers who commit to trials in developing a satisfactory product must be risk taking in their choice to do something radically new for the country, if not to the world (Nelson and Pack, 1999; Kim and Nelson, 2000). Such entrepreneurship is also necessary to participate in and originate technical change.

In comparison, technological dependence, such as learning-by-doing localization under an imported architecture, is completely different. This dependence is a self-continuing equilibrium, such as catching-up traps, that must be punctuated by exogenous technical change. However, a lack of architectural knowledge restricts latecomers' options in technical turbulence. A fundamental change in product design (technological paradigm) would make obsolete all technological accumulation under the old architecture (Dosi, 1982). Given technical change and derived threats, latecomers in dependence must either import the new technology, which leads to the circle of "import→lag behind→new import→lag again," or turns to a lower end in the value chain. Both choices ensure that latecomers remain dependent upon imported technologies and West-dominated architecture.

As a short summary of Section 2, the changing context of technological catching-up and industrialization makes learning-by-innovating, such as learning by developing products, possible and necessary for technological self-reliance. Product development here is not a linear succession of localization in the East Asian Model but the most creative and risky decision and leapfrog in technological learning.

3. COMPARATIVE CASE STUDY

To explain the divergence of industrial competitiveness and the decisive role of product development in technological self-reliance, this section provides a comparative case study in three sectors in China. These sectors are the telecommunication equipment sector and concrete machinery sector as successful stories, and the vehicle diesel engine sector as a failure. To execute the triangulation in case comparison, sources of data in this section were various and independent from each other. In the telecommunication case, our data were collected from several biographies of entrepreneurs and firms, internal memos (for example, the speech of Ren Zhengfei in Huawei) and technological letters (for example, internal letters in ZTE), and existing research. In the other two cases, in addition to those second-hand data sources, first-hand data were collected from substantive interviews with managers, engineers and retired leaders in related companies. Furthermore, a corresponding summary and comparison of these cases is shown in Figure 5.2.

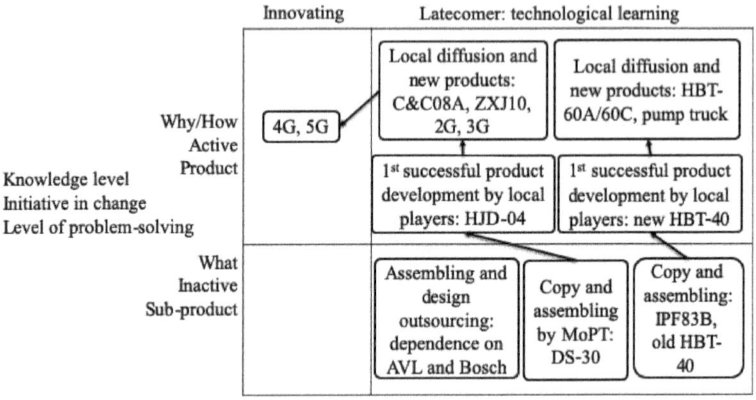

Figure 5.2 Positioning the case studies in the theoretical framework

3.1 Telecommunication Equipment

As the most successful hi-tech industry in China, the telecommunication equipment sector is a miracle. This miracle began with the successful development of Digital Program-Controlled Switches (DPCS) twenty years ago. This section shows the origin and its diffusion of the local product development, which led to technological self-reliance and global competitiveness in this sector.

3.1.1 Technological dependence: "eight trajectories from seven countries"

The telecommunication equipment sector began its "trading market for technology" in the early 1980s. Implementation of F150 (Fujitsu) DPCS in Fuzhou began MNCs' market penetration in China, and the network fragmentation made this penetration easier. Furthermore, the incitement on infrastructure development, which was known as "*to accomplish in one action*," combined with financial incentives from the home governments of MNCs, led the Chinese telecommunication equipment market into a mess; eight kinds of DPCSs from seven countries took over the core telecommunication network in China.

In addition to this infrastructure leapfrog, the Chinese government focused heavily on reducing the dependence on imported products in two directions. On the one hand, the government established joint ventures with foreign MNCs, such as Bell, to introduce DPCS product lines and to push the localization of crucial components. On the other hand, public research institutes were organized to copy imported products, particularly F150. A 2000-line copy was finally certificated by the Ministry of Post & Telecommunication (MoPT) in October 1986. Subsequently, the 10th Institute of MoPT in Xi'an developed 10000-line DPCS over a long period; this was completed in 1991 and was named DS-30 (Liu and Wang, 2007). Because of the difficult development of DS-30, MNCs propagated that China had minimal opportunity in high-capacity DPCS.

3.1.2 Product development and the resulting technological self-reliance

Copying and the resultant dependence stressed the Chinese government's patience. In the long wait for DS-30, certain new forces in product development experienced rapid growth. An R&D team at the PLA Institute of Information Engineering (PIIE) began its research on telecommunication equipment in 1983. These researchers' 1024-line PCS in 1986 piqued the interest of PTIC (China National Post and Telecommunications Industry Corporation), which funded 3 million to PIIE to develop DPCS. In the ensuing two years (November 1989–October 1991), the PIIE team developed 10000-line DPCS; this was called HJD04. Additionally, the processing capacity of HJD-04 was much higher than all the imported products.

Gaps in R&D efficiency between DS-30 and HJD-04 reflected the differences in computing capability, which was important in DPCS development. Localization conducted by MoPT was constrained by intellectual resources and key components. For example, MoPT could not obtain suitable ASICs because of the control from COCOM and thus chose Intel chips as a substitute. Comparatively, the PIIE team were not constrained by this behavior because of their experience on computer development, which was begun in 1968. The teams transferred their computing experience to DPCS easily. This transfer made original designs possible, and those local designs, such as distributed control and modular construction in HJD-04, led to a better performance.

At the same time, the telecommunication demand had also changed. The fragmented telecommunication network called for a powerful control. Therefore, MoPT decided to use Signal System No.7 (SS7) as a network controlling system, which would guarantee the communication quality and network control. Furthermore, this usage enabled the introduction of DPCS from different manufacturers into the networks. Compared with MNCs, domestic firms better utilized this opportunity and developed their demand knowledge of the rural market at the very beginning, which provided necessary access to the core network. ZTE and Huawei are the best players in this process of technological self-reliance and turnover of leadership.

ZTE was one of the earliest telecommunication equipment manufacturers in China and attained great success in the rural market in the early 1990s. ZTE began its development of 10000-line DPCS in September 1993 and moved their research center to Nanjing, which was more suitable for long-term product development than Shenzhen. In March 1995, ZTE developed its first 10,000-line DPCS, ZXJ10. ZXJ10 used SS7 in accordance with MoPT's regulation and borrowed HJD-04's system architecture and its modular construction, which enabled a flexible capacity by increasing switch modules. This design, combined with ZTE's understanding of rural demand, made ZXJ10 a blockbuster. Rural tele-networks bureaus, which realized that imported products were "backward in technology, too big in volume, electricity-consuming, and difficult to fit to the environment compared with domestic ones," turned to ZXJ10, which was suitable to both current and future needs. Furthermore, because of its advanced design, "ZXJ10 needs no air conditioning, while imported counterparts can't work without it" (Hua, 1998: 5).

Compared to ZTE, Huawei, founded in 1988, was a latecomer in DPCS. The company needed to cede ASDS in 1993 because of a dead end in its infrastructure leapfrog. Huawei decided to develop both 2000-line and 10000-line DPCS at the same time. Huawei greatly benefited from the success of HJD-04 by various means,[1] which finally shaped Huawei's product design. Based on its understanding of the rural market, Huawei launched the 2000-line DPCS, Chinese-UI C&C08, which was very practical for rural customers. The market success of C&C08 allowed Huawei to focus on the development of a 10000-line DPCS, C&C08A. The key technology in C&C08A was to link those 2000-line modules together. In accordance with the rural context in China, engineers in Huawei proposed connecting multiple modules with optical fiber rather than use the dominant design of MNCs. After repeated experiments, this new product design experienced large market success because of its efficiency and flexibility.

Encouraged by the success of HJD-04 and other favorable conditions, local firms such as ZTE and Huawei began their technological learning through product development. This learning-by-innovating process and the resulting knowledge base enabled the researchers to absorb new technologies, which was a paradigmatic shift to 2G to 3G, and expand product lines. Finally, these product development firms became competent players in the global market.

3.2 Construction Equipment: Concrete Machinery

Two examples of the sectoral transition in concrete machinery are two leading construction machinery manufacturers, Zoomlion and Sany. In contrast to DPCS, whose first successful local development was derived from cross-sector diffusion, technological self-reliance in concrete machinery was rooted in intra-sector accumulation.

3.2.1 Technological dependence

Acceleration in construction in the 1990s called for high-quality concrete. However, in 1992, nearly all concrete pumps in China were imported from Japan and Germany, which placed a heavy burden on foreign exchange. The Chinese government had to appoint Hubei Factory of Construction Machinery to import and assemble IPF85B concrete pumps in Ishikawa. However, the localization of key components, such as hydraulic parts, was difficult, and customers' operation knowledge was poor. Both factors resulted in frequent malfunction, inefficient imitation and heavy losses for the Hubei factory. Furthermore, frequent malfunctions pushed customers to imported brands such as Schwing and Putzmeister. Therefore, concrete machinery was one of the two sub-sectors of construction machinery in China in the trade deficit in the early 1990s. Once imported pumps broke, it would be more difficult to replace the malfunctioning components.

3.2.2 Zoomlion: pioneer in this product development

Zoomlion was a spin-off of CCMI (Changsha Construction Machinery Institute), which was previously the design institute for all Ministry of Construction factories in the central planned economy.

Zoomlion was founded on 28 September 1992; it finally chose the concrete pump as its first product because of the company's earlier experience with this product and its simplicity in assembly. Comparatively, system design, such as system design to integrate different sub-systems, is more crucial. Furthermore, obstacles regarding core components and user knowledge were improved. "Rexroth components could be imported since then. Moreover, they (official programs in localization) gradually created a domestic market by training customers" (interview in Zoomlion).

Zoomlion launched its first HBT-40 concrete pump on 1 July 1993, at the price of RMB 800,000 (RMB 1,200,000 for imported pumps). However, the first product went wrong quickly. Engineering practices such as "machines running while workers shifting" and hot weather in summer led to many problems with the HBT-40, which imitated a European product. Zoomlion was required to cease compliance and assembly immediately and solve problems such as heat dissipation. This product development was successful after a six-month deficit.

Ensuring that the improved pump was well-designed, CCMI began technology diffusion. This success also inspired product development in the whole sector. Furthermore, the trivial role of the Chinese market in the 1990s and their limited interactions with Chinese customers made MNCs unaware of such turbulence in the Chinese market. Thus, local enterprises led by Zoomlion regained the domestic market when the window of opportunity opened, while other MNCs ignored these changes.

3.2.3 Sany: product development and diversification

Sany was a latecomer in concrete pumps. The company bought the blueprint of the improved HBT-40 from CCMI in 1993 and was able to design a concrete pump, HBT-60A, indigenously in 1995. Thereafter, Sany began its learning by innovating the concrete pump. In June 1996, Sany developed its new concrete pump, 60C. This new product inherited the technological trajectory of better heat dispersion created by HBT-40 and HBT-60A. It changed the design of a closed hydraulic sub-system to an open one, which was good at heat dispersion and completely fit the engineering demand and climate variations. This led to a good reputation and large revenues for Sany.

To capitalize on the surging development of taller buildings, Sany decided to develop the first 37-meter-arm concrete pump truck in 1997. At that time, CCMI designed the first 36-meter pump truck in 1996, the Hubei Factory of Construction Machinery copied imported 28-meter pump trucks, and international brands, such as Schwing and PM, sold 30 or 32-meter pump trucks in China.

Change in arm length would lead to many changes in design and engineering, including fundamental parameters such as pressure and stability. Therefore, it was said that “any change in arm length is even more difficult than to fly in the sky,” and whether arms could be designed and produced independently was an important criterion in pump truck competition. Based on these considerations, Sany surveyed the domestic market and consuming habits:

> Our operators were not so literate … that their operating abilities were low. But users who spent 3 million to buy an advanced machine would not like to have too many use constraints. The machine had better run around the whole country … and not be so picky but pump all kinds of cement. Imported machines ... are very strict on load, working time and raw materials. (interview in Sany)

This orientation made Sany design their pump truck from the very beginning. The company began to order steel, hydraulic components and welding materials from international suppliers when the new architecture had been finished.

In April 1999, the first 37-meter-arm concrete pump truck in China was produced by Sany. Henceforth, with the increasing popularity of tall buildings in China, Sany strengthened their market advantage by continuous product development.

3.3 Vehicle Diesel Engine

The case of the diesel engine sector revealed the importance of product development and technological self-reliance. The historical path of this sector that determines the capability gap in product design, which has been enlarged by unstable technical progress. This made domestic manufacturers believe in MNCs' first-mover advantage and build long-term cooperation with these leaders, such as professional design consultants who make low-cost design possible and international suppliers of key components, such as Bosch and Denso. Both R&D outsourcing and dependence on key components are harmful to the emergence, diffusion and improvement of product development in local firms.

3.3.1 Technological dependence rooted in the central planned economy

To understand the source of technological dependence, we must retrace the history of the diesel engine industry in China. The division of this sector in the command economy, which was designed in 1952, deprived manufacturers of autonomy in product design. All factories were confined to product adjustments and blueprint management until the 1980s. Since the early 1980s, several design-capability building programs were forced to give up for different reasons, including administrative reforms that dramatically weakened the industrial administration. Therefore, these Chinese engine manufacturers, whose development capacities were poor, experienced a furious price war in the 1990s to explore a fast-growing market. The decade after 1998 witnessed a rapid growth of more than 240 percent in power, which concealed the capability gap on product design. So-called R&D tasks before the ICT revolution developed product series based on a given design. These tasks were nothing but adjustments in injection angles and crankcases in mechanical pumps, which was so easy that "experienced craftsmen could finish by trial-and-error in less than one week" (interview in SDEC, Shanghai Diesel Engine Corporate).

3.3.2 Western leaders and their dominance in division of knowledge

Because of the historical inertia, Chinese domestic diesel manufacturers had no preparation to embrace the increasingly tough environmental regulations and integrate new technologies, such as CR (Common Rail) injection and EGR (Exhaust Gas Recycling, a post-processing technology), into new products under the ICT paradigm. This enlarged the capability gap and led these manufacturers to depend on Western leaders in both product design and key components.

The dominant design forces that Chinese firms relied on were international professional consultancies, including AVL (Austria), Ricardo (UK), FEV (Germany) and SWRI (Southwest Research Institute, USA). In their cooperation, Chinese firms chose a market segment first and told their international partners their target market. Thereafter, the foreign consultants concentrated their endeavors in those engineering-intensive system integrations, such as an IPR portfolio, 3D modeling and system optimization. That meant that the Chinese firms outsourced the fundamental tasks in product development and thus ceded their autonomy in technical change. At the same time, international firms sold design software to their Chinese customers, who were inexperienced in product design and thus could not obtain a creditable optimization curve, however perfect the software. Additionally, continuous software upgrading made Chinese enterprises doubt themselves. "Can we design it by ourselves? Maybe we must buy a new product from Ricardo/AVL/FEV" (interview in CICEIA, China Internal Combustion Engine Industry Association).

What about the key components? Because of the institutional outsourcing (Steinfeld, 2010) of the Chinese government in environment regulations, there was no suitable supplier of CR injection systems or post-processing systems (PPS) whose products met EU IV emissions standards. This lack of supply opened windows of opportunity to key component suppliers, such as Bosch and Denko, generally, and consultants would recommend that the diesel manufacturers share their emission and safety requirements to a specific supplier. Then, mechanical components in the diesel engines would be designed and produced by the Chinese firms, while the electrical components were designed and produced by the international suppliers.

Such a division of knowledge among Chinese manufacturers, design consultants and suppliers of key components led to the Chinese firms' dependence on foreign knowledge from the very beginning of a new product at both the product and component levels. That meant that "there are only two product development platforms for Chinese manufacturers, one of which is built on the CR system of Bosch, and the other on Denso" (interview in SDEC in 2011). Because of this powerful advantage and system incompatibility, both Bosch and Denko priced their products extremely high; the CR system and PPS represent two-thirds of the total cost of the engine (Li, 2008).

It is interesting to note that Chinese diesel manufacturers have obtained great benefits from the market expansion that has occurred since 1998; however, the most profitable diesel firms spent no money on product development in the mid-2000s. All these manufacturers heavily relied on R&D outsourcing and component suppliers because of historical inertia and a lack of confidence, given hundreds of millions in R&D input. Thus, the technological dependence in the diesel sector became a self-continuing equilibrium.

4. CONCLUSIONS AND POLICY IMPLICATIONS

In this chapter, we define technological self-reliance as a specification of technological learning based on the theoretical framework of technical change. Theoretical discussions on "what is technological self-reliance" enables an analysis of the importance of product development through a comparative case study in China. Now it is possible to briefly summarize the topic of technological self-reliance.

First, it is interesting to further discuss the theoretical implications of this topic. Technological self-reliance, as an independent concept that depicts the middle stage between technological dependence and innovating, is a useful tool for understanding the logic and paths of capability-building in catching-up. This self-reliance enables us to catch the essence of "indigenous innovation" in the East Asian Model and China. A large component of indigenous innovation in these latecomers is to learn Western-based technologies (Amsden, 1989), an innovation that is something new to followers rather than to the world or marketplace (Hobday, 2000). Therefore, indigenous innovation contains both the active pattern of technological learning, such as technological self-reliance and Schumpeterian innovation. This explanation is also rational because of the blurred boundary between technological self-reliance and innovating, which is determined by the similarities and accumulation in several facets of product development.

Managers and students in management can also borrow insights from the discussion on technological self-reliance. For example, our discussion and case research show the crucial role of product development in technological learning, such as "learning by innovating." Additionally, this finding also explains the fundamental difference between technological dependence and self-reliance, which reveals a fundamental divergence in the learning strategies. One strategy is the popular learning-by-doing strategy, which is useful for the first-movers in the West (Lieberman and Montgomery, 1998) but may not be as direct for latecomers when they do not master product design from the very beginning and the design knowledge cannot be learned solely by doing. The other strategy is the so-called learning-before-doing strategy (Pisano, 1996). This strategy shows the possibility and importance for latecomers to master design knowledge at the product level directly rather than by the traditional OEM path. This finding also explains the difficulties for those export-oriented enterprises in East China whose businesses lead to minimal knowledge in product development and thus a self-continuing technological dependence. In addition, learning before doing, such as product development, is the very strategy used by companies to halt this dilemma and upgrade their businesses.

The discussion of technological self-reliance hints at the policy implications of findings. One of the core issues in China is the necessity of a multi-level policy system based on divergent industrial competitiveness. For those sectors in dependence, it is important to recognize the bottlenecks hindering local latecomers' product development. Our empirical research reveals two kinds of bottlenecks. One bottleneck is related to radical technical change and increasing difficulties in reverse engineering; the other is derived from the crowding-out effect of FDI, which suppresses local players' productive investment and technological capability-building. In comparing those sectors in technological self-reliance and innovating, the pivotal policy issue is improving the pluralism, rivalry and ex post selection in technological development while continuing traditional product development (Nelson, 1990).

NOTE

1. Key designs of Huawei and ZTE's DPCS followed HJD-04's trajectory. Wu of the HJD-04 team continued to remember that engineers from Huawei requested help in the 1990s. Other research on business history noted that many HR managers went to Zhengzhou to seek experienced engineers on the PIIE team with higher salaries (Zhang, 2009).

REFERENCES

Abernathy, W. and J. Utterback (1978), 'Patterns of industrial innovation', *Technology Review*, **80**(7), 40–47.

Amsden, A. (1989), *Asia's Next Giant: South Korea and Late Industrialization*, New York and Oxford: Oxford University Press.

Arthur, B. (2007), 'The structure of invention', *Research Policy*, **36**(2), 274–287.

Bell, M. and K. Pavitt (1993), 'Technological accumulation and industrial growth: contrasts between developed and developing countries', *Industrial and Corporate Change*, **2**(1), 157–210.

Chamarik, S. and S. Goonatilake (eds.) (1994), *Technological Independence: The Asian Experience*, Tokyo, New York and Paris: United Nation University Press.

Christensen, J. and B.A. Lundvall (eds.) (2004), *Product Innovation, Interactive Learning and Economic Performance*, Bingley, UK: Emerald.

Cohen, W. and D. Levinthal (1990), 'Absorptive capacity: a new perspective on learning and innovation', *Administrative Science Quarterly*, **35**(1), 128–152.

Dore, R. (1984), 'Technological self-reliance: sturdy ideal or self-serving rhetoric', in M. Fransman and K. King (eds.), *Technological Capability in the Third World*, London and Basingstoke: Macmillan, pp. 65–80.

Dosi, G. (1982), 'Technological paradigms and technological trajectory', *Research Policy*, **11**(2), 147–162.

Dosi, G. (1988), 'Sources, procedures, and microeconomic effects of innovation', *Journal of Economic Literature*, **26**(3), 1120–1171.

Dosi, G. and R. Nelson (2010), 'Technical change_and industrial dynamics as evolutionary processes', in B. Hall and N. Rosenberg (eds.), *Handbook of Economics of Innovation*, Amsterdam: Elsevier, pp. 52–127.

Forbes, N. and D. Wield (2002), *From Followers to Leaders; Managing Technology and Innovation*, London and New York: Routledge.

Gao, X. (2003), *Technological Capability Catching up: Follow the Normal Way or Deviate*, Published PhD Dissertation, MIT.

Gao, X. (2005), '"Latecomers' unfavorable position" and the development strategies of emerging technology for firms in China' (in Chinese), *Chinese Journal of Management*, **2**(3), 291–294.

Gu, S. (2000), 'Learning models and technology strategy in catching-up', paper presented on the DRUID Summer Conference, Rebild, Denmark, June 2000, accessed 12 December 2013 at http://www.druid.dk/uploads/tx_picturedb/ds2000-103.pdf.

Herstatt, C., R. Tiwari, D. Ernst and S. Buse (2008), 'India's national innovation system: key elements and corporate perspectives', *Working paper No. 51 of Hamburg University of Technology*, www.tu-harburg.de/tim.

Hikino, T. and A. Amsden (1994), 'Staying behind, stumbling back, sneaking up, soaring ahead: late industrialization in historical perspective', in W. Baumol, R. Nelson and E. Wolff (eds.), *Convergence of Productivity: Cross-national Studies and Historical Evidence*, New York: Oxford University Press, pp. 285–315.

Hobday, M. (1995), *Innovation in East Asia: The Challenge to Japan*, Aldershot, UK and Brookfield, VT: Edward Elgar Publishing.

Hobday, M. (2000), 'East versus Southeast Asian innovation systems: comparing OEM- and TNC-led growth in electronics', in L. Kim and R. Nelson (eds.), *Technology, Learning and Innovation: Experiences of Newly Industrializing Economies*, New York: Cambridge University Press, pp. 129–169.

Hua, T. (1998), 'ZTE: a bright future' (in Chinese), *Communications Weekly*, **3**(31), 4–5.

Kim, L. (1993), 'National system of industrial innovation: dynamics of capability building in Korea', in R. Nelson (ed.), *National Innovation Systems: A Comparative Analysis*, New York and Oxford: Oxford University Press, pp. 357–383.

Kim, L. (1997), *Imitation to Innovation: The Dynamics of Korea's Technological Learning*, Boston: Harvard Business School Press.

Kim, L. and R. Nelson (2000), 'Introduction', in L. Kim and R. Nelson (eds.), *Technology, Learning and Innovation: Experiences of Newly Industrializing Economies*, New York: Cambridge University Press, pp. 1–9.

Krishnan, R. T. (2003), 'The evolution of a developing country innovation system during economic liberalization: the case of India', *Globelics Conference paper*, http://www.globelics.org.

Lee, Keun and C. Lim (2001), 'Technological regimes, catching-up and leapfrogging: findings from the Korean industries', *Research Policy*, **30**(3), 459–83.

Li, M. (2008), 'Technological roadmap to Euro-IV heavy diesel and implementation advice' (in Chinese), *Modern Components*, **11**, 44–47.

Lieberman, M. and D. Montgomery (1998), 'First-mover (dis)advantage: retrospective and link with the resource-based view', *Strategic Management Journal*, **19**(12), 1111–25.

Liu, J. and Y. Wang (2007), 'Technological learning and catching-up of China's telecom-equipment industry: an analysis on the technical factors' (in Chinese), *Management on Innovation and Entrepreneurship*, **3**, 1–24.

Lu, F. and L. Mu (2011), 'Learning by innovating: lessons from China's digital video player industry', *Journal of Science and Technology Policy in China*, **2**(1), 27–57.

Lu, F. and Y. Yu (2013), '"Double-surplus", capability gap and innovation: a macro-and micro-perspective on the transformation of the Chinese mode of economic development', *Social Sciences in China*, **34**(3), 76–100.

Malerba, F. and S. Mani (eds.) (2009), *Sectoral Systems of Innovation and Production in Developing Countries*, Cheltenham, UK and Northampton, MA, USA: Edward Elgar Publishing.

Malerba, F. and R. Nelson (eds.) (2012), *Economic Development as a Learning Process: Variation across Sectoral Systems*, Cheltenham, UK and Northampton, MA, USA: Edward Elgar Publishing.

Mathews, J. and D.-S. Cho (2000), *Tiger Technology: The Creation of a Semiconductor Industry in Asia*, New York: Cambridge University Press.

Nassif, A. (2007), 'National Innovation System and Macroeconomic Policies: Brazil and India in Comparative Perspective', *UNCTAD discussion paper*, https://unctad.org/en/docs/osgdp20073_en.pdf

Nelson, R. (1990), 'Capitalism as an engine of progress', *Research Policy*, **19**(3), 193–214.

Nelson, R. (1993), *National Innovation Systems: A Comparative Analysis*, New York and Oxford: Oxford University Press.

Nelson, R. and H. Pack (1999), 'The Asian miracle and modern growth theory', *The Economic Journal*, **109**(457), 416–436.

Nelson, R. and S. Winter (1982), *An Evolutionary Theory of Economic Change*, Cambridge, MA: Belknap Press of Harvard University.

Odagiri, H. and A. Goto (1993), 'The Japanese system of innovation: past, present and future', in R. Nelson (ed.), *National Innovation Systems: A Comparative Analysis*, New York and Oxford: Oxford University Press, pp. 76–114.

Pack, H (2000), 'Research and development in the industrial development process', in L. Kim and R. Nelson (eds.), *Technology, Learning and Innovation: Experiences of Newly Industrializing Economies*, New York: Cambridge University Press, pp. 69–94.

Pavitt, K. (2005), 'Innovation processes', in J. Fagerberg, D. Mowery and R. Nelson (eds.), *The Oxford Handbook of Innovation*, New York and Oxford: Oxford University Press, pp. 86–114.

Pisano, Gary (1996), 'Learning-before-doing in the development of new process technology', *Research Policy*, **25**(7), 1097–1119.

Samuels, R. (1994), *Rich Nation, Strong Army: National Security and the Technological Transformation of Japan*, New York: Cornell University Press.

Steinfeld, E. (2010), *Playing Our Game: Why China's Rise Doesn't Threaten the West*, New York: Oxford University Press.

Suarez, F. (2004), 'Battles for technological dominance', *Research Policy*, **33**(2), 271–286.

Sun, Xi and Feng Lu (2015), 'From technological self-reliance to innovating: a conceptual framework of technological learning', *Studies in Science of Science*, **33**(7), 975–984 and 1016.

Utterback, J. (1994), *Mastering the Dynamics of Innovation*, Boston, MA: Harvard Business School Press.

Utterback, J. and F. Suarez (1993), 'Innovation, competition and industry structure', *Research Policy*, **22**(1), 1–21.

Xiao, Y., A. Tylecote and J. Liu (2013), 'Why not greater catch-up by Chinese firms? The impact of IPR, corporate governance and technology intensity on late-comer strategies', *Research Policy*, **42**(3), 749–764.

Zhang, G. (2009), *Four Faces of Huawei* (in Chinese), Guangzhou: Guangdong Economy Publishing House.

6. Chinese multinational enterprises bridging technologies across home and host regions

Vito Amendolagine, Elisa Giuliani, Arianna Martinelli and Roberta Rabellotti

INTRODUCTION

This chapter explores the technological characteristics of medium- and medium–high-tech Chinese multinational enterprises (MNEs) undertaking cross-border acquisitions in the EU, USA and Japan. There are interesting issues to explore, because China recently has become an important global investor: in 2015 it was the third largest in the world after the USA and Japan, and the third main foreign direct investment (FDI) destination after the USA and Hong Kong. China's outstanding investment stock amounts to US$1010 billion, which is around 4 percent of world outward FDI (UNCTAD, 2016). The largest share of Chinese FDI stock is located in developing countries (84 percent including Hong Kong, which receives 58 percent). Advanced country destinations include the EU (6 percent of total Chinese FDI stock) and the USA (3 percent), which registered a strong and continuous increase between 2003 and 2012, of some 77-fold for FDIs in Europe and 47-fold for FDI to the US (UNCTAD, 2016).

Since the second half of the first decade of the 2000s, most of this increase has been in the form of cross-border acquisitions (CBAs), which have risen in both value and world share, peaking in 2013 at more than US$50 billion, corresponding to about 20 percent of all acquisitions worldwide and almost 50 percent of total outflows from China (UNCTAD, 2016) (Figure 6.1). In 2015, China's CBAs represented 34 percent of its total FDI outflows and, according to UNCTAD (2016), a number of cross-border megadeals, such as Haier's acquisition of GE Appliances in the USA, ChemChina's purchases of Pirelli in Italy and Syngenta in Switzerland, and Cosco's deal for Piraeus Port, have reinforced the perception of China as a leading investor in developed economies.

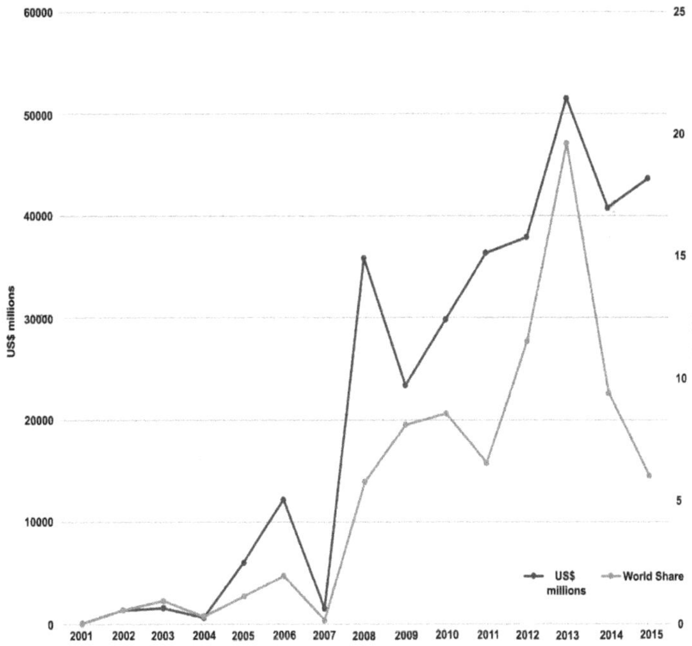

Source: UNCTAD (2016).

Figure 6.1 Chinese cross-border acquisitions (value and %)

In general, CBAs of companies located in advanced countries are considered the fastest and most effective means of accessing firm-specific strategic assets and key capabilities (Chung and Alcacer, 2002). Several empirical studies conducted on large samples of firms find that Chinese MNEs invest in developed countries mainly for knowledge-seeking reasons (see, among others, Amighini et al., 2013) and this is confirmed by case studies of well-known companies such as Haier, the world-leading Chinese company specialized in white goods (Duysters et al., 2009).

The strategic assets obtained via acquisitions provide Chinese MNEs with reputation and allow them to acquire and control the resources needed to access local and global markets. In addition, in principle, acquisitions could enable Chinese MNEs to rapidly close their technology gap by facilitating the development of new skills and R&D competences, and providing opportunities for organizational, managerial, marketing and technological learning (Amendolagine et al., 2015).

Acquisitions allow Chinese multinationals not only to access firm-specific assets from the target company but also provide the opportunity to access knowledge and other relevant technological assets embedded in the home region of the acquired firm. The latter often is accomplished through the development of formal and/or informal networks with local actors, such as suppliers, customers, universities and research centres, in the target region (Cantwell and Mudambi, 2011; Li et al., 2012; Piscitello et al., 2015). Thus, regions with strong technological bases and extensive knowledge assets provide Chinese MNEs with opportunities to tap into these knowledge pools and upgrade their technological capabilities and skills (Awate et al., 2015). The absorption of relevant knowledge and technologies is not automatic and depends on the presence of several conditions; the most important, according to the literature, being the absorptive capacity of the acquiring MNE (Cantwell and Mudambi, 2011; Crescenzi et al., 2016). The ability to understand, absorb and apply external knowledge acquired through acquisitions is affected by internal factors such as the MNE's prior knowledge, R&D spending and human skills, and also by external factors, which include the external knowledge environment in the MNE's home region. Chapters 7 and 8 also address similar issues of acquisitions and internationalization, through case studies of specific Chinese firms.

In this chapter, we consider Chinese MNEs as nodes, connecting the home and host regions, which are characterized by several 'knowledge bases' based on their accumulated technological specialization. We operationalize these as the technological classes in the patents awarded to the actors in the focal regions. We assume that the location of Chinese MNEs at the interface between the home and host regions, gives them access to different pieces of knowledge, which may (or may not) contribute to their learning and technological capabilities building processes. To take account of the (possibly) different technological specializations of the home and host regions, we introduce the notions of technologically distant regions (TDRs) to describe the situation where the home and host regions have knowledge bases specialized in very different technological areas, and technologically proximate regions (TPRs) to describe the situation when the home and host regions' knowledge and technology bases are similar. We ask what types of innovative activities (in terms of technological specialization, experience of patenting, patent portfolio size and involvement in international collaborations) are undertaken by Chinese MNEs that invest in more (or less) technologically distant regions. The focus is on Chinese MNEs investing in Europe, Japan and the USA.

The chapter is organized as follows. The next section provides information on the data and methodology, and a description of cross-border acquisition host countries and regions and industry specializations. We present the findings of our empirical analysis before the final section which discusses some conclusions.

DATA AND METHODOLOGY

Data on acquisitions by Chinese MNEs come from two sources: Zephyr (Bureau van Dijk - BvD) and SDC Platinum (Thomson Reuter),[1] both of which provide the name and location of the acquirer and target company, deal status (such as, 'completed', 'rumoured', 'pending'), percentage of the ownership transferred from target to investor, and date of the project. Our analysis focuses on all completed majority stake deals during 2003–2011[2] and, following previous studies on the effects of acquisitions on patenting (Ahuja and Katila, 2001; Cloodt et al., 2006; Valentini and Di Guardo, 2012), we focus on medium- and high-tech manufacturing and service industries based on NACE code classifications.[3] The final sample includes 95 acquisitions of European, Japanese and US target firms.

Data on acquisitions are matched and harmonized at the investor and target firm levels; for both target and acquiring firm, we collected information on the ownership structure of the acquiring Chinese MNE, the exact location of domestic and foreign subsidiaries, industry specialization and patenting activity. The data for these additional variables come from the Orbis database, published by Bureau van Dijk.

To classify home and host regions as either TDRs or TPRs, we use a Technology Proximity Index (TPI), calculated using the Patent Convention Treaty (PCT) applications contained in the OECD REGPAT Database (Maraut et al., 2008). The TPI is calculated as the correlation coefficient of two technological vectors, whose elements are the number of a region's patents in each four-digit level technological class (Jaffe, 1986; Bottazzi and Peri, 2003). The index is equal to zero if two regions hold patents in completely different technological classes and is equal to 1 if two regions apply for patents in the same technological classes.[4] We measure the technology proximity between the home and host regions for the 95 deals in our sample and assign them to the corresponding TDR or TPR category depending on whether the value for technological distance is below or above the median value.

The analysis employs a subsample of 37 deals involving a Chinese MNE that had applied for at least one patent before the CBA. For these firms, we consider a number of patent-related variables that are likely to capture some features of the innovative activities undertaken by these firms, measured using the EPO-PASTAT database and defined as follows.[5]

Technological specialization considers that each patent can be assigned to a technological class and, therefore, also to a technological area[6] and to a specific industry sector (NACE Rev. 2).[7] We calculate three indicators:

1. Average scope of patent, measured as the number of IPC classes referred to in the patent documents in the Chinese MNE patent portfolio: the higher the number of the technological classes, the greater the technological breadth of the patent (Lerner, 1994);
2. Share of patents in the same sector as the acquirer (primary NACE code);
3. Herfindahl–Hirschman Index (HHI) of patent portfolio diversification, calculated as the sum of the squares of the share of the acquirers' patents in different technologies. High values indicate a patent portfolio characterized by concentration in few technological areas; lower values indicate a patent portfolio with no dominant technological focus.

Patent experience, measured as the year in which the Chinese MNE applied for its first patent.
Patent portfolio size, measured as the number of patent applications filed by the Chinese MNE before the acquisition. We distinguish between the number of applications filed at the State Intellectual Property Office (SIPO) of the People's Republic of China and the number of patents filed at the United States Patent and Trademark Office (USPTO).
Non-collaborative patents, defined as the number of patents applied for by the Chinese MNE involving only Chinese inventors (domestic patents) and the number involving only foreign inventors (foreign patents).
Collaborative patents, measured as the number of patents applied for by the Chinese MNE involving foreign inventors from developed countries (i.e. European and Chinese inventors, US and Chinese inventors).

CHINESE ACQUISITIONS IN EUROPE, JAPAN AND THE USA

In the period 2003–2011, Chinese CBAs in medium- to high-tech industries increased substantially following the general trend depicted in Figure 6.1. Since 2007, despite a downturn in 2010, this rise has been quite significant. Figure 6.2 shows the increasing role of European countries in Chinese acquisitions, and the continuing stable role of Japan. Table 6.1 provides information on the geographical distribution of Chinese acquisitions in the EU, Japan and the USA. Between 2003 and 2011, the countries most targeted for acquisitions were the USA (32 percent of the total number of acquisitions), followed by Germany (21 percent), the UK and Japan (9 percent each) and the Netherlands (8 percent). Other attractive target countries were France and Italy.

Table 6.1 Chinese acquisitions: geographical distributions and main sectors of specialization (#, % and main destination regions)

	Chemicals & pharma	Electronic & electric products	Machinery & equipment	Motor vehicles & other transport equipment	Other manufacturing industries	Computer programming & consultancy	Other service industries	Total
Austria				1 (7.14)				1 (1.05)
Belgium	2 (18.18)							2 (2.11)
Denmark		1 (4.17)			1 (20.0)			2 (2.11)
France	1 (9.09) Ile de France		1 (8.33)	2 (14.29) Alpes Cote d'Azur		1 (14.29)	1 (4.55)	6 (6.32)
Germany		4 (16.67) Baden Wurttemberg	8 (66.67) Baden Wurttemberg & Bavaria	4 (28.57) Bavaria	1 (20.0)		3 (13.64)	20 (21.05)
Italy		2 (8.33) Lombardy	2 (16.67) Lombardy		1 (20.0) Lombardy			5 (5.26)
Japan	1 (9.09) Southern Kanto	3 (12.5) Southern Kanto			1 (20.0)	2 (28.57) Southern Kanto	2 (9.09)	9 (9.47)
Netherlands	2 (18.18)	2 (8.33)	1 (8.33)	1 (7.14)			2 (9.09)	8 (8.42)
Portugal	1 (9.09)							1 (1.05)
Sweden				1 (7.14)			1 (4.55)	2 (2.11)

	Chemicals & pharma	Electronic & electric products	Machinery & equipment	Motor vehicles & other transport equipment	Other manufacturing industries	Computer programming & consultancy	Other service industries	Total
United Kingdom	3 (27.27) Yorkshire			3 (21.43) Greater London		1 (14.29)	2 (9.09)	9 (9.47)
USA	1 (9.09)	12 (50.0) California & Hawaii		2 (14.29) Michigan	1 (20.0)	3 (42.86) Washington	11 (50.0) California	30 (31.58)
Total	11 (100)	24 (100)	12 (100)	14 (100)	5 (100)	7 (100)	22 (100)	95 (100)

Source: BvD Zephyr and SDC Platinum.

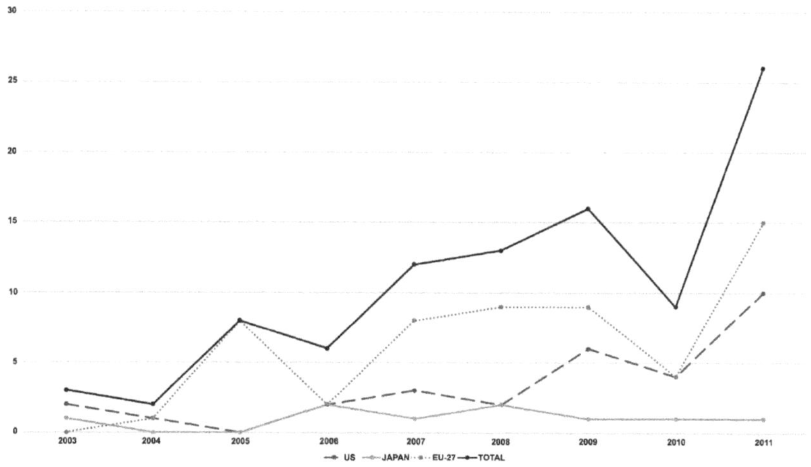

Source: BvD Zephyr and SDC Platinum.

Figure 6.2 *Number of Chinese high-tech cross-border acquisitions in EU, Japan and USA (2003–2011).*

Table 6.1 shows also that almost 70 percent of Chinese acquisitions were in the manufacturing sector, and among them 25 percent were in electronics and electric products, followed by the automotive and machinery and equipment industries. In the service industry, 32 percent of the acquisitions were in the computer and programming sector with the remaining 68 percent in a variety of sectors including publishing activities, information services and telecommunications.

It is interesting that most electronics industry acquisitions are concentrated in the USA, particularly California and Hawaii. Acquisitions in Germany are mainly in the automotive sector with investments going to Bavaria, a key specialized cluster, and machinery to Bavaria and Baden Wurttemberg, both highly specialized in machinery. In the automotive sector, Chinese companies have acquired firms in the UK, France and the USA, in regions with strong specialization in the automotive sector such as Michigan and the southern Alpine region of France. Finally, in computer programming and consultancy acquisitions have been undertaken in the USA in Washington State and in Japan in the Tokyo region.

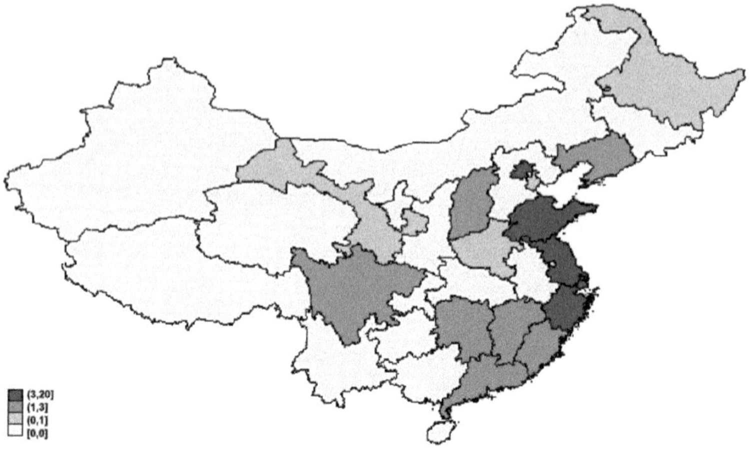

Source: BvD Zephyr and SDC Platinum.

Figure 6.3 *Geographical origin of Chinese high-tech cross-border acquisitions (2003–2011)*

Figure 6.3 presents the geographical origin of Chinese acquiring MNEs, showing that more than 60 percent of them were distributed across four main provinces: Beijing (accounting for 23 percent of Chinese MNEs undertaking cross-border acquisitions), Hong Kong (14 percent),[8] Shanghai (13 percent) and Zhejiang (South of Shanghai) (11 percent). Other important provinces include Jiangsu (North of Shanghai), the neighbouring provinces of Beijing: Shanxi and Shandong, Sichuan and Guangdong on the border with Hong Kong.

TECHNOLOGICAL DISTANCE BETWEEN HOME AND HOST COUNTRY REGIONS

In this section, we explore the differences between Chinese MNEs that connect TDRs (defined as regions with a TPI below the median) and those that connect TPRs (TPI above the median). We focus on the subset of 37 deals where the acquirers were involved in patenting activity before making acquisitions in the EU, Japan or USA, and we investigate the heterogeneity in the knowledge bases of the groups identified above. Table 6.2 presents the main results of our analysis, which are discussed below.

First, we examine acquirers' technological specialization (Table 6.2, Column 1). We expect specialized and diversified firms to have different preferences about the degree of technological similarity of the regions in which they choose to invest. For Patent Scope (Table 6.2, Column 1a), we find that the inventions developed by acquirers who choose to invest in TDRs, span more technologies compared to the group, which chooses to invest in TPRs. However, the difference is not statistically significant.

Table 6.2, Column 1b reports the Share of Patents in the Same Industry as the acquirer firm. Acquirers investing in TDRs are less interested in the technology related to their main specialization than the other group. This indicates that MNEs undertaking acquisitions in TDRs have technological competences that go beyond their own industry (not statistically significant difference).

Finally, the HHI (Table 6.2, Column 1c) indicates that MNEs investing in TDRs are those that, prior to the acquisition, exhibited a stronger pattern of diversification in their innovation activities (the difference between TDRs and TPRs is statistically significant). The higher HHI for companies investing in TPRs implies that their patent portfolios are concentrated in fewer technological competences than the patent portfolios of the other group. Overall, we find that Chinese investors with more technologically diversified patent portfolios target TDRs. There are two possible explanations for this stylized fact. On the one hand, investors with some experience in investing in unfamiliar sectors are more likely to search for acquisitions in regions that will extend their technological horizon and bring new knowledge competences. On the other hand, the location of target companies in technologically advanced host regions, might provide a stronger motivation for the acquisition and more opportunities to access new technologies and diverse knowledge (Cantwell and Iammarino, 2001; Meyer et al., 2011; Beugelsdijk and Mudambi, 2013; Dau, 2013; Iammarino and McCann, 2013).

Table 6.2, Column 2 presents the results for Patent Experience and, although the differences between Chinese MNEs undertaking acquisitions in TDR and TPRs are not statistically significant, we observe that firms investing in TDRs have longer experience of patenting activity. This suggests that more experienced MNEs seek for investments in regional contexts that differ technologically from their home region. In this case, the acquisition can be considered to be more challenging since it exposes the acquirer company to new technological knowledge.

Table 6.2, Column 3 shows that Chinese MNEs connecting TDRs have a larger Patent Portfolio Size, measured by both SIPO and USPTO patents (both statistically significant). In addition, the difference in magnitude between SIPO and USPTO patents is notable, which can be attributed to both the effect of recent Chinese policies to encourage domestic patenting (Hu and Jefferson, 2009) and the quality of Chinese inventions, which would be unlikely to stand

Table 6.2 Patent portfolio characteristics by regional technological similarity of the deal

	1) Technological Specialization			2) Patent Experience	3) Patent Portfolio Size		4) Non-Collaborative Patents		5) Collaborative Patents		
	(a) Patent Scope	(b) % Patents in the same sectors	(c) HHI		(a) # SIPO	(b) # USPTO	(a) Domestic	(b) Foreign	(a) Total	(b) China–EU	(c) China–USA
	1.48	0.003	0.10	2005.10	43.79	0.21	23.95	2.26	0.10	0.00	0.10
TPRs	2.14	0.001	0.04	2003.54	187.38	2.77	76.38	6.77	0.23	0.08	
TDRs											0.15
Diff	2.23	0.35	3.69*	1.01	3.44*	3.02*	4.54**	4.06*		1.48	0.07
Group1–									0.45		
Group2											

Note: * p<0.10; ** p<0.05

up to examination at a foreign patent office (Eberhardt et al., 2011). Anderson et al. (2015) confirm the strong increase in domestic patenting activity and show that, often, Chinese acquisitions are aimed at reverse transfer of technologies that can be put into production quickly in the domestic market. Given the more stringent examination procedures in the USPTO compared to the SIPO, the difference between patent portfolio size measured using USPTO patents can be interpreted also as a qualitative difference. The (on average) larger USPTO patent portfolio of acquirers investing in TDRs indicates higher level technological competences compared to the other group.

Our finding that Chinese MNEs investing in TDRs have larger patent portfolios suggests that firms with stronger knowledge bases are more likely to risk investment in more technologically distant regions. This result is consistent qualitatively with the literature that finds an inverse-U shaped relation between innovation success and technological distance (Ahuja and Katila, 2001). It emphasizes that very innovative and experienced firms understand that investing in regions that are technologically distant can be difficult from the point of view of knowledge integration.

In the last two columns of Table 6.2, we examine the extent of external collaboration between the two groups of acquirers MNEs. Table 6.2, Columns 4 and 5 respectively, report the average number of non-collaborative and collaborative patents. Note that Non-Collaborative Patents, which involve only domestic or only foreign inventors, are far more frequent than Collaborative Patents involving Chinese and foreign inventors from the EU, Japan or the USA – a result that is in line with Branstetter et al. (2015) and Giuliani et al. (2016). International collaborations involving co-inventions (or cross-border inventions) constitute valuable channels for the transfer of knowledge from developed to emerging countries (Montobbio and Sterzi, 2011) because they frequently are characterized by intensive knowledge sharing over extended periods of time, and by face-to-face interactions among inventors with different levels of technological competence, both features that facilitate international knowledge spillovers. The limited engagement of Chinese MNEs in international collaborations and co-patenting suggests that they may, nevertheless, not be able to take advantage of this channel to improve their innovative capacity, accumulate technological capabilities and catch-up with the more advanced countries (Agrawal et al., 2006; Alnuaimi et al., 2012).

However, it seems that Chinese MNEs connecting TDRs have a significantly higher number of patents involving foreign investors, meaning that these companies employ foreign inventors. A limitation of patent data is that they do not reveal the mechanisms through which such foreign patents emerge (such as labour mobility, foreign subsidiary, foreign consultants); however, this result is in line with the more intense patenting activity of Chinese MNEs investing in TDRs, discussed earlier.

CONCLUSIONS

In this chapter, we explored the differences between Chinese MNEs that connect technologically distant regions (TDRs) and those connecting regions with more similar technological bases (TPRs). We used firm-level data on high- and medium-tech acquisitions undertaken by MNEs in Europe, Japan and the USA. Our descriptive analysis suggests that Chinese MNEs with a strong knowledge base, measured as more diversified and larger patent portfolios, invest more in TDRs and exploit their cross-border acquisitions to extend their knowledge and capabilities to new sectors in order to expand their technological horizons. We found also that, although this type of MNE is more involved with foreign inventors (for instance, through consultancies, external experts, foreign workforce), they are not more likely than other Chinese MNEs to establish international patenting collaborations. The number of collaborative patents among the companies considered in our analysis is limited, which might suggest that, while Chinese MNEs are rapidly expanding their operations and production activities abroad, they are internationalizing their innovative activities to a lesser extent. Much of their innovation and patenting activity seems to be confined to the home country territories and, likely, is aimed mainly at reverse knowledge transfer of international technologies to the domestic market.

Our research suggests that Chinese policy-makers should develop and strengthen policies oriented towards technological capability building in the domestic market (Lema et al., 2015). This can be achieved in various ways such as increasing the country's attraction for MNEs from advanced countries; learning from advanced country MNEs can be a viable first step for laggard multinationals from emerging countries to enhance their technological capabilities (Li et al., 2012). Policy-makers should aim also at increasing investment in higher education and creating incentives for return migration of engineers, scientists and managers (World Bank, 2010). In general, measures aimed at strengthening the national system of innovation should be continued (Lundvall et al., 2009), but with more attention paid to the development of local innovation systems. Crescenzi et al. (2012) show that innovation activity in China is spatially concentrated and innovative regions generate few knowledge spillovers to other regions. In the next few years, China must promote dispersal of production and urbanization, and, also, innovation.

The analysis in this chapter has some limitations, which suggest that our results should be interpreted with caution. First, we are not able to investigate whether the technological distance between the home and host regions is an antecedent to or a cause of some of the characteristics of Chinese MNEs observed here. Also, despite the temporal lag, we cannot account for reverse causality. However, we believe that the observed differences are reasonable considering the setting of our analysis and the conventional wisdom that, to be able to identify and absorb diverse international knowledge, requires the prior accumulation of specific knowledge. Second, we do not look at the outcomes of the investigated international connections: do Chinese MNEs connecting TDRs show more successful performance or higher levels of innovation after a CBA compared to those connecting TPRs? Do the former MNEs learn faster than the latter? Third, a natural extension to this study would be to include in the empirical analysis other characteristics, such as financial indicators, of the Chinese MNEs and target firms. Fourth, our focus on patents is a major limitation since they may not be suited to measuring innovation in the context of an emerging country such as China. We are unable to observe learning processes and innovative outcomes that do not result in patent applications. All these issues represent areas for future research.

NOTES

1. The overlap between the two databases is partial: 28 percent of the acquisitions appear only in Zephyr, and 31 percent appear only in SDC Platinum.
2. The start year is 2003 because, according to UNCTAD (2015), most outward foreign investments from emerging to advanced countries occurred after that date.
3. The 2-digit NACE codes are 20, 21, 26, 27, 28, 29 and 30 (for manufacturing) and 59, 60, 61, 62, 63, 64, 65, 66, 69, 70, 71, 72, 73, 74, 78 and 80 (for services). The SDC classification applies to deals taken from the SDC-Platinum database.
4. This measure is also referred to as 'cosine distance' since it can be interpreted as the cosine of the angle between the two technological vectors. When the vectors are orthogonal (i.e. the two regions innovate in completely different technological areas), the cosine is equal to 0.
5. For a more detailed description of the indicators see Squicciarini et al. (2013).
6. The technological classification is the same as used to calculate the TPI.
7. The EPO-PATSTAT Database (2016) provides a table linking the patent applications to NACE Classification, based on the concordance table developed by Van Looy et al. (2015).
8. We include in our database those acquisitions originating in Hong Kong, undertaken by companies from Mainland China.

REFERENCES

Agrawal, A., I. Cockburn and J. McHale (2006), 'Gone but not forgotten: Labor flows, knowledge spillovers, and enduring social capital', *Journal of Economic Geography*, **6**, 571–91.

Ahuja, G. and R. Katila (2001), 'Technological acquisitions and the innovation performance of acquiring firms: A longitudinal study', *Strategic Management Journal*, **22** (3), 197–220.

Alnuaimi, T., J. Singh and G. George (2012), 'Not with my own: Long-term effects of cross-country collaboration on subsidiary innovation in emerging economies versus advanced economies', *Journal of Economic Geography*, **12** (5), 943–68.

Amendolagine, V., C. Cozza and R. Rabellotti (2015), 'Chinese and Indian multinationals: A firm-level analysis of their investments in Europe', *Global Economic Review*, **44** (4), 452–69.

Amighini, A., R. Rabellotti and M. Sanfilippo (2013), 'China's outward FDI: An industry-level analysis of host-country determinants', *Frontiers of Economics in China*, **8** (3), 27.

Anderson, J., D. Sutherland and S. Severe (2015), 'An event study of home and host country patent generation in Chinese MNEs undertaking strategic asset acquisitions in developed markets', *International Business Review*, **24** (5), 758–71.

Awate, S., M. M. Larsen and R. Mudambi (2015), 'Accessing vs sourcing knowledge: A comparative study of R&D internationalization between emerging and advanced economy firms', *Journal of International Business Studies*, **46** (1), 63–86.

Beugelsdijk, S. and R. Mudambi (2013), 'MNEs as border-crossing multi-location enterprises: The role of discontinuities in geographic space', *Journal of International Business Studies*, **44**, 413–26.

Bottazzi, L. and G. Peri (2003), 'Innovation and spillovers in regions: Evidence from European patent data', *European Economic Review*, **47** (4), 687–710.

Branstetter, L., L. Guangwei and F. Veloso (2015), 'The rise of international co-invention', in A. Jaffe and B. Jones (eds), *The Changing Frontier: Rethinking Science and Innovation Policy*, Chicago: University of Chicago Press, pp. 135–68.

Cantwell, J. and S. Iammarino (2001), 'EU regions and multinational corporations: Change, stability and strengthening of technological comparative advantages', *Industrial and Corporate Change*, **10** (4), 1007–37.

Cantwell, J. A. and R. Mudambi (2011), 'Physical attraction and the geography of knowledge sourcing in multinational enterprises', *Global Strategy Journal*, **1** (3–4), 206–32.

Chung, W. and J. Alcacer (2002), 'Knowledge seeking and location choice of foreign direct investment in the United States', *Management Science*, **48**, 1534–54.

Cloodt, M., J. Hagedoorn and H. Van Kranenburg (2006), 'Mergers and acquisitions: Their effect on the innovative performance of companies in high-tech industries', *Research Policy*, **35** (5), 642–54.

Crescenzi, R., A. Rodríguez-Pose and M. Storper (2012), 'The territorial dynamics of innovation in China and India', *Journal of Economic Geography*, **12** (5), 1055–85.

Crescenzi, R., C. Pietrobelli and R. Rabellotti (2016), 'Regional strategic assets and the location strategies of emerging countries' multinationals in Europe', *European Planning Studies*, **24** (4), 645–67.

Dau, L. A. (2013), 'Learning across geographic space: Pro-market reforms, multinationalization strategy, and profitability', *Journal of International Business Studies*, **44** (3), 235–62.

Duysters, G., J. Jacob, C. Lemmens and J. Yu (2009), 'Internationalization and technological catching up of emerging multinationals: A comparative case study of China's Haier Group', *Industrial and Corporate Change*, **18** (2), 325–49.

Eberhardt, M., C. Helmers and Z. Yu (2011), 'Is the dragon learning to fly? An analysis of the Chinese patent explosion', *University of Nottingham Research Paper* No. 2011/16.

Giuliani, E., A. Martinelli and R. Rabellotti (2016), 'Is co-invention expediting technological catch up? A study of collaboration between emerging country firms and EU inventors', *World Development*, **77**, 192–205.

Hu, A. G. and G. H. Jefferson (2009), 'A great wall of patents: What is behind China's recent patent explosion?', *Journal of Development Economics*, **90** (1), 57–68.

Iammarino, S. and P. McCann (2013), *Multinationals and Economic Geography: Location, Technology and Innovation*, Cheltenham, UK and Northampton, MA, USA: Edward Elgar Publishing.

Jaffe, A. (1986), 'Technological opportunities and spillovers of R&D: Evidence from firms' patents, profits and market value', *The American Economic Review*, **76**, 984–1001.

Lema, R., R. Quadros and H. Schmitz (2015), 'Reorganising global value chains and building innovation capabilities in Brazil and India', *Research Policy*, **44** (7), 1376–86.

Lerner, J. (1994), 'The importance of patent scope: An empirical analysis', *The RAND Journal of Economics*, **25**, 319–33.

Li, J., Y. Li and D. Shapiro (2012), 'Knowledge seeking and outward FDI of emerging market firms: The moderating effect of inward FDI', *Global Strategy Journal*, **2**, 277–95.

Lundvall, B. A., K. J. Joseph, C. Chaminade and J. Vang (eds) (2009), *Handbook of Innovation Systems and Developing Countries*, Cheltenham, UK and Northampton, MA, USA: Edward Elgar Publishing.

Maraut, S., H. Dernis, C. Webb, V. Spiezia and D. Guellec (2008), 'The OECD REGPAT database: A presentation', *STI Working Paper 2008/2*, Paris: Organisation for Economic Co-operation and Development.

Meyer, K. E., R. Mudambi and R. Narula (2011), 'Multinational enterprises and local contexts: The opportunities and challenges of multiple embeddedness', *Journal of Management Studies*, **48** (2), 235–52.

Montobbio, F. and V. Sterzi (2011), 'Inventing together: Exploring the nature of international knowledge spillovers in Latin America', *Journal of Evolutionary Economics*, **21** (1), 53–89.

Piscitello, L., R. Rabellotti and V. Scalera (2015), 'Chinese and Indian acquisitions in Europe: The relationship between motivation and entry mode choice', in A. Risberg, D. King and O. Meglio (eds), *The Routledge Companion to Mergers and Acquisitions*, London: Routledge, pp. 114–29.

Squicciarini, M., H. Dernis and C. Criscuolo (2013), 'Measuring patent quality: Indicators of technological and economic value', *Science, Technology and Industry Working Paper No. 2013/03*, Paris: Organisation for Economic Co-operation and Development.

United Nations Conference on Trade and Development (UNCTAD) (2015), *World Investment Report*, Geneva: UNCTAD.

United Nations Conference on Trade and Development (UNCTAD) (2016), *World Investment Report*, Geneva: UNCTAD.

Valentini, G. and M. C. Di Guardo (2012), 'M&A and the profile of inventive activity', *Strategic Organization*, **10** (4), 384–405.

Van Looy, B., C. Vereyen and U. Schmoch (2015), *IPCV8-NACE Rev.2 Update (version 2.0)*, Brussels: EUROSTAT.

World Bank (2010), *Innovation Policy: A Guide for Developing Countries, The International Bank for Reconstruction and Development*, Washington DC: The World Bank.

7. Internationalisation for technological capability building: from production to innovation in a case study of Goldwind Technology

Ju Liu

1. INTRODUCTION

This chapter investigates the 20-year-long process of Goldwind Technology, a Chinese wind energy company, and its internationalisation for technological capability building. It focuses on the role of cross-border technological learning through human mobility between its headquarters and its foreign counterpart in the process of technological capabilities building. There are two common arguments about Chinese firms' internationalisation for technological capability building. First, they are mainly driven by technological learning rather than technological innovation (Di Minin et al., 2012). The firms usually do not possess superior technological resources when they go abroad (Mathews, 2006; Li, 2010; Peng, 2012). The purpose of their internationalisation is not to exploit the technologies that they possess but to access and gain those that they do not have. Second, their internationalisation for technological capability building has been primarily in the form of acquisition, often high-profile acquisitions (Peng, 2012; Sun et al., 2012). Scholars argue that the firms with few technological capabilities tend to acquire innovative firms in developed countries rather than to build up their own. The advantages are obvious. Acquisition provides substantially more and quicker access to resources than green-field investment, which can serve a fast market entry. Further, success is more likely particularly when the acquisition is combined with the firm's low-cost-based production capacity. On top of that, acquisition can help the firm to overcome the following disadvantages: their poor-quality image, the lack of locally embedded assets and the lack of international exposure.

Nevertheless, technological learning through international acquisition is more likely to fail than to succeed. When going abroad, Chinese firms' technological disadvantages suggest their weak absorptive capacity for learning.

It also implies weak bargaining power in the pre-acquisition stage and a high probability of failure in the post-acquisition period. No clear evidence shows that Chinese EMNCs' acquisition for technology performs better than the global average.

Despite many failures, there are successful cases. These firms not only successfully actualised technological learning, but they also gradually evolved from production into technological innovation in the later stage by combining foreign technology and their home R&D capability (Di Minin et al., 2012; Si et al., 2013). The more general question about why and how the firms can build technological capability through the internationalisation processes are interesting ones, with related questions addressed in Chapters 8 and 9.

This chapter is an in-depth case study of a successful Chinese wind energy firm, Xinjiang Goldwind Science and Technology Co., Ltd. (Goldwind). Although it was previously a spin-off of a public research institute in 1988, the firm was listed as one of the world's most innovative firms by MIT in 2012. In 2015, Goldwind became the world's largest wind turbine producer, surpassing many leading firms such as Vestas (Denmark), Siemens (Germany), and GE (USA). Goldwind acquired the German wind turbine technology firm Vensys in 2008, after 12 years of doing business with German firms. The acquisition later is proved to be the turning point in Goldwind's technological capability-building process. Since then, Goldwind has gradually moved from production to innovation. Ru et al. (2012) find that public policy was a driving force for the evolution of innovation modes, within the Chinese wind turbine manufacturing industry. Slepniov et al. (2015) analyse the relationships between entrepreneur and national innovation system, as the Goldwind company expands internationally. Tan and Mathews (2015) argue that Goldwind was able to use resource leveraging, in order to accelerate the speed of internationalisation. Hansen and Lema (2019) analyse the relationship between learning sources and technological capabilities, also using Goldwind as one of their case studies to argue that late-comers can move from production to innovation.

Similar to previous research, this chapter addresses two research questions in relation to trust and building capacities: 1) What is the process of internationalisation for technological capability building in the case company? 2) How did the case company make the transition from production to innovation?

Our analysis defines a specific process, by showing that the firm has a three-phase process of internationalisation for technological capability building, namely import phase, co-development phase and integration phase. Cross-border technological learning through human mobility between its headquarters and its foreign counterpart facilitated the case firm's transition from production to innovation. The cross-border technological learning was enabled by cross-border relationship building with mutual trust based on long-term personal relationships among the key managers from both parties.

2. ANALYTICAL FRAMEWORK

One distinctive characteristic of the internationalisation of EMNCs is their explorative motive (Meyer, 2015). This is different from other forms of internationalisation such as market-seeking, efficiency-seeking and natural resource-seeking, as distinguished in internationalisation literature (Dunning, 1998; Makino et al., 2002; Buckley et al., 2007). The internationalisation of emerging multinational companies (EMNCs) aims at accessing, obtaining or creating strategic assets – usually knowledge and technology – that these firms do not possess. This is different from the conventional multinational companies' (MNCs) internationalisation, which aims at exploiting technologies they already own by taking advantage of the host countries' cheap labour, abundant natural resources or profitable local market. The internationalisation aiming at strategic technology assets to build up a company's technological capability has been discussed in different strands of research with different perspectives, such as the asset-seeking perspective (Makino et al., 2002; Ivarsson and Jonsson, 2003), the knowledge-seeking perspective (Chung and Alcácer, 2002), the springboard perspective (Luo and Tung, 2007) and the learning perspective (Mathews, 2006; Li, 2010). In the early stage of these strands of research, scholars focused more on the internationalisation of MNCs from advanced countries (such as Kogut and Chang, 1991; Almeida, 1996; Shan and Song, 1997); later the focus shifted to internationalisation of EMNCs (Chen and Chen, 1998; Kumar, 1998; Hoesel, 1999; Makino et al., 2002; Mathews, 2006), particularly, in recent decades, EMNCs from China (Rui and Yip, 2008; Deng, 2009; Li et al., 2012; Cui et al., 2014; Anderson et al., 2015).

The explorative motive of Chinese firms' internationalisation implies the great importance of learning for innovation (Makino and Inkpen, 2003). The learning-based view sees MNCs' internationalisation as a cross-border learning process (Mathews, 2006; Li, 2010). It is argued that when technologically disadvantaged EMNCs go abroad, first, they need to link up with the incumbents in the advanced countries. Second, they leverage (or acquire) and internalise the incumbent firms' knowledge and technology into their own systems. Third, after rounds of such internalisation, learning happens and technological capability is built. Besides the great contribution of understanding the distinctive characteristics of the internationalisation of EMNCs, scholars with the learning perspective have not yet offered a satisfying answer about how the EMNCs link up with the incumbents in the developed countries and when and why the incumbents are willing to "teach" the emerging country firms (Liu and Lema, 2015). Hence, foreign direct investment can be a source of learning (Liu, 2019).

The great importance of learning in the internationalisation for technological capability building raises another important question about relationship building for learning (Beeby and Booth, 2000; Li, 2005; Manolova et al., 2010; Liu, 2012). Learning emphasises the repeated application of linking up with incumbents and internalising the incumbents' knowledge. Such learning will not be completed in one stroke. Rather, it takes a long time to accomplish. It requires one to establish, to maintain and to sustain a long-term relationship with the incumbent firms in the advanced countries.

Therefore, the chapter proposes to use the analytical framework as shown in Figure 7.1, in order to study the process of the internationalisation for technological capability building in the case firm. The framework includes the analysis of: 1) the process of technological learning, which is expected to facilitate the transition from production to innovation; and 2) the process of inter-organisational relationship building, which is expected to enable the 20-year-long technological learning to build up the firm's technological capability.

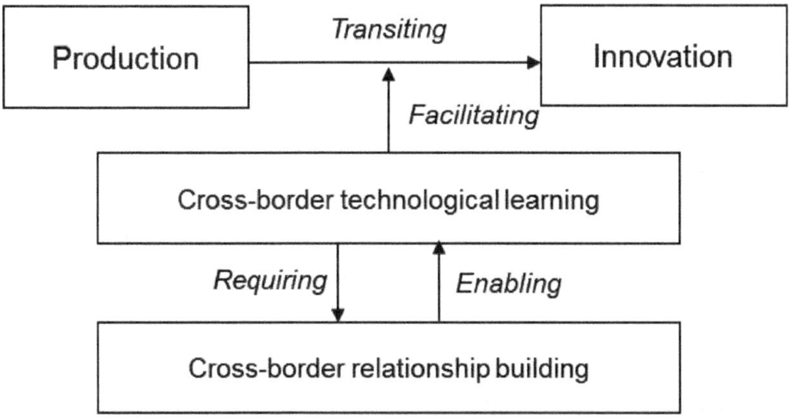

Figure 7.1 A framework for understanding the process of internationalisation for technological capability building

3. METHOD

This chapter adopts an in-depth case study method, which is an empirical inquiry that investigates a contemporary phenomenon within its real-life context when the boundaries between phenomenon and context are not clearly defined (Yin, 2013).

The chapter uses the process tracing technique to recall the internationalisation process, including the key events, the main measures and the main outcomes of the different phases over time. Process tracing is a qualitative technique of working backwards to identify the intervening cause process between different variables (George and Bennett, 2005). Both the process of cross-border technological learning and relationship building are analysed.

Multiple data sources were used in the case study, including semi-structured interviews with managers and experts, the firm's annual reports and internal documents, industrial reports, policy documents, press news, and academic publications about the case firm and industry. Multiple evidences improve the accuracy of information and the robustness of the results (Jick, 1979). The interviews were conducted between 2013 and 2014 in the headquarters of the case firm in Beijing, China, and its German counterpart in Neunkirchen, Germany. We interviewed the top management team members, including the vice president of Goldwind International and the key managers on the German side. In 2014 and 2015, to follow up the previous research, the author also interviewed the case firm's suppliers as well as industrial experts in other cities in China. Some of the interviews were done via phone calls.

Potential informant bias was addressed in four ways. First, we selected highly knowledgeable informants with either over ten years of work experience in the case firms and/or informants who were the key persons in the internationalisation process. Second, we focused on factual accounts by using a "courtroom questioning" technique (Lipton, 1977; Huber and Power, 1985). We asked the informants to specify what kinds of activities are carried out and what kinds of outcomes are produced during a specific strategic process so as to ensure that they did not mix up what has been done and what should have been done or planned to have been done. Third, we granted anonymity to the informants. Fourth, we triangulated the information collected during the interview with archives, websites, internal reports, internal documents, press news, and scientific publications about the case firms. We also triangulated the information provided by different informants on the same issue. Nevertheless, the limited number of interviews conducted seriously limits the extent to which the observed patterns can be generalised with other firms; consequently, this study can only be considered explorative.

4. THE CHINESE CASE FIRM AND ITS GERMAN COUNTERPART

The Chinese firm Xinjiang Goldwind Science & Technology Co., Ltd. was previously a spin-off of the Xinjiang Institute of Water Resources and Hydro

Power Research, which was affiliated to the Xinjiang provincial government until 1988. In 1998, the company was formally established and renamed as Goldwind. It is now one of the world's leading wind power firms, providing integrated wind energy solutions, including R&D; manufacturing; sales; wind farm investment and service, such as wind resource assessment; EPC (engineering, procurement and construction); contracting; and so on. The company has more than 6,000 employees globally, with two headquarters – Xinjiang and Beijing, China – and three international subsidiaries – Chicago, USA; Neunkirchen, Germany; and Sydney, Australia. Further, Goldwind has one R&D centre in China and one in Germany. The company was listed by IAM – the world's leading IP business media platform – as one of the China IP champions, whose intellectual property management and value creation strategies meets those of global leaders. It also holds the title of one of the 50 Most Innovative Firms in 2012 by MIT Technology Review. In 2015, the company became the world's largest wind turbine original equipment manufacturer, according to the 2015 reports from FTI Consulting and Bloomberg New Energy Finance (BNEF), respectively.

The most important foreign partner in Goldwind's internationalisation for technological capability building is Vensys, a German-based wind turbine design company. Vensys started as a small engineering bureau that emerged from an R&D centre at the University of Saarbrücken, and it has been operating commercially in Germany since 2000, whereas the R&D activities at the university started about ten years earlier. It conducts R&D in the fields of direct drive wind turbine, energy efficiency, rotor design, larger wind turbines, low wind speed areas, extreme climatic conditions such as extreme heat, coldness, winds and grid instability. The permanent magnet direct drive (PMDD) is considered Vensys' most important innovation. Though Vensys' business model was licensing to partners, licensing poses risks of IPR infringements, provides only limited financial benefit and offers only limited contacts and networks. In 2001, two top managers of another German wind energy company, RePower, joined Vensys and brought with them their contact with Goldwind. Later, Goldwind bought the license from Vensys and started producing Vensys' models. After several years of collaboration on production, Goldwind finally acquired Vensys. Since then, it has given Vensys access to the Chinese market and contacts. At the same time, Goldwind guaranteed its access to Vensys' knowledge and technologies.

5. THE THREE-PHASE PROCESS OF INTERNATIONALISATION FOR TECHNOLOGICAL CAPABILITY BUILDING

The chapter identifies three phases in the process of internationalisation for technological capability building through which Goldwind has gradually gained the technological capability for production to adaptation engineering and further to advanced design.

5.1 The Import Phase (1996–2005)

Import refers to buying technology from abroad, such as obtaining wind turbines, key components, licenses, patents, and so on. Between 1996 and 2005, Goldwind mainly adopted this strategy to gradually build up its technological capability for production through learning by imitating and reverse engineering. It was called "liangtou zainei, zhongjian zaiwai", which literally means two-ends-inside-and-the-middle-outside. The two ends refer to the planning and managing of the wind farms. The middle refers to manufacturing the wind turbines, particularly the key components. The import of foreign technology was for the development of the technological capability for basic production.

The key event in this phase was the import of 600kW wind turbines in 1996 from the German company Jacobs Energy. This paved the way for Goldwind's internationalisation. As a result of its dealings with Jacobs Energy, Goldwind became friendly with the then owner as well as his business partner. Subsequently, Goldwind has built up a 20-year-long relationship with these two key persons, one of which recalled:

> I founded Jacobs Energy together with my business partner in 1991 … In 1996, a 600kW station was sold to Goldwind … Soon Goldwind asked for a production license for China, and Jacobs Energy granted this license; and they also trained Goldwind staff in Germany. In 2000, the name of Jacobs Energy was changed to Repower. The then Chairman of the Board wanted another partner than Goldwind. It was a bigger one, Dongfeng, a state-owned company. But I told him that Goldwind would be the best partner they could imagine. The chairman did not agree, so I and my business partner left RePower and joined Vensys in 2001. We continued to work with Goldwind since after.

During the import phase, the collaboration between Goldwind and its German counterparts was mainly exporting and importing. The outcomes of the import phase were Goldwind's manufacturing a 600kW wind turbine in 1999, scaling up production capacity to 200 units per year in 2002 and adding a 750kW wind turbine to its product portfolio in the same year. At the end of the import phase, Goldwind was ready to start its own R&D. In 2004, it tried to develop a new model of a 1.2MW wind turbine alone, and it successfully produced a prototype in 2005. However, this model was not put into production.

5.2 The Co-Development Phase (2006–2008)

This phase involved Goldwind co-developing new models of wind turbines with its German counterpart. The co-development on Goldwind's side was mainly adapting Vensys' theoretical design to industrial mass production. It also entailed the development of the technological capability for adaptation and engineering.

There were two key events in this phase. The first was Goldwind in 2006 building a factory alongside Vensys in Neunkirchen, Germany, with the purpose of co-developing Vensys' newly designed turbines and producing them for the European market. The second was Goldwind in 2008 acquiring a 70 per cent share of Vensys for 41.24 million Euros, thereby becoming the major shareholder of the company.

Reasoning as to why building a factory particularly for Vensys' design, Goldwind's chairman said:

> The Germans are doing their business with full heart. They simply love manufacturing. I asked the Vensys staff: "What is your biggest dream?" They told me that Vensys is a design company, and they had never manufactured a turbine that they designed. Their biggest dream is to produce by their own hands a turbine that is designed by themselves. So we spent less than six months to build up a factory for them. I want to show them our sincerity and determination of collaboration. I helped them to realise their dreams.

The co-development phase was the accelerating period of Goldwind's technological capability building. Talking about the impact of the acquisition on Goldwind's technological capability, a minority shareholder of Vensys reported:

> After the acquisition, the Chinese headquarters mastered the Getriebelose station technology. The training and qualification of Chinese suppliers for Goldwind headquarters was done by the staff from Vensys. It can be assumed that without the acquisition this qualification would not have been done by Vensys.

Our informants from both the Beijing headquarters and Vensys confirmed that the acquisition was to "avoid the risk of being cut off from the collaboration in the case of some other firms buying Vensys".

In this phase, the personnel exchange between the Beijing headquarters and Vensys became more and more intense. Before the acquisition, more Vensys staff went to China mainly for transforming their design to mass production and adaption to the Chinese market. However, the situation started to reverse after the acquisition. More staff from the Beijing headquarters went to visit and work in Vensys, Germany. There was an annual exchange of between 10 to 20 R&D staff and sometimes marketing staff. Usually, they stayed in the counterpart's sites for at least one year.

The outcome of the co-development phase was the successful co-development of the 1.5MW and the 2.5MW wind turbines. In 2008, Goldwind produced and installed 111 units of this model on a wind farm in Inner Mongolia, China. The successful co-development with Vensys enhanced Goldwind headquarters' technological capability, while the acquisition secured the technological assets that Goldwind gained from Vensys.

5.3 The Integration Phase (2009–2013 and beyond)

Integration refers to actively involving the acquired foreign company's R&D activities into the strategic R&D portfolio of the parent company. The company's Beijing headquarters and its German counterpart operated through the common source of strategic control, but they had clear labour division focusing on different strategic areas. Goldwind did not consider Vensys as its German subsidiary. Instead, it considered Vensys as an independent company of strategic importance, one that it was the majority shareholder of. After the acquisition, Vensys continued to develop high-end products with higher technological sophistication for the European market, while Goldwind mainly developed wind turbines for the Asian, African and South American markets, where cost was given a higher priority. Goldwind's technological capability building in this phase targeted advanced design technology.

The two key events of this phase were the establishment of a Vensys factory in Germany in 2009, for which Goldwind invested 5 million Euro and the assignment of Vensys' CEO as the CTO of Goldwind in 2010.

At this phase, the headquarters in China had built up certain technological capability through years of importing German technology and co-developing new products with Vensys. The company was able to independently conduct R&D of advanced wind turbines. Goldwind started to broaden its technology portfolio to further enhance its technological capabilities. Explaining the integrating strategy, the vice president of Goldwind International stated:

> What I mean by integrating is that, for instance, maybe some kinds of technologies are not in the future direction of Goldwind, but we try to develop them as a different part of the company's technology portfolio. One example can be that in 2012 Goldwind developed the 3M semi-PMDD technology without the direct participation of Vensys, who focus only on PMDD. This technology is developed to solve the oversize problem of PMDD. We need to have certain technology reserve and test it

against the risk of technology change. Integrating does not mean to replace Vensys but to support each other.

By integrating Vensys into the Goldwind R&D strategy, Goldwind further enhanced its technological capabilities to a new level. The VP of Goldwind International conveyed:

> After the acquisition, we are able to do advanced innovation. In 2013, we successfully developed the 6MW offshore wind turbine, which marks Goldwind's leading position in the world's wind energy technology field. The newly developed patents are shared between Goldwind and Vensys… Even though the potential of integrating has not been 100 per cent realised, we have definitely improved our technological capability thanks to the integration of Vensys.

In this phase, multiple measures were taken to create the synergy between the Beijing headquarters and its newly bought German counterpart. For example, Goldwind adopted the "Can Sha Zi" approach, which literally means mixing sand into cement, a metaphor of injecting new blood into an inflexible organisation to spur change. In order to transfer knowledge and technology, Goldwind created opportunities to bring together the R&D staff from its Beijing headquarters and that of Vensys. Moreover, it assigned the CEO of Vensys as the CTO of Goldwind, which marked the integration of Goldwind and Vensys' R&D strategy.

The outcome of the integration phase was the successful development of the 3MW semi-PMDD wind turbine in 2009, the ultra-low-speed GW93/1500 wind turbine in 2012, and the 6MW PMDD wind turbine in 2013.

6. CASE ANALYSIS OF GOLDWIND

6.1 The Process of Cross-border Technological Learning

Along the three phases of internationalisation for technological capability building, Goldwind experienced three different types of cross-border technological learning (see Figure 7.2). They are as follows: 1) unilateral learning to produce and produce efficiently; 2) bilateral learning to improve products and to co-develop new products; and 3) multilateral learning to independently develop new products.

The import of foreign technologies was the starting point of Goldwind's technological learning. By assembling, installing and revising the engineering of foreign imported wind turbines, Goldwind accumulated experience, concrete know-how, and craft and practical skills for wind turbine manufacturing. Initially, the technological learning was mainly for producing; thereafter, it was for producing efficiently. It was more unilateral, which means knowledge

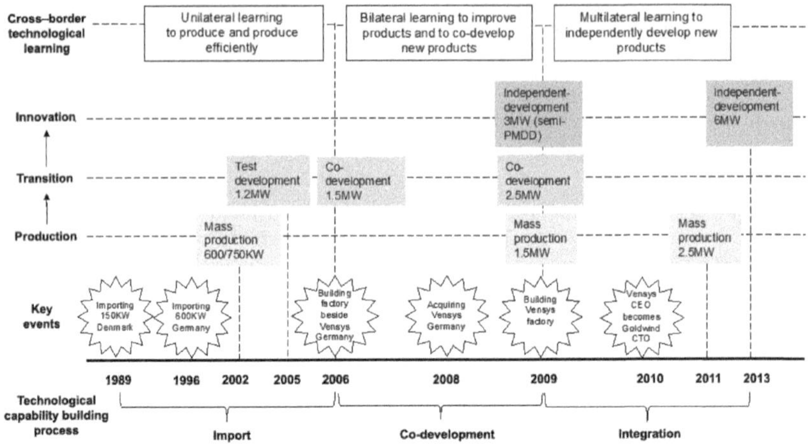

Figure 7.2 *The cross-border technological learning along the process of internationalisation for technological capability building*

that was embedded in the physical equipment and components, the technical documents, and the after sales service transferred from foreign firms to Goldwind in a one-way manner.

During the co-development phase, the technological learning became bilateral between Goldwind's Beijing headquarters and Vensys. In the beginning, the learning was mainly for improving products and later on for co-developing new products. Operational knowledge, design knowledge and management knowledge were bilaterally transferred between Goldwind, Beijing, and Vensys, Germany. Nevertheless, the scale, scope and direction of the knowledge transfer kept changing over time. For example, the operation knowledge – including technical information about the product, customers' requirement and feedback – flowed from Goldwind, Beijing, to Vensys, and design knowledge – such as design criteria and specifications, theoretical tools, and design procedures – flowed in the opposite direction. Managerial knowledge, such as portfolio management and project management, was transferred from Goldwind, Beijing, to Vensys, Germany, while technological management knowledge was transferred conversely.

Until the integration phase, Goldwind's technological learning was multilateral, that is, among its Beijing headquarters, Vensys and its collaborators in Europe, as well as other newly joined international technology providers, component manufacturers and technology consultants, such as Switch (Finland), GL Garrad Hassan (UK), Swancor (Taiwan), Siemens (Germany) and Risö Lab (Denmark). The learning was mainly for the purpose of independent R&D.

To a great extent, the cross-border technological learning was actualised by human mobility between Goldwind's Beijing headquarters and its German counterpart through thousands of occasions for training, work site visits, job rotation and project co-developing involving different levels of managers and engineers. This is in line with the arguments in management literature about the dynamic role of human resources, which influence the strategic technological capability building (Song et al., 2003; Liu et al., 2009). Firms and organisations ultimately learn via their individual members (Kim, 1998), and learning happens when people are involved and interact.

The cross-border technological learning facilitated the transition from production to innovation. The transition started in the strategic phase of co-development, and it was in this phase that Goldwind acquired Vensys. Before acquiring Vensys, Goldwind had spent 20 years moving from "learning to produce" to "learning to produce efficiently" through imitating and revising engineering. One could hardly maintain that without the acquisition of Vensys in 2008, Goldwind would never have been able to accomplish such a transition. Nevertheless, the author argued in another paper (Liu and Lema, 2015) that the acquisition of Vensys played the role of an accelerator in the company's accumulative process of learning for innovation.

6.2 The Process of Cross-border Relationship Building

Along the import, co-development, and integration phase of internationalisation for technological capability building, the cross-border relationship between Goldwind and its German counterpart also evolved from the relationship as 1) importer and exporter to 2) external collaborators and further to 3) internal partners (see Figure 7.3).

In this process, human mobility between Goldwind's Beijing headquarters and its German counterpart, Vensys, was increasingly intensified. The cross-border relationship was gradually built up through the inter-person interaction among engineers and managers from both sides.

During the interviews at Goldwind's Beijing headquarters and Vensys in Germany, trust was frequently mentioned as the most important influential factor for the success of the acquisition, besides that of the technological complementation. Importantly, the trust does not come from nowhere. It is fostered by the long-term interaction between hundreds of managers and engineers from both parties. Furthermore, it is particularly embedded in the long-term strong personal relationship between Goldwind's top management and the two German key managers, regardless of all the turbulence in business and the changes in personal careers.

Noticeably, the chapter finds that the cross-border relationship building demonstrates a helix-like pattern, that is, building-confirming and further-building–further-confirming through different activities such as gaining familiarity and demonstrating commitment, securing ownership and re-confirming commitment, and so on. It shows that the higher level the relationship is, the higher the level the commitment and trust are.

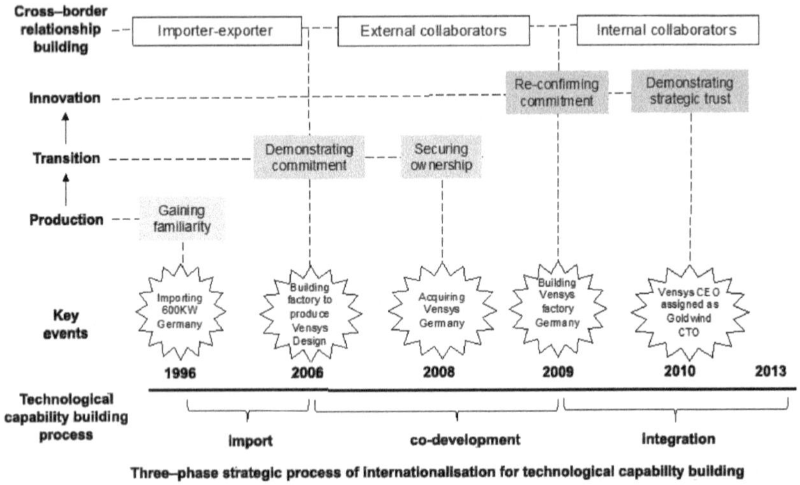

Figure 7.3 *The cross-border relationship building in the process of internationalisation for technological capability building*

7. CONCLUSION

This chapter has provided an in-depth case study about a Chinese wind energy firm, which is analysed in terms of an internationalisation process for technological capability building. As compared to previous research (Ru et al., 2012; Slepniov et al., 2015; Tan and Mathews, 2015; Hansen and Lema, 2019), this chapter puts more emphasis on trust and managing cross-border relationships, during processes of globalisation and innovation.

In recounting the case study, this chapter identifies and categorises the firm's history into three phases of the process: the import phase, the co-development phase and the integration phase. Furthermore, our analysis is that internationalisation played a great role in its technological capability building and helped its successful transition from production to innovation. Such a transition was facilitated by the cross-border technological learning, which was enabled by the cross-border relationship building between the case firm's headquarters and its foreign counterpart over years.

More specifically, in this case study, we find that when cross-border technological capability building shifts from production to transition and to innovation, then also the cross-border relationship building must evolve at the same pace from the importer/exporter to external collaborators and further to internal partners. This may suggest that an interesting proposition for future research is whether the greater technological capability is targeted, then the closer the cross-border relationship is needed for technological learning. Moreover, the development of the domestic Chinese wind energy industry was developed at the same time as the wind turbine and general wind energy technology was expanded at Chinese university departments and research institutes. Future research should combine the perspectives of cross-border technological learning with the within-border technological learning to see the global–local interaction and its role in the firm's technological capability building.

ACKNOWLEDGEMENT

The chapter is based on the research project *The Challenge of Globalization: Technology Driven Foreign Direct Investment (TFDI) and its Implications for the Negotiation of International (bi and multilateral) Investment Agreements* funded by the Swedish Foundation for Humanities and Social Science. Great thanks to project partner Ping Lv, Eva Dantas, and Niclas Meyer for organising interviews.

REFERENCES

Almeida, P. (1996), 'Knowledge sourcing by foreign multinationals: Patent citation analysis in the US semiconductor industry', *Strategic Management Journal*, **17**, 155–65.

Anderson, J., D. Sutherland and S. Severe (2015), 'An event study of home and host country patent generation in Chinese MNEs undertaking strategic asset acquisitions in developed markets', *International Business Review*, **24**(5), 758–71.

Beeby, M. and C. Booth (2000), 'Networks and inter-organizational learning: A critical review', *The Learning Organization*, **7**(2), 75–88.

Buckley, P. J., L. J. Clegg, A. R. Cross, X. Liu, H. Voss and P. Zheng (2007), 'The determinants of Chinese outward foreign direct investment', *Journal of International Business Studies*, **38**, 499–518.

Chen, H. and T. Chen (1998), 'Network linkages and location choice in foreign direct investment', *Journal of International Business Studies*, **29**(3), 445–67.

Chung, W. and J. Alcácer (2002), 'Knowledge seeking and location choice of foreign direct investment in the United States', *Management Science*, **48**, 1534–54.

Cui, L., K. Meyer and H. Hu (2014), 'What drives firms' intent to seek strategic assets by foreign direct investment? A study of emerging economy firms', *Journal of World Business*, **49**, 488–501.

Deng, P. (2009), 'Why do Chinese firms tend to acquire strategic assets in international expansion?', *Journal of World Business*, **44**, 74–84.
Di Minin, A., J. Zhang and P. Gammeltoft (2012), 'Chinese foreign direct investment in R&D in Europe: A new model of R&D internationalization?', *European Management Journal*, **30**(3), 189–203.
Dunning, J. H. (1998), 'Location and the multinational enterprise: A neglected factor?', *Journal of International Business Studies*, **29**, 45–66.
George, A. L. and A. Bennett (2005), *Case Studies and Theory Development in the Social Sciences*, Cambridge, MA: MIT Press.
Hansen, U. and R. Lema (2019), 'The co-evolution of learning mechanisms and technological capabilities: Lessons from energy technologies in emerging economies', *Technological Forecasting and Social Change*, **140**(March), 241–57.
Hoesel, R. (1999), *New Multinational Enterprises from Korea and Taiwan*, London: Routledge.
Huber, G. and D. Power (1985), 'Research notes and communications retrospective reports of strategic-level managers: Guidelines for increasing their accuracy', *Strategic Management Journal*, **6**(2), 171–80.
Ivarsson, I. and T. Jonsson (2003), 'Local technological competence and asset-seeking FDI: An empirical study of manufacturing and wholesale affiliates in Sweden', *International Business Review*, **12**, 369–86.
Jick, T. D. (1979), 'Mixing qualitative and quantitative methods: Triangulation in action', *Administrative Science Quarterly*, **24**(4), 602–11.
Kim, L. (1998), 'Crisis construction and organizational learning: Capability building in catching-up at Hyundai Motor', *Organization Science*, **9**(4), 506–21.
Kogut, B. and S. J. Chang (1991), 'Technological capabilities and Japanese foreign direct investment in the United States', *The Review of Economics and Statistics*, **73**(3), 401–13.
Kumar, N. (1998), 'Emerging outward foreign direct investment from Asian developing countries: Prospects and implications', in N. Kumar (ed.), *Globalization, Foreign Direct Investment and Technology Transfers*, London: Routledge, pp. 177–94.
Li, J., Y. Li and D. Shapiro (2012), 'Knowledge seeking and outward FDI of emerging market firms: The moderating effect of inward FDI', *Global Strategy Journal*, **2**, 277–95.
Li, L. (2005), 'The effects of trust and shared vision on inward knowledge transfer in subsidiaries' intra-and inter-organizational relationships', *International Business Review*, **14**(1), 77–95.
Li, P. P. (2010), 'Toward a learning-based view of internationalization: The accelerated trajectories of cross-border learning for latecomers', *Journal of International Management*, **16**, 43–59.
Lipton, J. P. (1977), 'On the psychology of eyewitness testimony', *Journal of Applied Psychology*, **62**(1), 90–95.
Liu, C. L. (2012), 'An investigation of relationship learning in cross-border buyer–supplier relationships: The role of trust', *International Business Review*, **21**(3), 311–27.
Liu, J. (2019), 'The roles of emerging multinational companies' technology-driven FDIs in their learning processes for innovation', *International Journal of Emerging Markets*. Published online 21 January 2019.
Liu, J. and R. Lema (2015), 'The roles of emerging multinational companies' technology-driven FDIs in their learning processes for innovation: A dynamic and contextual perspective', *Papers in Innovation Studies*: *2015/50*, Lund, Sweden.

Liu, J., B. Angathevar and S. Li (2009), 'Building technological innovation based strategic capabilities at firm level in China: A dynamic resource-based-view case study', *Industry and Innovation*, **16**(4–5), 411–34.

Luo, Y. and R. L. Tung (2007), 'International expansion of emerging market enterprises: A springboard perspective', *Journal of International Business Studies*, **38**, 481–98.

Makino, S. and A. C. Inkpen (2003), 'Knowledge seeking FDI and learning across borders', in M. Easterby-Smith and M. Lyles (eds), *The Blackwell Handbook of Organizational Learning and Knowledge Management*, Hoboken: Blackwell, pp. 231–52.

Makino, S., C.-M. Lau and R.-S. Yeh (2002), 'Asset-exploitation versus asset-seeking: Implications for location choice of foreign direct investment from newly industrialized economies', *Journal of International Business Studies*, **33**, 403–21.

Manolova, T. S., I. Manev and B. Gyoshev (2010), 'In good company: The role of personal and inter-firm networks for new-venture internationalization in a transition economy', *Journal of World Business*, **45**(3), 257–65.

Mathews, J. A. (2006), 'Dragon multinationals: New players in 21st century globalization', *Asia Pacific Journal of Management*, **23**, 5–27.

Meyer, K. (2015), 'What is "strategic asset seeking FDI"?', *The Multinational Business Review*, **23**, 57–66.

Peng, M. W. (2012), 'The global strategy of emerging multinationals from China', *Global Strategy Journal*, **2**(2), 97–107.

Ru, P., Q. Zhi, F. Zhang, Z. Zhong, J. Li and J. Sun (2012), 'Behind the development of technology: The transition of innovation modes in China's wind turbine manufacturing industry', *Energy Policy*, **43**, 58–69.

Rui, H. and G. S. Yip (2008), 'Foreign acquisitions by Chinese firms: A strategic intent perspective', *Journal of World Business*, **43**, 213–26.

Shan, W. and J. Song (1997), 'Foreign direct investment and the sourcing of technological advantage: Evidence from the biotechnology industry', *Journal of International Business Studies*, **28**, 267–84.

Si, Y., I. Liefner and T. Wang (2013), 'Foreign direct investment with Chinese characteristics: A middle path between Ownership–Location–Internalization model and Linkage–Leverage–Learning model', *Chinese Geographical Science*, **23**(5), 594–606.

Slepniov, D., A. H. Lassen, S. Haakonsson and M. McKelvey (2015), 'Understanding innovation spaces through emerging multinational enterprises in China: An explorative case study of a Chinese wind turbine manufacturer', in M. McKelvey and S. Baghchi-Sen (eds), *Innovation Spaces in Asia*, Cheltenham, UK and Northampton, MA, USA: Edward Elgar Publishing, 103–123.

Song, J., P. Almeida and G. Wu (2003), 'Learning-by-hiring: When is mobility more likely to facilitate interfirm knowledge transfer?', *Management Science*, **49**(4), 351–65.

Sun, S. L., M. Peng, B. Ren and D. Yan (2012), 'A comparative ownership advantage framework for cross-border M&As: The rise of Chinese and Indian MNEs', *Journal of World Business*, **47**(1), 4–16.

Tan, H. and J. Mathews (2015), ‘Accelerated internationalization and resource leverage strategizing: The case of Chinese wind turbine manufacturers’, *Journal of World Business*, **50**(3), 417–27.

Yin, R. K. (2013), *Case Study: Research Design and Methods* (the fifth edition), Thousand Oaks: Sage Publications.

8. Technology transfer and the internationalization process of the emerging market firm: a case study of the acquisition of Volvo Car Corporation by Zhejiang Geely Holding Group

Claes G. Alvstam and Inge Ivarsson

1. INTRODUCTION

This chapter focuses upon how a Chinese multinational company globalizes through acquisitions. The aim is to describe and analyse how the acquisition of a global prestigious branded consumer product by an emerging market multinational enterprise (EMNE) affects the process of knowledge and technology transfer within the global value chain between the acquired firm and companies belonging to the acquiring group. As in Chapters 5 and 12, we analyse a Chinese firm in the automobile and transportation industries. We use the takeover in 2010 of the former Swedish automobile manufacturer, Volvo Car Corp. (VCC) by the Chinese Zhejiang Geely Holding Group (ZGH) from American Ford Motor Corp. as a case study. We have previously called these "hybrid emerging market multinational enterprises" (Alvstam and Ivarsson, 2014, 2017). In this chapter, the case study illustrates our main arguments about how the rapidly growing outward foreign direct investment from China is under transition from the initial resource-seeking activities to the seeking of strategic assets aiming at transfers of cutting-edge technology and knowledge back to China in order to build up a solid and internationally competitive manufacturing platform for the domestic market, but later also for the upgrading of exports from China.

2. THEORETICAL PLATFORM FOR ANALYSIS

This chapter uses two different theoretical approaches in order to better understand how technology and knowledge transfers, initially generated through inward foreign direct investment (FDI) from foreign multinational enterprises (MNEs), are used to support the internationalization process of firms from emerging markets. First is whether the rise and success of EMNEs can be explained by conventional internationalization theory, or if they should be considered as a new form, requiring a complementary set of explanations. In this context we also use institutional theories of political embeddedness to argue for the need to complement the conventional theory in order to better understand and explain the new patterns that have emerged recently, particularly those related to Chinese outward FDI. Second, we have been inspired by the literature around how technology and knowledge transfers from foreign MNEs can be used for the upgrading of local host-market suppliers in emerging markets, and become an important component in the building up of "national champions", which in the next step are prepared for a successful expansion into the global market. It shall be observed, though, that supplier upgrading is only one element in the larger picture of how two firms cooperate. The EMNE internationalization process and its technology and knowledge asset-seeking abroad is closely interconnected and reciprocal with the explanation of the process of technology and knowledge transfers between home- and host-market firms, but are nevertheless often isolated from each other in the literature. Our ambition is therefore to put these strands of theories together in a more comprehensive way in a common explanatory synthesis.

2.1 Emerging MNEs

The vast and growing literature on outward investment from EMNEs has to a large extent been focused on whether a new theory regarding EMNEs is required or not, and if the category of "emerging markets" in itself qualifies for a novel common theory (Mathews, 2006; Luo and Tung, 2007; Buckley and Casson, 2009; Gammeltoft et al., 2010; Narula, 2012; Ramamurti, 2012; Aharoni, 2014; Cuervo-Cazurra and Ramamurti, 2014; Pedersen and Stucchi, 2014; Williamson, 2014; Alvstam et al., 2020). In particular, the large inner variations between various emerging markets have called for a debate as to whether China should be treated as a special case due to its size, potential and state-managed economic system with a growing number of private entrepreneurs involved (Child and Rodrigues, 2005; Rugman and Li, 2007; Rui and Yip, 2008; Luo et al., 2010; Deng, 2012; Zhang et al., 2012; Amighini and Franco, 2013; Tsai, 2013; Williamson and Raman, 2013; Alvstam and

Ivarsson, 2014). We argue that the "springboard approach" (Luo and Tung, 2007; Ramamurti, 2012) is still a useful starting-point to understand China's new phase of outward FDI, since it casts the limelight on the domestic market impacts on outward FDI, i.e. that the internationalization process is to a large extent an instrument to build up a solid domestic platform. At the same time, the internationalization theories have – not least in China – to be complemented and supported by a better understanding of the institutional systems at various administrative geographic levels (Thun, 2006; Witt and Redding, 2014), and by a more explicit focus on the interaction and competition between these levels, as being highlighted in spatially oriented theories (Buckley and Ghauri, 2004; Meyer et al., 2011; Beugelsdijk and Mudambi, 2013; Iammarino and McCann, 2013; Parrilli et al., 2013), and theories regarding how national production networks to an increasing extent are integrated in global value chains (GVCs) within global production networks (Alcacer and Chung, 2007; Sturgeon and van Biesebroeck, 2011; Coe and Yeung, 2015). In the Chinese context the "springboard" should in particular be assessed from a local and regional perspective, i.e. in the interaction between on one hand the integration into global production networks that favours further regional concentration to the already more advanced coastal provinces in order to be closer to global suppliers and markets, and, on the other hand, the active official policies to provide for better balance between different regions in China. The focus should not only be on the final stages of the value chain, which involve the foreign MNEs and their local partners, but the whole supply system, including suppliers and sub-contractors in different parts of the country. The springboard approach assumes that the objective to increase international competitiveness through promotion of exports and outward FDI is to a large extent aiming at enhancing the domestic power base, and that investment abroad is followed by even larger domestic investment. These investments are, though, not geographically blind, but deliberately used by government institutions in a combination of sticks and carrots to "advise" the company to direct investment capital to regions that fulfil the criteria to be supported within the framework of the national regional development policy. Furthermore, private as well as semi-public and public actors at the provincial and local levels in China have during the 2000s become increasingly powerful when it comes to promoting their own interests, and have been given larger freedom to implement these interests, as far as they do not directly collide with the national priorities. This freedom is particularly apparent when it comes to providing financial resources for foreign acquisitions and joint ventures through various forms of "state asset operations" and investment companies, controlled by regional and local governments or separate ministries at the national level. Accordingly, an outward FDI from an EMNE is in this context not only an instrument to build up national champions, but also to provide for reducing the gaps between richer and poorer regions in the home country. We propose that the process of international technology and knowledge transfers, usually viewed from the viewpoint of the traditional MNE perspective, takes a different trajectory when EMNEs are involved, particularly in the cases when Chinese companies are expanding abroad, and suggest that new theoretical approaches are needed in order to better explain the logics of this process.

2.2 Technology and Knowledge Transfers from Foreign MNEs to Host Country Suppliers and Partners

The second pillar under our theoretical platform is constituted by the literature regarding upgrading in the global supply chain with focus on how technology and knowledge is transferred from foreign MNEs to local host country suppliers. In this context it is relevant to extend the focus to also incorporate "family members", i.e. previously competing or independent firms, which have become related through an acquisition. The literature can be sub-divided into evolutionary approaches to technology spillovers (Nelson and Winter, 1982; UNCTAD, 2001), emphasis on technology improvements through linkages, leverage and learning (Mathews, 2006), supplier upgrading and the rise and proliferation of global production networks (Gereffi et al., 2005; UNCTAD, 2013; Gereffi, 2014; Coe and Yeung, 2015), and geographical proximity (Malecki, 1997; Scott-Kennel, 2007). It complements the abovementioned theories around emerging market outward FDI in the sense that it helps us to explain how EMNEs are building technology and knowledge capacity upstream in order to gain a higher international competitive edge. It is demonstrated in a number of previous empirical studies carried out by the authors (Ivarsson and Alvstam, 2005a, 2005b, 2009, 2010, 2011) that the improved technology and knowledge level of local suppliers, initially provided through the support from foreign MNEs, also can become an opportunity for domestic competitors to the foreign MNE to raise quality levels in the long-term strategic mission to become "national champions" and in the next step also to become a global actor within their business field. Within the GVC framework, four types of upgrading are identified, which are process upgrading, product upgrading, functional upgrading, and chain or inter-sectoral upgrading. The process upgrading transforms inputs into outputs more efficiently by reorganizing the production system or introducing superior technology. The product upgrading is moving into more sophisticated product lines. The functional upgrading entails acquiring new functions (or abandoning existing functions) to increase the overall skill content of the activities, while during the process of chain or inter-sectoral upgrading, firms move into new but often related industries. The upgrading trajectory is in this context seen to run from assembly through original equipment manufacturing (OEM) status, original design manufacturing (ODM) to original brand manufacturing (OBM). The process of upgrading can be observed in both producer- and consumer-driven sectors of industry, although through different trajectories. The improved capabilities can, along with existing literature, be divided into operational, duplicative, adaptive and innovative capabilities. The technology transfer by the MNE was shown to contribute to improving the adaptive capacity of the local suppliers. This happened through gaining a deeper technological understanding of how to enhance know-how that was originally developed in co-operation with their MNE customer, and was made possible through offering improved and adapted product and process technology, also to other customers, and through increased exports to existing and new customers. Since the foreign MNEs establish closer long-term business relations with their local suppliers, resulting in more efficient sourcing of products, and technology-upgrading among suppliers, the usually applied typologies of governance structures of value chains were in our previous studies complemented by a "developmental" category, specifically addressing the dynamic and evolutionary nature of the way to manage and govern the GVC. There is, however, according to our knowledge, limited research regarding how the reciprocal process of technology and knowledge transfers between the foreign MNE and its host country suppliers is affected by a situation where the foreign MNE has been acquired by a host country firm with its own supply chain. The acquisition of the foreign MNE is in such a context also used to enhance upgrading along the whole value chain in the host-market firm, and a slow but evident integration process between the two systems of suppliers is presumed to be emerging.

3. RESEARCH METHOD

For the collection of material regarding the empirical example, we have mainly adopted a longitudinal qualitative approach, consisting of frequent interviews and other forms of personal communication with key actors within VCC in Gothenburg, Shanghai, Chengdu, Zhangjiakou and Daqing during the whole period from the acquisition in 2010 up to May 2016. In addition, key actors in Geely have been interviewed during visits at the Headquarters in Hangzhou as well as at the plants in Chengdu and Cixi between 2011 and 2014. Finally, interviews have been undertaken with representatives of China Euro Vehicle Technology (CEVT) in Gothenburg, a wholly owned engineering and development centre, owned by ZGH, with the task to develop and design future cars for the Geely Group and a new common platform of VCC and Geely for the C-segment small cars. The specific information in the case is mainly derived from interviews with Volvo and Geely managers in China and Sweden, carried out at many different occasions between 2011 and 2016.

4. THE ACQUISITION OF VOLVO CAR CORP. BY ZHEJIANG GEELY HOLDING GROUP

The spectacular acquisition of Volvo Car Corporation by the Chinese Zhejiang Geely Holding Group from American Ford Motor Corp. in 2010 was the first major acquisition of a brand in the premier car segment by a private company, listed and incorporated outside China, but financed by a mix of private and local public interests in China (Alvstam and Ivarsson, 2014, 2017).

The acquisition can be seen as the result of "seizing the opportunity" to buy a prestigious global brand and at the same time to invest in future technology and knowledge transfer within automotive manufacturing. The final bid was initiated by a self-made businessman, Mr Li Shufu, the founder of ZGH, founded in 1986. Since the first car production in 1998, ZGH has grown through an aggressive expansion policy, including 12 assembly plants for the Geely brand in China and an annual production volume of 1.5 million cars, including the brands Geometry and Lynk&Co, but also through a couple of foreign acquisitions, e.g. British Manganese Bronze, Malaysian Proton, the sports car Lotus, and the Australian automatic transmission maker DSI. The ZGH was listed in Hong Kong. After the merger, VCC's new board of management announced immediately highly ambitious expansion plans – from about 370,000 units annually in 2010 to 800,000 units in 2015, later moved forward to 2020, with production in China becoming the third pillar in the geographical distribution of their assembly (Alvstam and Ivarsson, 2014, p.227; Alvstam et al., 2020). The Chinese sales of VCC amounted in 2010 to about 30,000 units, mainly the models assembled in Chongqing. The sales target in China for 2015 was set at 200,000 cars, or about 20 per cent of China's premium segment (ibid., p.228). Even though this target was viewed as unrealistic already from the beginning, it signalled the ambitious vision of expansion in China, and set an optimistic standard for the development of the new VCC, not least in Sweden where the acquisition had been received with mixed feelings. The fear that the production gradually was to move from Europe to China was thus met with an expansion plan that aimed at keeping the Gothenburg and Ghent plants at least at the existing levels, but also allowing for growth in production and employment, while the largest share of expansion was to take place in new plants in China. In 2019, VCC sold 705,000 cars, of which 155,000 were in China.

The major challenge for the management board of the "new" VCC was to provide for a subtle balance between the Volvo and Geely brands, where Volvo was a global prestigious brand with an emphasis on values like "quality", "safety" and "environmental responsibility", while Geely was a low-end actor in the Chinese market with limited exports, mainly to emerging markets. Would Volvo soon end up as a Geely brand and thus ruin its global status? On the other hand, would it be financially sustainable not to take advantage of the obvious synergy effects of coordinating the supply and distribution systems between the two brands, and to develop new platform technologies together? The mantra – Volvo is Volvo and Geely is Geely – that has been expressed at numerous occasions by the majority owner has so far been kept, and VCC has been given considerable freedom to sustain and to develop its own corporate identity. Relatively small adaptations to the Chinese markets have been made when the new platform, the Scalable Product Architecture (SPA) was launched in 2014. The only visible difference is the addition of the letter "L" in the Chinese-built models, symbolizing a slightly longer version, compared to the global standard.

5. THE PROCESS OF TECHNOLOGY AND KNOWLEDGE TRANSFERS IN THE GEELY–VOLVO CASE

The intrinsic, intricate relation of reciprocal enhancement of technological competence and innovation capacity that has been built up during ten years of a less-than-arm's-length relationship between Geely and Volvo Cars can be followed along at least six separate trajectories. First, the rapid building up of integrated greenfield plants in China for the production of Volvo Cars; second, the collaboration regarding a new engine plant, to be served by several brands in the family; third, through various forms of coordination and co-operation of the respective supply systems; fourth, the integration of management and engineering resources, and fifth, through joint R&D ventures. These five forms of co-operation are finally synthesized in the common development of a joint platform for the C-segment (small cars), Compact Module Architecture (CMA), and a joint new plant for these cars under a third "neutral" brand (Lynk & Co), that was launched in 2017, which is the sixth trajectory. All of these contribute to ZGH having gradually upgraded its process, product, functional and production capacity, and achieved its upgrading in the value chain, as mentioned in Section 2.

5.1 The Integrated Plants

One of the first decisions by the new management after the acquisition in 2010 was to build two new integrated plants for Volvo in China with a potential production capacity of up to 200,000 cars each: one in Chengdu, Sichuan province, and the other in Daqing, Heilongjiang province. The Chengdu venture was prioritized, partly due to the opportunity to take advantage of a site already owned by Geely. The development of Chengdu is also given high priority by the national government as a part of the "One Belt One Road" framework, in which both the city and the entire province is an important node. The new plant, opened in 2013, became accordingly a close neighbour to an existing Geely operation. During the first years the two companies also shared office space. In addition, a couple of large foreign car brands were already established in the vicinity, so the opportunities to take advantage of a local cluster of suppliers, technical competence and trained labour were good. The Chengdu operations were furthermore prepared to gradually take over the assembly of Volvo cars in the abovementioned joint Ford plant in nearby Chongqing. The venture in Daqing was a larger challenge. Daqing is one of the most remote cities in north-eastern China, located 1,400 km north of Beijing, and has no previous history of automotive manufacturing. Instead, the oil industry has been the key sector in the region. The ambitions of its massive investment to own 37 per cent of VCC of the local industrial development body, Daqing State Asset Operation, were to build a modern car manufacturing plant in the city in order to transform and broaden its economic structure and to promote better opportunities for highly skilled labour. The VCC project can in this context be seen as one element in a grand plan for technology and knowledge upgrading in the city. The projecting and building of the plant, which is a copy of the Chengdu works, was accordingly urged on by the local government. It was officially erected and equipped in 2014, despite that at this time there was no opportunity to utilize it at its technical capacity. There was also in this case an active priority at the national level to support the transformation and technology-upgrading of the Northeast, and to further develop the existing automotive cluster along the central road and railway from Dalian in the south via Shenyang, Changchun and Harbin to Daqing and Qiqihar in the north.

5.2 The Engine Plant

An initial condition of the establishment of Volvo production in China was that the cars should be equipped with original Volvo engines, developed within the new Volvo Engine Architecture (VEA), and in this respect being totally separated from the Geely engine production system, which rested on local and Japanese technology. Due to the larger investment need, the decision to also build an engine plant in China took a longer time, and was not finally made until 2012. While the establishment of an integrated plant with a production capacity of 200,000 units, including stamping, bodyshop, paintshop and final assembly requires an initial investment of about 250 million Yuan, an engine plant to support the Chengdu and Daqing operations would cost about 1.5 billion Yuan, i.e. corresponding to six integrated factories. The location at the city of Zhangjiakou, Hebei province, roughly half-way between Chengdu and Daqing, can be seen as a result of the active contacts between Chairman Li and the local authorities. The collaboration with Geely concerns joint operation of the premises, where VCC is the minority owner, and the production and development of a common engine for small-sized cars based on the CMA platform.

5.3 Supplier Systems

Through the active influence of the third VCC owner, Shanghai Jiaerwo Investment Company, wholly owned by Shanghai Jiading Corporation, the office for coordination of management activities – product development, purchasing, supply-chain management and human resource management – was set up at the City of Jiading, in the north-western part of Metro Shanghai. It is emphasized by both parties that the upstream co-operation between the Volvo and Geely brands along the supply chain should be entirely based on arm's-length business conditions, and that all sub-contracting involving VCC should meet Volvo's technical specifications, but there are in reality clear advantages for each side to exchange information regarding potential suppliers and to coordinate purchasing deals. Geely's existing domestic network of supplier contacts was thus traded with Volvo's global sourcing experiences. The long-term ambition is to increase the local content of a Volvo that is produced in China, and in this respect Volvo's unconditional requirement to maintain and to enhance its global standards is also used to improve the quality of the Geely cars. The coordination of purchasing has during the first years mainly taken place regarding low-end plastic, metal and rubber materials, but also within a number of other items and input components that are not "visible" to the driver, e.g. in gearboxes. Gradually, the share of joint inputs has accordingly become higher. The big steps of supplier coordination in the next years are to be taken within the field of engine production, and in the implementation of the CMA platform, in which the VEA also will become the standard for the new Geely models, as well as for joint brands, built on the CMA platform technology.

5.4 Management and Engineering Resources

The Jiading office in Shanghai acts as the coordination centre for VCC's activities in China, while Geely is managed from its headquarters in Hangzhou, Zhejiang province. It was natural during the first years of the building up of VCC to recruit staff from both Europe and China, and a number of key functions, both in Jiading and at the Chengdu and Daqing plants, were served by former Geely managers. A number of domestic recruitments did also have experiences from other foreign car manufacturers before they were employed by VCC. The product development operations at Jiading were initially mainly devoted to local adaptation of Volvo cars to the Chinese market, e.g. to the slightly longer version, but has gradually continued to also include tasks within the global production system with a mix of Chinese, Swedish and international engineers. A system of "matched pairs" of double management functions was initially introduced to abridge the cultural gap and to facilitate the integration of VCC in a Chinese context, but was later relaxed and transformed into a more conventional line organization model. The number of Swedish/European managers and engineers has gradually declined to a few key positions only (Yakob, 2018, 2019).

5.5 Technical Co-operation and Joint R&D Ventures

The process of knowledge and technology transfers between Volvo in Europe and its Chinese operations was initially dominated by the European units, in which the design and running of the production in Chengdu followed VCC's global standards, although the degree of robotization in the plants is considerably lower in China. It should be particularly noted, however, that the Chengdu project was the first opportunity in decades for VCC to build up a new plant completely from zero, which is why the experiences from this venture were also used for further improvements of the operations in Sweden and Belgium. The labour turnover in a Chinese plant is normally higher than in Europe, and a large number of the newly employed workers were recruited from the adjacent Geely plant, as well as from neighbouring foreign-owned car plants. There is also a flow of labour back to other plants in the vicinity, although the VCC's labour turnover is lower than the local average. There were, especially during the first two years of operations, a number of examples of practical technical co-operation between the Volvo and Geely plants, although these were kept at a low level. When the Daqing plant was projected and built, the Chengdu design was followed, and there were a number of engineers as well as middle managers that moved from Chengdu to Daqing to take part in the preparation of operations. The experiences gained by the building up of two completely new plants in China have also been used for the project to launch the first Volvo plant in USA, located at Charleston, SC, that started operations in 2018.

5.6 Common Production Platform

However, the long-term most strategic co-operation accomplishment between the Volvo and Geely brands regards the common development of the CMA platform. This project is organized in the China Euro Vehicle Technology, located at Lindholmen Science Park in central Gothenburg and opened in late 2013. It is an R&D and product development centre for Geely cars and employs a mix of Chinese, Swedish and internationally recruited engineers. It has rapidly expanded to about 2,000 employees and external consultants in

Sweden and a further 300 in China. While it is legally a wholly owned Geely company, it is nevertheless currently led by a Swedish CEO with a deputy from Geely. The symbolic importance of this project cannot be underestimated. The location to Gothenburg, close to VCC's main production and R&D site, was important to emphasize and maintain the Volvo influence in the project, even though the cars will be manufactured in a new joint plant in China from 2017. Even though the initial objective was the CMA development, intended for a new joint production site, owned by Geely but run by Volvo at Taizhou/ Luqiao in Zhejiang province, that opened in 2018, Geely has gradually moved a larger share of its R&D and design development functions for its own brand to Gothenburg, and has since 2019 also established an independent Innovation Center, at Lindholmen. The CMA project is also used for further development of electric cars, and driverless technologies, both for China and the global market. Furthermore, it will enhance the development of shared component development between Volvo and Geely, by creating technical solutions that are applicable to both brands.

6. SUMMARY AND CONCLUSIONS

This chapter has described how the acquisition of Volvo Cars by Zhejiang Geely has given rise to an intensive development of the company. This process has transformed VCC from being a "Eurocentric" manufacturer with its main markets in North America and Europe, although with global ambitions to become a "Euro-Chinese" "hybrid" company with China as its main market and a growing home base for manufacturing in China. The EMNE demonstrates a number of different modes of expansion compared with the traditional internationalization theories. In this respect EMNEs expanding from China should be seen as a specific case, in which internationalization is an element to build up a solid domestic base and to support "national champions"; see also the discussion in Chapter 9 in the book, the connecting role of Chinese EMNEs between host and home countries. There is in the Chinese example of internationalization strategies a strong component of policy coordination between the balance and mix of domestic production capacity, not only at the national, but also at the regional and local levels, combined with technological and knowledge upgrading through acquisitions of leading global companies, and market expansion abroad. We suggest that this kind of complex mutual relationship between government policy coordination, state-owned enterprises, private entrepreneurship with both a domestic and foreign leg, and global industry, seems to have become a role model for China's innovation and technology policy.

We have given examples of how Geely's technological competence and innovation capacity, both domestic and abroad, has been enhanced through

ZGH's acquisition of Volvo Cars. This process is characterized by several parallel strands: first, technology transfer through the building up of the latest and most modern production plants at home, such as the manufacturing plants in Chengdu and Daqing; second, upgrading of host-market suppliers through direct and indirect co-operation between the foreign and the domestic brand regarding purchasing and requirements of technical specifications to meet global standards, such as the integrated and upgraded supply systems; third, through establishment of joint R&D projects between the foreign and the local brand, located where the cutting-edge technical competence can be recruited, rather than at home, for instance CEVT and Geely's Innovation Center in Gothenburg.

Compared with the existing literature regarding technology and knowledge transfers from foreign MNEs to local industry, this case study does illustrate a trajectory, where the process of transfers is driven by the acquisition of the foreign MNE. In this respect we suggest that the "developmental" category of GVC upgrading capability, aimed at complementing the operational, duplicative, adaptive and innovative capabilities within the forms of process, product, functional, chain/intersectoral categories (Ivarsson and Alvstam, 2010, 2011), is particularly useful when it comes to understanding the dynamic and evolutionary process of technology transfer when the co-operation is also connected to ties of formal ownership and control.

The technology transfer process between global MNEs and ambitious EMNEs, which aim to build up a position to become a national champion in their home market in parallel with a rapid expansion abroad, is normally multi-faceted and contradictory. A new situation has emerged where EMNEs, particularly those from China, speed up the internationalization process by acquiring prestigious global MNEs. Such acquisitions open up for a long-term, comprehensive reciprocal process of interchange that differs in size and scope from traditional cases. Since it can be assumed that this phenomenon will grow strongly in the future as an effect of more Chinese firms becoming global actors, the lessons from the ZGH-VCC example regarding how knowledge and technology transfers are managed in a new corporate constellation need to be studied closely and brought to a broader theoretical understanding.

REFERENCES

Aharoni, Y. (2014), 'Theoretical debates on multinationals from emerging economies', in A. Cuervo-Cazurra and R. Ramamurti (eds), *Understanding Multinationals from Emerging Markets*, Cambridge: Cambridge University Press, pp. 15–30.

Alcacer, J. and W. Chung (2007), 'Location strategies and knowledge spillovers', *Management Science*, **53**(5), 760–776.

Alvstam, C.G. and I. Ivarsson (2014), 'The "hybrid" emerging market multinational enterprise: The ownership transfer of Volvo Cars to China', in C.G. Alvstam, H.

Dolles and P. Ström, *Asian Inward and Outward FDI: New Challenges in the Global Economy*, Houndmills, Basingstoke: Palgrave Macmillan, pp. 217–242.

Alvstam, C.G. and I. Ivarsson (2017), 'Becoming a "national champion", yet remaining a "global player": The acquisition of Volvo Car by Zhejiang Geely', in M. Fuchs, S. Henn, M. Franz and R. Mudambi, *Organization and Culture in Cross-border Acquisitions*, Abingdon: Routledge, pp. 61–69.

Alvstam, C.G., I. Ivarsson and B. Petersen (2020), 'Are multinationals from emerging markets configuring global value chains in new ways?' *International Journal of Emerging Markets*, **15**(1), 111–130.

Amighini, A. and C. Franco (2013), 'A sector perspective of Chinese outward FDI: The automotive case', *China Economic Review*, **27**, 148–161.

Beugelsdijk, S. and R. Mudambi (2013), 'MNEs as border-crossing multi-location enterprises: The role of discontinuities in geographic space', *Journal of International Business Studies*, **44**(5), 413–426.

Buckley, P.J. and M.C. Casson (2009), 'The internalization theory of the multinational enterprise: A review of the progress of a research agenda after 30 years', *Journal of International Business Studies*, **40**(9), 1563–1580.

Buckley, P.J. and P. Ghauri (2004), 'Globalisation, economic geography and the strategy of the multinational enterprise', *Journal of International Business Studies*, **35**(2), 81–98.

Child, J. and S.B. Rodrigues (2005), 'The internationalization of Chinese firms: A case for theoretical extension', *Management and Organization Review*, **1**(3), 381–410.

Coe, N.M. and H.W.-C. Yeung (2015), *Global Production Networks: Theorizing Economic Development in an Interconnected World*, Oxford: Oxford University Press.

Cuervo-Cazurra, A. and R. Ramamurti (2014), *Understanding Multinationals from Emerging Markets*, Cambridge: Cambridge University Press.

Deng, P. (2012), 'The internationalization of Chinese firms: A critical review and future research', *International Journal of Management Reviews*, **14**(10), 408–427.

Gammeltoft, P., H. Barnard and A. Madhok (2010), 'Emerging multinationals, emerging theory: Macro- and micro-level perspectives', *Journal of International Management*, **16**(2), 95–101.

Gereffi, G. (2014), 'Global value chains in a post-Washington Consensus world', *Review of International Political Economy*, **21**(1), 9–37.

Gereffi, G., J. Humphrey and T. Sturgeon (2005), 'The governance of global value chains', *Review of International Political Economy*, **12**(1), 78–104.

Iammarino, S. and P. McCann (2013), *Multinationals and Economic Geography: Location, Technology and Innovation*, Cheltenham, UK and Northampton, MA, USA: Edward Elgar Publishing.

Ivarsson, I. and C.G. Alvstam (2005a), 'The effect of spatial proximity on technology transfer from TNCs to local suppliers in developing countries: The case of AB Volvo's truck and bus plants in Brazil, China, India and Mexico', *Economic Geography*, **8**(1), 83–111.

Ivarsson, I. and C.G. Alvstam (2005b), 'New TNC-strategies and international technology transfer to developing countries: The case of Volvo Global Trucks and their component suppliers in India 2001', *World Development*, **33**(8), 1325–1344.

Ivarsson, I. and C.G. Alvstam (2009), 'Local technology linkages and supplier upgrading in global value chains: The case of Swedish engineering TNCs in emerging markets', *Competition and Change*, **13**(4), 368–388.

Ivarsson, I. and C.G. Alvstam (2010), 'Upstream control and downstream liberty of action? Interdependence patterns in global value chains, with examples from producer-driven and buyer-driven industries', *The Review of Market Integration*, **2**(1), 43–60.
Ivarsson, I. and C.G. Alvstam (2011), 'Upgrading in global value-chains: A case study of technology learning among IKEA suppliers in China and South East Asia', *Journal of Economic Geography*, **11**(4), 731–752.
Luo, Y. and R.L. Tung (2007), 'International expansion of emerging countries enterprises: A springboard perspective', *Journal of International Business Studies*, **38**(4), 481–498.
Luo, Y., Q. Xue and B. Han (2010), 'How emerging market governments promote outward FDI: Experiences from China', *Journal of World Business*, **45**(1), 68–79.
Malecki, E.J. (1997), *Technology and Economic Development: The Dynamics of Local, Regional and National Competitiveness*, 2nd ed. Harlow: Longman,
Mathews, J.A. (2006), 'Dragon multinationals: New players in 21st century globalization', *Asia-Pacific Journal of Management*, **23**(1), 5–27.
Meyer, K.E., R. Mudambi and P. Narula (2011), 'Multinational enterprises and local contexts: The opportunities and challenges of multiple embeddedness', *Journal of Management Studies*, **48**(2), 235–252.
Narula, R. (2012), 'Do we need different frameworks to explain infant MNEs from developing countries?', *Global Strategy Journal*, **2**(3), 188–204.
Nelson, R.R. and S.J. Winter (1982), *An Evolutionary Theory of Economic Change*, Cambridge, MA: Harvard University Press.
Parrilli, M.D., K. Nadvi and H.W.C. Yeung (2013), 'Local and regional development in global value chains, production networks and innovation networks: A comparative review and the challenges for future research', *European Planning Studies*, **21**(7), 967–988.
Pedersen, T. and T. Stucchi (2014), 'Business groups, institutional transition, and the internationalization of firms from emerging economies', in A. Cuervo-Cazurra and R. Ramamurti (eds), *Understanding Multinationals from Emerging Markets*, Cambridge: Cambridge University Press, pp. 224–241.
Ramamurti, R. (2012), 'What is really different about emerging market MNEs?', *Global Strategy Journal*, **2**(1), 41–47.
Rugman, A.M. and J. Li (2007), 'Will China's multinationals succeed globally or regionally?', *European Management Journal*, **25**(5), 333–343.
Rui, H. and G.S. Yip (2008), 'Foreign acquisitions by Chinese firms: A strategic intent perspective', *Journal of World Business*, **43**(2), 213–226.
Scott-Kennel, J. (2007), 'Foreign direct investment and local linkages: An empirical investigation', *Management International Review*, **47**(1), 51–77.
Sturgeon, T.J. and J. van Biesebroeck (2011), 'Global value chains in the automotive industry: An enhanced role for developing countries?', *International Journal of Technological Learning, Innovation and Development*, **4**(1–3), 181–205.
Thun, E. (2006), *Changing Lanes in China: Foreign Direct Investment, Local Governments and Auto Sector Development*, Cambridge: Cambridge University Press.
Tsai, H.-T. (2013), 'Towards a Guanxi-based theory of internationalization: Chinese, Taiwanese and evolving MNEs', *Chinese Management Studies*, **7**(1), 111–126.
UNCTAD (2001), *World Investment Report: Promoting Linkages*, Geneva and New York: United Nations Conference on Trade and Development.

UNCTAD (2013), *World Investment Report: Global Value Chains: Investment and Trade for Development*, Geneva and New York: United Nations Conference on Trade and Development.

Williamson, P.J. (2014), 'The global expansion of EMNCs: Paradoxes and directions for future research', in A. Cuervo-Cazurra and R. Ramamurti (eds), *Understanding Multinationals from Emerging Markets*, Cambridge: Cambridge University Press, pp. 155–168.

Williamson, P.J. and A.P. Raman (2013), 'Cross-border M&As and competitive advantage of Chinese EMNEs', in P.J. Williamson, R. Ramamurti, A. Fleury and M.T. Leme Fleury (eds), *The Competitive Advantage of Emerging Market Multinationals*, Cambridge: Cambridge University Press, pp. 260–277.

Witt, M.A. and G. Redding (eds) (2014), *The Oxford Handbook of Asian Business Systems*, Oxford: Oxford University Press.

Yakob, R. (2018), 'Augmenting local managerial capacity through knowledge collectivities: The case of Volvo Car China', *Journal of International Management*, **24**(4), 386–403.

Yakob, R. (2019), 'Context, competencies, and local managerial capacity development: A longitudinal study of HRM implementation at Volvo Car China', *Asian Business and Management*. https://doi.org/10.1057/s41291-019-00080-4

Zhang, Y., G. Duysters and S. Filippov (2012), 'Chinese firms entering Europe: Internationalization through acquisitions and strategic alliances', *Journal of Science and Technology Policy in China*, **3**(2), 102–123.

9. Ideal types of reverse innovation for firms without overseas R&D centers: case studies of Chinese firms

Jun Jin, Min Guo, Maureen McKelvey and Zhengyi Zhang

1. INTRODUCTION

The purpose of this chapter is to develop the taxonomy of ideal types of reverse innovation for firms from developing countries. We develop this taxonomy based on an analysis of Chinese firms, but suggest it is more widely applicable. We define reverse innovation as the process by which the original idea of a technology or product is created in developing countries and/or a new technology or product first developed for markets in developing countries, then the idea or technology or product is diffused and implemented in advanced countries. The aim of this chapter is thus to develop a new map of global innovation flows about reserve innovation based upon how firms from developing countries can act.

In the era of globalization, developing countries have become an important engine of global economy growth. The increasing importance of R&D centers in developing countries by multinational enterprises (MNEs) from advanced countries means China, India, and other developing countries have gradually become the global innovation hubs (Li and Kozhikode, 2009), while more and more emerging market multinational enterprises (EMNEs) conduct their R&D in advanced countries (Li and Kozhikode, 2009; Jin et al., 2014). Chapters 5, 6, and 13 also address the development of technology and innovation within large Chinese multinational firms.

With the increasing role and strategic position of R&D centers of MNEs from advanced countries in developing countries, especially in China and India, MNEs from advanced countries start to transfer innovation and technology from developing countries to advanced countries, which was defined as "reverse innovation" by Immelt et al. (2009). Since then, the process of reverse innovation whereby innovation and technology transferred from developing countries to advanced countries has attracted attention from academia, industries, and government agencies. However, the previous research focuses on the reverse innovation of MNEs from advanced countries, which is MNEs from advanced countries transfer innovation and technology from their R&D centers in developing countries to their subsidiaries or headquarters in advanced countries (Govindarajan and Ramamurti, 2011; von Zedtwitz et al., 2015). In addition, von Zedtwitz et al. (2015) propose 16 types of global innovation and find 10 typical types of reverse innovation.

However, Chinese high-speed rail technology (Chen and Huang, 2011; Zheng and Chen, 2014) and BYD Company (Zhen, 2012) to advanced countries are not completely the same as the types proposed by von Zedtwitz et al. (2015). Of course, these researches on Chinese firms do not describe types of reverse innovation of Chinese firms well because only a single case was used in their researches. Moreover, what are ideal types of reverse innovation of firms from developing countries without global R&D centers? This chapter attempts to answer this research question.

2. LITERATURE REVIEW

This chapter examines existing research and further develops it in order to introduce a revised matrix framework. We use the matrix to analyze our case study, including describing different types of reverse innovation (from the perspective of firms from developing countries), and we also propose new ideal types, based on Chinese cases.

2.1 Reverse Innovation

This section provides definitions of reverse innovation and reverse engineering, as well as suggesting why this phenomenon is now visible. With the development of trade internalization, overseas R&D investment in MNEs has been growing fast since the 1980s (Gassmann and von Zedtwitz, 1998, 1999), and more and more MNEs operate their R&D outside their home countries (Gassmann and von Zedtwitz, 1999; Boutellier et al., 2008). Globalization increases "a high (and increasing) degree of interdependency and interrelatedness among different and geographically dispersed actors" (Archibugi and Iammarino, 2002: 99). Thus, the global innovation provides more interaction and cooperation chances between firms from advanced countries and those from developing countries. With the growing global R&D centers built by MNEs in developing countries (von Zedtwitz, 2005), R&D in emerging markets has an impact on innovation in advanced economies.

Based on research about the knowledge transfers to and from newly acquired subsidiaries in three transition economies in Central and Eastern

Europe, Yang et al. (2008) discuss the determinants of reverse knowledge flows. Later, Immelt et al. (2009) initially put forward the concept of "reverse innovation" through the case of GE's portable ultrasonic imaging instrument, which was developed and sold in the Chinese market at first, but then successfully accepted and used in the American market. The authors describe reverse innovation as the opposite of the traditional globalization process (technology and/or trade from advanced countries to developing countries) (Immelt et al., 2009). Govindarajan and Ramamurti (2011) characterize reverse innovation as the process by which an innovation is adopted first in poor countries before trickling up to advanced countries. Each phase in the innovation flow from concept ideation, product development, first primary market introduction after the product development, and to subsequent secondary market introduction, can take place in different geographical locations, advanced countries or emerging countries (von Zedtwitz et al., 2015). Adopting the concepts proposed by Govindarajan and Ramamurti (2011) and von Zedtwitz et al. (2015), this research emphasizes the concept of global technology flows among different geography locations. In this research, reverse innovation refers to how technology innovation accepted and diffused in advanced countries is initiated in developing countries as an innovation idea or research result or the first implementation of innovation and technology.

Since the concept of reverse innovation was proposed in 2009, it is often confused with reverse engineering. Reverse engineering means the processes of extracting the knowledge of a product or equipment and reproducing it or any others based on the extracted information (Chikofsky and Cross, 1990). Reverse engineering is widely accepted as a strategy which contributes to the development of innovation capabilities in developing countries, like China, especially as one part of a strategy of imitation to innovation. But it is not a process relative to globalization. Reverse innovation is recognized as a stage of global innovation from the aspect of MNEs from advanced countries, which is from globalization to localization then to reverse innovation.

In the research on reverse innovation, much literature concentrates on reasons why reverse innovation happens. For instance, the low cost in developing countries and niche market in advanced countries are recognized as two critical reasons why reverse innovation can be achieved (Govindarajan and Ramamurti, 2011; Brem and Ivens, 2013; Zeschky et al., 2014). Because of the advantage of cost, the research on reverse innovation is combined with research on frugal innovation or inclusive innovation (Govindarajan and Ramamurti, 2011; Brem and Ivens, 2013; Zeschky et al., 2014).

In addition, most of the existing research on reverse innovation takes MNEs from advanced countries as research targets, such as German MNEs (Agarwal and Brem, 2012), Swiss MNEs (Zeschky et al., 2014), and American MNEs (Govindarajan and Ramamurti, 2011; von Zedtwitz et al., 2015), especially reverse innovation in the health care industries (Govindarajan and Euchner, 2012; DePasse and Lee, 2013; Syed et al., 2013), analyzing the transfer of ideas from their R&D centers in developing countries to advanced countries. There is limited research on reverse innovation of Chinese firms (Dong and Chen, 2010; Zhen, 2012; Zheng and Chen, 2014) and Indian firms (Lim et al., 2013). Thus, the reverse innovation conducted by firms from developing countries, such as China, needs further research.

2.2 Theories of Countries' Catching-up Through Technology

In the research on catching-up and taking-off of developing countries, the transition from imitation to innovation is widely accepted as a process for developing countries since proposed by Kim in 1997. Firms from developing countries can improve their technological capabilities and achieve catching-up and even leapfrog through a process from acquisition to assimilation to improvement and finally to innovation (Kim, 1997; Lee and Kim, 2001; Jin and von Zedtwitz, 2008). In 2006, the Chinese government proposed an indigenous innovation policy which included three strategies to foster the technological capabilities and competitiveness of China including absorption to innovation, innovation based on the integration of existing technologies, and original innovation. Additionally, the Chinese government emphasized the critical role of original innovation in these three strategies,[1] which highlights the original innovation by Chinese organizations beyond the imitation.

There is limited research on reverse innovation of firms from developing countries, such as the growth and internationalization of China South Locomotive and Rolling Stock Corporation Limited (CSR) on the high-speed train (Zheng and Chen, 2014), the internationalization of Chinese firms in the environmental technology industry (Dong and Chen, 2010), and the development of the Indian firm, Tata (Lim et al., 2013). All of these cases suggest that reverse innovation contributes to the improvement of technological capabilities (Lim et al., 2013), achieving catching-up and leapfrog development for latecomers (Zhen, 2012; Lim et al., 2013), and the globalization of latecomers (Dong and Chen, 2010; Zheng and Chen, 2014). In contrast to literature which focuses upon product development flows in the global value chain, this chapter focuses upon analyzing ideal types of reverse innovation from the perspective of internationalization and catching-up strategies.

Based on the above literature review, we conclude here by proposing a typology of ideal types of reverse innovation for firms from developing countries without overseas R&D centers. We do so by using and modifying the ideas of innovation strategies of firms from developing countries and location concepts proposed by von Zedtwitz et al. (2015).

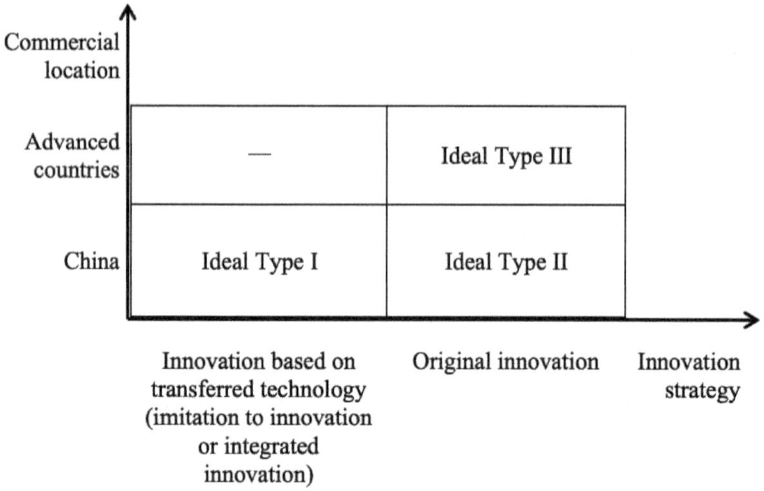

Figure 9.1 *Three ideal types of reverse innovation for firms from developing countries without overseas R&D centers*

On the y-axis, the two labels indicate whether the commercial location of the firm is in China or in advanced countries. We simplify the commercial locations in the process of product development (the primary target market introduction, and the subsequent secondary market (von Zedtwitz et al., 2015)) into the location of innovation commercialization. On the x-axis, the two labels indicate whether the innovation strategy of the firm is based upon transferred technology or original innovation. For transferred technology, we include aspects such as imitation in order to innovate and integrated innovation, and thus include situations where the original technology or idea is transferred to a firm in the commercial location.

There are four quadrants in this framework. One quadrant is blank here, because we are not investigating reverse innovation in the quadrant of innovation based on transferred technology and commercialization in advanced countries. The three ideal types found in Figure 9.1 are defined as follows:

Ideal Type I: Reverse innovation based on transferred technology. Technology is transferred from advanced countries at first, and then the enterprise in developing countries re-innovates and implements new technology in developing countries; finally products are exported to advanced countries.

Ideal Type II: Original reverse innovation. The enterprise in developing countries conducts original innovation and commercializes its own technologies

in developing countries. Products for developing countries are welcomed in advanced countries too.
Ideal Type III: Original reverse innovation (front-end technology). The leading technology is invented in developing countries, which is utilized and introduced in advanced countries.

3. RESEARCH METHODOLOGY

Previous research on reverse innovation indicates that case study methodologies are widely used in this field, in order to identify the key dimensions used to propose new typologies. Our focus is on firms in China, so using a multi-case study is appropriate. Because most of the firms from developing countries do not have their R&D centers overseas, how can they undertake reverse innovation? Therefore, this chapter focuses on firms from developing countries without overseas R&D centers. Our aim with this research design is to enlighten and explain multiple-level phenomena that may be too complex for tightly structured designs or pre-specified data sets (Yin, 2009). In addition, a case study is suitable for unraveling concepts (Yin, 2009). Therefore, this research employs multi-case studies as a method to illustrate the types of reverse innovation in China and we use the multi-case studies in order to illustrate the ideal types identified through our framework of the ideal types of reverse innovation.

Three firms are selected as case studies in order to illustrate the three ideal types found in our framework, and based on the following criteria. First, firms do not have overseas R&D centers for the studied technologies although they have cooperation with foreign organizations. Second, their innovation processes of the studied technology match one of the strategies in the framework. Third, the markets of the studied technology provided by the case firms at least include the market in advanced countries. The firms are called U-Company, N-Company, and P-Company in this research according to the requirement of firms.

The case descriptions of ideal types are based on in-depth interviews with senior managers of the case firms, such as founders of companies and vice-presidents, seminars and presentations given by senior managers of the case firms, and field visiting. The interviews as well as site visits were conducted in 2010, 2013, and 2014. The interview length for each individual was between one and two hours. Furthermore, public information from websites and companies' introduction documents were used as additional information and to triangulate the data. In addition, the information on N-Company was updated based on two further interviews in 2016 and 2017.

3.1 Introducing Firms in the Multi-Case Study

As a public high-tech company listed on the Shenzhen Stock Exchange, U-Company is committed to the development of the rail transportation business and energy and environment protection business, with an expectation to contribute to society through the substantial supply of environment-friendly technology, engineering, and equipment-manufacturing services. In the field of rail transportation, U-Company makes an effort to localize the construction of orbit traffic electromechanical systems. U-Company cooperates with national and international partners to advance technologies in rail transportation in various modes, such as public–private partnerships. Apart from that, U-Company also introduces, absorbs and digests professional signal technologies from Europe, so as to provide customers with a reliable service and solutions in the field of trams, intercity lines, and heavy haul railways.

Since its establishment in 2007 with patents of its founder, N-Company is devoted to developing a world-leading technology for providing the highest quality and the largest selection of uniformly sized nano- and microspheres (micro-particles). N-Company has the capability to supply monodisperse particles of almost any size ranging from 5 nanometers to 1000 microns of different materials, structures, and functionalities. N-Company has built 13 000 square-meter manufacturing plants and research centers in the Suzhou Industrial Park. N-Company sells its products in the markets of China, Korea, Europe, the USA, and other countries and regions. Additionally, N-Company offers an extensive line of media for pharmaceutical and biopharmaceutical separation by reversed phase, normal phase, ion exchange, affinity, size exclusion, and hydrophobic interaction chromatography. Nearly 40 percent of employees at N-Company work in R&D under the supervision of the founder of N-Company, one of the leading scientists in the Chinese nanotech field. N-Company cooperates with many Chinese universities and institutes in the research of nanotechnology. With its strong research team, N-Company has applied for more than 40 invention patents, and been granted 20 patents in China.

As a high-tech company leading the world in the field of air-cooling and self-humidification proton exchange membrane fuel cells (PEMFC), since its establishment in 2006, P-Company commits to the commercialization of fuel cells. P-Company has made prominent progress in several key-technology fields in fuel cells and in the development, manufacturing, and application of fuel cell systems of low and medium power. The close cooperation relationships with many well-known colleges and institutes at home and abroad, such as Imperial College (UK), University of Birmingham (UK), University of City of London (UK), University of New Haven (USA) contributes to the R&D of P-Company. P-Company has been granted more than 30 Chinese patents and two international patents. As the pioneer in the hydrogen technical industry, over 60 percent of the sales volume of P-Company comes from the European and American markets. P-Company's products have been used in the engines of motors, base-construction of telecoms, and so on.

4. CASE STUDIES OF REVERSE INNOVATION

4.1 Ideal Type I: Case of Railway Signal Control System of U-Company

U-Company signed an agreement of international scientific and technological cooperation with BBR from Germany on computer security core technology in 2010. The technology was mainly used in the rail transportation control system. After the introduction of BBR's key technology on the safety computer platform, U-Company gradually mastered the core technology of computer design, development, application, and certification. Then, via mutual cooperation, they successfully developed a new signal control system with patents of U-Company, and obtained a bidder for two projects with a contract value of 1440 million euros in the international rail traffic signal system market in Europe. This new signal control system was exported successfully, with certification and recognition from international evaluation agencies. The reverse innovation process of U-Company is summarized in Figure 9.2.

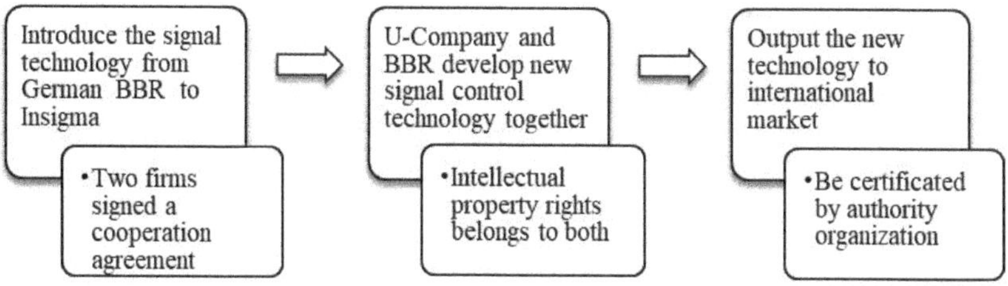

Figure 9.2 Reverse innovation process of U-Company

Figure 9.2 identifies three key steps, namely: first, the introduction of the signal technology, where both firms signed a cooperation agreement; second, a collaborative phase of developing technology where both were assigned international property rights (IPR); third, the Chinese firm being able to sell and output their technology to the international market, with a certification. During the process of reverse innovation, U-Company cooperated with universities and other organizations too, when they innovated based on the transferred technology from the German partner. In addition, the new patents which U-Company applied indicate that U-Company has innovation capabilities to assimilate and improve the transferred technology. Therefore, we argue that the open innovation (the use of external resources, cooperation and market activities) and innovation ability (the ability of absorption and innovation) played an important role for U-Company. The occurrence of reverse innovation can be considered as the market demand for a signal control system for rail transportation both at home and abroad, and the practice in the large Chinese market.

In addition, the research results that Chinese firms could achieve reverse innovation through the process of first introduction, then digestion and absorption, and finally re-innovation based on the case of BYD China (Zhen, 2012) confirms the existence of other possible cases of Ideal Type I of reverse innovation for firms in developing countries.

In summary, the case of U-Company suggests that firms from developing countries can develop new technologies and products with new technologies after absorbing and assimilating transferred technology for markets in developing countries, and finally export those technologies or products to advanced countries. It can be seen as a type of catching-up and involvement in the global industrial network. Since FDI and international technology transfer is encouraged in many developing countries, this type of reverse innovation can be seen as an ideal type, a type of reverse innovation based on transferred technology.

4.2 Ideal Type II: Case of Nano-Micron Ball Materials of N-Company

With its strong technology capabilities and cooperation with universities and institutes, N-Company has become one of the leading firms in the world to have the ability to produce some kinds of nano- and microsphere materials. N-Company's products, especially nano- and microspheres, not only quickly occupied the domestic market, but also successfully entered the international market, such as the American market. The overseas market contributes to about 20 percent of the annual sales of N-Company. For example, N-Company became the second firm in the world to produce nano-micron ball materials for flat panel display, which broke the monopoly of a Japanese firm. In the market of spacers of flat panel display, N-Company has around 40 percent of the Chinese market. In addition, thanks to its accuracy control of the ball size, N-Company has gradually exported its ball materials to the European market. In addition, a pharmaceutical firm in Europe purchased N-Company's technology, materials, and processes as one of its manufacturing processes to replace those provided by a Japanese firm before. In fact, because the process technology provided by N-Company is different from that of the Japanese firm, the European firm had to invest in the new process technology. The reason why the European firm would like to invest in the replacement of the process technology is because of the significant reduction in the operation cost (for example, the materials used in this process could be reduced from 13 000 liters to 3000 liters), and the increase in the purity of products. The reverse innovation process of N-Company is summarized in Figure 9.3.

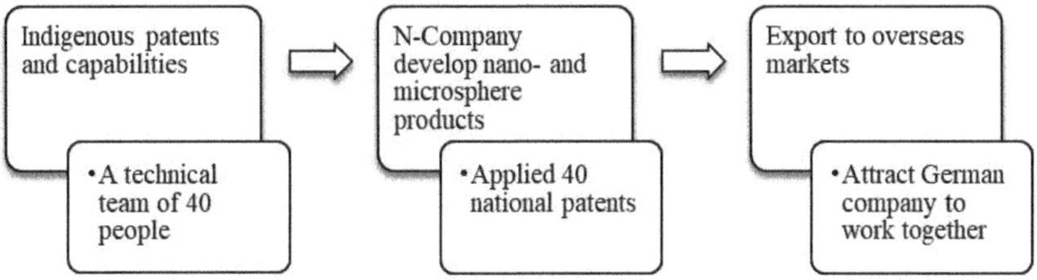

Figure 9.3 Reverse innovation process of N-Company

Figure 9.3 indicates a flow from the indigenous patents and capabilities of the Chinese firm, based on a technical team, to their development of products and national patents, to export to overseas markets, including foreign collaborators. In this case study, the leading original innovation ability of N-Company is an important engine to push its internationalization and reverse innovation. In addition, international cooperation brings wider and deeper opportunities to it as well. Nano technology is an emerging technology and its market is a growing market in the world, perhaps because the emerging technology provides opportunities for firms from developing countries to achieve the type of reverse innovation. The growth of biotechnology in Cuba can be seen as an example of Ideal Type II, original reverse innovation too.

In short, the example of N-Company illustrates that the Ideal Type II of reverse innovation, the original reverse innovation, exists, that firms from developing countries can develop technology and products from developing countries to advanced countries. Our suggestion is that this ideal type is likely to happen when firms from developing countries have the capabilities to compete with MNEs in emerging industries.

4.3 Ideal Type III: Case of Hydrogen Fuel Cell of P-Company

P-Company is engaged in the creation of hydrogen fuel cells with low cost and high efficiency. After years of R&D, P-Company finally developed the core technology of a membrane coated with catalyst. This kind of fuel cell was gas cooling without a water-cooling device, which not only reduced the battery's volume, price and cost, but also improved its efficiency. Given this, business opportunities that were previously neglected appeared. Because of difficulties in the acceptance of this technology in the Chinese market, P-Company developed the hydrogen fuel cell e-bicycles in Europe with their international partners. With an Italian enterprise Acta, P-Company jointly developed a whole solution with hydrogen fuel for bicycles, which was applied successfully in the European market. In addition, P-Company cooperates with Imperial College London to provide fuel cells for intelligent racing cars. The reverse innovation process of P-Company is summarized in Figure 9.4.

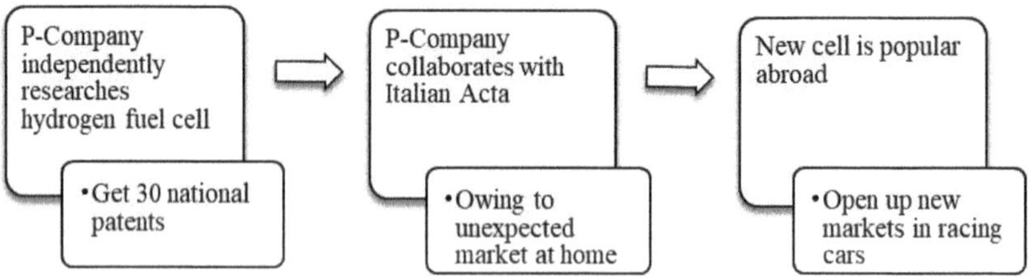

Figure 9.4 Reverse innovation process of P-Company

Figure 9.4 shows the flow from the firm's independent research, and associated patents, to collaborating with a foreign partner, to the high popularity of the product including new markets. In this case, P-Company has the strong capability of original innovation to develop front-end technologies in the world, which benefits cooperation with international partnerships and work on the global market. The advanced emerging technologies and market segmentation of advanced countries push P-Company to successfully implement their technologies in advanced countries. As in the case of N-Company, the technology and industry in the case of P-Company is also an emerging technology and industry.

In summary, the case of P-Company illustrates the Ideal Type III, where the original reverse innovation (front-end technology or leading technology) is an ideal type of reverse innovation for firms from developing countries with front-end technology and leading technological capabilities in emerging industries.

Taken together, these three cases illustrate new ways of thinking about reverse innovation for firms from developing countries, especially for those without overseas R&D centers. We suggest that these case studies indicate that reverse innovation could be a strategy and a criterion for firms in developing countries to improve innovation capabilities and global competitiveness. However, without R&D investment and enough internal innovation capabilities, firms could not achieve the stage of reverse innovation, as in the cases of U-Company, N-Company and P-Company. Moreover, all case study firms have cooperated with different organizations during their innovation and product development. Thus, our study suggests that even without overseas R&D centers, firms from developing countries can be encouraged to be involved in the global network and cooperate with partners. Our findings about cooperation suggest the important role of open innovation during reverse innovation, which confirms the research findings of Hossain (2013) for firms to adopt open innovation to stimulate the reverse innovation.

5. REFLECTIONS FOR FUTURE RESEARCH

We have proposed a framework of ideal types of reserve innovation, and illustrated this through a multi-case study of Chinese firms without overseas R&D centers. We proposed and validated the existence of three ideal types of reverse innovation: (1) Ideal Type I, reverse innovation based on transferred technology: technology transferred from advanced countries–learn and implement new tech in developing countries–export to advanced countries; (2) Ideal Type II, original reverse innovation: Innovate in developing countries–implement in developing countries–export to advanced countries; (3) Ideal Type III, original reverse innovation (front-end technology/leading technology): Innovate in developing countries–implement in advanced countries–sale to advanced countries.

In doing so, our research results illustrate the importance of internal firm capabilities for technology and innovation. Despite the fact that two types of the original categorization of reverse innovation and reverse innovation were based on transferred technology, our case studies suggest that the firms' innovative capability still plays a critical role in the process of reverse innovation. International cooperation will provide more chances for firms in the process of reverse innovation.

Like MNEs from advanced countries, EMNEs also build their R&D centers in other developing countries too, as seen in Chapters 8 and 13. For instance, Huawei has set its R&D centers in several advanced countries, such as Sweden, Germany, the USA, and Japan, as well as developing countries, such as India and Turkey. There are more options available. Taking strategies of reverse innovation, leading EMNEs could have more explicit strategies to use resources and capabilities also from other developing countries. Reverse innovation (the low cost, inclusive innovation, and so on) can bring new competitive advantages and development advantages for firms, so succeeding with it can bring value for firms from developing countries. This may be one pathway for Chinese firms to develop technologies, access global market shares and realize internationalization. More could be done on these topics.

Future research should also use mixed methods to explore the characteristics of these types of reverse innovation and the reasons why these firms succeed in reverse innovation. In addition, the determinants and drivers in reverse innovation and reverse innovation strategies could be analyzed in the future. Moreover, the connection between reverse innovation and open innovation, between reverse innovation and disruptive innovation, between reverse innovation and frugal innovation, and their interactions could be study fields in the future. Furthermore, other theories in the research of globalization, such as the global value chain (Morrison et al., 2008), organization research in innovation phases (Schmitz and Strambach, 2009), technological capabilities (Jin and von Zedtwitz, 2008), the organizational decomposition of the reverse innovation process and its impact on this process, the evolution of technological capabilities in the phases of reverse innovation, and so on, can be studies in the future.

Finally, we suggest that companies may follow different innovation strategies, dependent upon the underlying technologies. Technologies in the Ideal Types II and III are likely rapidly emerging ones in the world, such as nano technology and new energy technology, while technologies in the Ideal Type I are likely relatively mature technologies for advanced countries, such as technologies in high-speed trains. Taking the mature technology, we propose that the Ideal Type I will be a good strategy for firms in developing countries to achieve reverse innovation, while the Ideal Types II and III will be a strategy suitable to firms in developing countries to achieve reverse innovation in emerging technology and emerging market.

ACKNOWLEDGMENTS

This research is sponsored by project grants from the National Natural Science Foundation of China (NSFC: 71172111, 71232013, 71672172, U1509221) and Zhejiang Natural Science Foundation (ZJNSF: LY16G020010).

NOTE

1. The speech of President Hu Jingtao: http://theory.people.com.cn/GB/49169/49171/4012810.html

REFERENCES

Agarwal, N. and A. Brem (2012), 'Frugal and reverse innovation: Literature overview and case study insights from a German MNC in India and China'. In Engineering,

Technology and Innovation (ICE), 2012 18th International ICE Conference, 1–11, IEEE.

Archibugi, D. and S. Iammarino (2002), 'The globalization of technological innovation: definition and evidence', *Review of International Political Economy*, **9**(1), 98–122.

Boutellier, R., O. Gassmann and M. von Zedtwitz (2008), *Managing Global Innovation: Uncovering the Secrets of Future Competitiveness* (Third edition), Springer: Berlin.

Brem, A. and B. Ivens (2013), 'Do frugal and reverse innovation foster sustainability? Introduction of a conceptual framework', *Journal of Technology Management for Growing Economies*, **4**(2), 31–50.

Chen, J. and H. Huang (2011), 'Reverse innovation: A kind of new innovation model' (in Chinese), *Science and Technology Progress and Policy*, **28**(8), 1–5.

Chikofsky, E. and J. Cross (1990), 'Reverse engineering and design recovery: A taxonomy', *Software, IEEE*, **7**(1), 13–17.

DePasse, J. and P. Lee (2013), 'A model for reverse innovation in health care', *Globalization and Health*, **9**(1), 1–7.

Dong, Y. and J. Chen (2010), 'Backtracking innovation in ecological field' (in Chinese), *Technique Economics*, **29**(1), 9–12.

Gassmann, O. and M. von Zedtwitz (1998), 'Organization of industrial R&D on a global scale', *R&D Management*, **28**(3), 147–161.

Gassmann, O. and M. von Zedtwitz (1999), 'New concepts and trends in international R&D organization', *Research Policy*, **28**(2–3), 231–250.

Govindarajan, V. and J. Euchner (2012), 'Reverse innovation', *Research Technology Management*, **55**(6), 13–17.

Govindarajan, V. and R. Ramamurti (2011), 'Reverse innovation, emerging markets, and global strategy', *Global Strategy Journal*, **1**, 191–205.

Hossain, M. (2013), 'Adopting open innovation to stimulate frugal innovation and reverse innovation'.

Immelt, R., V. Govindarajan and C. Trimble (2009), 'How GE is disrupting itself?', *Harvard Business Review*, **87**(10), 56–65.

Jin, J. and M. von Zedtwitz (2008), 'Technological capability development in China's mobile phone industry', *Technovation*, **28**(6), 327–334.

Jin, J., Y. Wang and W. Vanhaverbeke (2014), 'Patterns of R&D internationalization in developing countries: China as a case', *International Journal of Technology Management*, **64**(2–4), 276–302.

Kim, L. (1997), *Imitation to Innovation: The Dynamics of Korea's Technological Learning*, Boston, MA: Harvard Business Press.

Lee, K. and C. Lim (2001), 'Technological regimes, catching-up and leapfrogging: Findings from the Korean industries', *Research Policy*, **30**(3), 459–483.

Li, J. and R.K. Kozhikode (2009), 'Developing new innovation models: Shifts in the innovation landscapes in emerging economies and implications for global R&D management', *Journal of International Management*, **15**(3), 328–339.

Lim, C., S. Han and H. Ito (2013), 'Capability building through innovation for unserved lower and mega markets', *Technovation*, **33**(12), 391–404.

Morrison, A., C. Pietrobelli and R. Rabellotti (2008), 'Global value chains and technological capabilities: A framework to study learning and innovation in developing countries', *Oxford Development Studies*, **36**(1), 39–58.

Schmitz, H. and S. Strambach (2009), 'The organizational decomposition of innovation and global distribution of innovative activities: Insights and research agenda', *International Journal of Technological Learning, Innovation and Development*, **2**(4), 231–249.

Syed, S., V. Dadwal and G. Martin (2013), 'Reverse innovation in global health systems: Towards global innovation flow', *Globalization and Health*, **9**(1), 1.
von Zedtwitz, M. (2005), 'International R&D strategies in companies from developing countries – the case of China', in UNCTAD (ed.), *Globalization of R&D and Developing Countries*, Geneva and New York: United Nations, pp. 117–140.
von Zedtwitz, M., S. Corsi, P. Soberg and R. Frega (2015), 'A typology of reverse innovation', *The Journal of Product Development and Management*, **32**(1), 12–28.
Yang, Q., R. Mudambi and K. Meyer (2008), 'Conventional and reverse knowledge flows in multinational corporations', *Journal of Management*, **34**(5), 882–902.
Yin, R. (2009), *Case Study Research: Design and Methods*, Sage: Thousand Oaks.
Zeschky, M., S. Winterhalter and O. Gassmann (2014), 'From cost to frugal and reverse innovation: Mapping the field and implications for global competitiveness', *Research-Technology Management*, **54**(7), 20–27.
Zhen, W. (2012), 'Research on reverse innovation pattern in the case of BYD' (in Chinese), *Science and Technology Progress*, **29**(5), 18–22.
Zheng, Z. and J. Chen (2014), 'Reverse innovation in China: A case study of CSR Qingdao Sifang' (in Chinese), *Science Technology and Innovation*, **34**(4), 3–8.

10. Indigenous Chinese innovation and the influence of global markets

Astrid Heidemann Lassen

1. INTRODUCTION

This chapter addresses knowledge-intensive innovative entrepreneurship (KIE) in high-tech industries. The focus is primarily on the development of in-house capabilities in relation to technological/scientific knowledge, business knowledge and market knowledge. In the context of this book, these can be seen as corresponding to the different dimensions of the innovative capabilities of these firms, and they are needed to act upon innovative opportunities.

International technology transfer through foreign direct investment (FDI) has long been regarded as a major engine of economic development in developing countries. As such, many developing countries have operated with the expectation that acquisition of advanced technological knowledge can drive technological upgrading in their countries. Such thoughts have in particular long fuelled the catch-up strategies of many Asian countries, creating a strong reliance on and influence of global markets and global investments as drivers of development (Gong, 2011). Fagerberg and Godinho (2004) discuss the role of inward FDI in successful catching-up economies, and explain how Asian catch-up gets access to foreign technology.

Hence, much of the technological effort in developing countries is oriented towards the acquisition of technological capabilities from global markets. Evidence has shown that industrial technology development in many developing countries is equal to the ability to become more efficient and competitive in the use of imported technologies (Li et al., 2010). As a consequence, Asian innovation efforts have often been associated primarily with efficient market exploitation rather than own development of unique technologies and products. Public policy has sought to change this. In 2006 the Chinese government focused particularly on indigenous innovation in its Medium- and Long-Term Plan for the Development of Science and Technology (2006–2020). In this connection "indigenous innovation" was primarily defined as the process of improving the quality and lowering the cost of world-leading technologies transferred from abroad (Liu et al., 2011; Lazonick and Li, 2012).

This is, however, in the process of changing, and greater emphasis is gradually being placed on indigenous innovation as a driver of the development of indigenous technological capabilities. In China this change is evident, for example in the rise of a generation of contemporary entrepreneurs (Liao and Sohmen, 2001), which correspond to modern definitions of knowledge-intensive entrepreneurs (Malerba and McKelvey, 2016; McKelvey and Lassen, 2013). According to Freeman (1995: 20), variation in national innovative performance depends on "institutional differences in the mode of importing, improving, developing and diffusing new technologies, products and processes". Entrepreneurship in China is becoming one of the significant mechanisms for achieving this, and has in particular over the past decade generated significant economic growth and job creation (Huang, 2008). This realization is also evident in the most recent national economic strategy. In April 2016, Premier Li Keqiang called explicitly for "mass entrepreneurship and innovation" and made it a significant part of the next five-year agenda for China's national economy.

Entrepreneurship is in this context primarily connected to technology-based knowledge in domains such as "Internet Plus", "sharing economy", "big data" and "Internet of Things" (Tse, 2016). This resonates well with the fact that China's new entrepreneurs tend to be younger and well-educated in areas such as science and technology (see also Chapter 2). The Global Entrepreneurship Monitor (GEM) 2012 finds that China has a high proportion of young entrepreneurs, with 57 per cent between 18 and 34 years of age (Xavier et al., 2013). Furthermore, they have the world's highest digital literacy, access to a Chinese internet market of more than 700 million users, and they are driven by the ambition to create highly significant careers through their entrepreneurial endeavours.

Internet entrepreneurs in particular started to emerge in China in the 1990s. Contemporary giants such as Alibaba, Tencent and Baidu were formed during this period. The number of entrepreneurs grew significantly throughout the 2000s, with founders of, for example, Xiaomi, JD.com and Qihoo 360 being globally recognized examples of China's internet entrepreneurs. Apart from the internet and mobile technology sectors, many entrepreneurs have also started to appear in industries such as energy, financial services and healthcare, where businesses are increasingly built based on the rapid growth of science and technology. This book thus contends that knowledge-intensive entrepreneurship – especially of this type – will likely become an important driver of the indigenous Chinese innovations in the future.

This is a highly interesting development, which also raises questions about what the influence of global markets will be in relation to innovation in a Chinese context in the future. This chapter shows ten Chinese KIE ventures in the development of their innovative capabilities to global markets and how this, in turn, impacts on the development of their KIE ventures.

2. RESEARCH DESIGN FOR ANALYSING TECHNOLOGICAL/SCIENTIFIC, MARKET AND BUSINESS KNOWLEDGE

The study has been carried out in collaboration with the Sino-Danish Center (SDC), which is a bilateral teaching and research program between eight Danish universities and the University of Chinese Academy of Sciences. This specific research project addresses the field of KIE in high-tech domains in China.

Given the exploratory nature of this research, qualitative case studies are chosen as the appropriate research method to apply (Yin, 1994). Ten cases were selected for the study, and these are regarded as revelatory cases to reach a deeper understanding of the phenomenon studied.

The case studies are used to illustrate and explain the perception of global markets expressed by Chinese high-tech entrepreneurs and how this relates to the development of their ventures. The criteria for selection of the cases were that they are knowledge-intensive entrepreneurial organizations, as defined theoretically and operationally in Malerba and McKelvey (2016 and 2018). The specific criteria included:

- The organizations had existed less than eight years (e.g. were in the new venture creation phase).
- The organizations competed based upon advanced knowledge, specifically technological/scientific knowledge, market knowledge and business knowledge, as proposed in McKelvey and Lassen (2013).
- The organizations operated in high-tech domains.
- The organizations worked with innovative technologies, products, or services.

The perception and influence of global markets is studied through a number of dimensions capturing the global influence on the technological/scientific, business, and market knowledge of the KIE ventures.

Through the development of an interview protocol, interviews were conducted with the owners or CEOs of the firms. The data collection was carried out following a similar interview protocol in all cases in order to create replication logic between the cases (Yin, 1994).

Fifteen in-depth interviews were carried out in total, resulting in approximately 40 hours of interview material. All interviews are partially transcribed allowing for clustering of emerging themes, and worked on across the team. An overview of the case organizations is presented in Table 10.1. Each case study has been written up descriptively, and then analysed according to the variables thought to capture the influence of global markets.

Table 10.1 Overview of knowledge-intensive entrepreneurial firms

	Year of establishment	Size: number of employees	Areas of innovation activity
A	2010	80	Development and sales of indigenous Chinese medical robots and supporting systems
B	2009	5	Networked R&D, service and investment company in the area of energy technologies
C	2014	130	Automotive online platform, combining sales, information, financing and insurance of cars
D	2015	1	Meet-up app development
E	2015	5	Mobile gaming platform
F	2012	4	3D antique visualization technology
G	2014	10	Mobile gaming platform
H	2006	90	Development and distribution of ophthalmic equipment and consumables
I	2012	90	Online banking technology
J	2013	137	Bitcoin trading platform

The ten companies selected for the study are all founded by entrepreneurs who were between 22 and 30 years old at the time of establishment. In this sense the age group corresponds very well to the segment of new entrepreneurs identified through the GEM study.

3. ANALYSIS OF KNOWLEDGE CAPABILITIES AND GLOBALIZATION

In the following, a short case description is provided of each of the ventures, focusing explicitly on the influence of global aspects in relation to the knowledge-base of the company, i.e. the technological/scientific knowledge, the business knowledge and the market knowledge of the ventures.

Venture A

The venture is a high-tech company, which has developed China's first indigenous orthopedic surgery robot, and an associated remote surgery service system. A certain awareness of global counterparts is expressed by the respondents, but they also emphasize that this has no direct influence on the technology development of the firm. All suppliers of product components are Chinese, and the human knowledge resources are Chinese. Regarding the influence of global markets on the business knowledge of the venture, this is also very limited. The founders express awareness of the price level of a French counterpart, and explain that this has helped them position the target price of their own technology and service system. However, international sales are not prioritized at this point in time, so the global markets have very little significance. The focus of the venture is primarily to develop an eco-system of Chinese hospitals requesting the technology they provide.

Venture B

The venture is a network organization which develops knowledge and technologies based on close collaboration with five Chinese research environments and one German R&D company in the domains of automation and industrial IT. The Chinese partners are primarily involved in technology development, whereas the German partner is engaged in technology testing. The founder of the venture has a strong global interest and follows the developments of the European Industry 4.0 and the American Advanced Manufacturing initiatives very closely. His interest is to utilize the knowledge to identify and stimulate opportunities in the area of the indigenous Chinese initiative on industrial revolution. In the interviews, the global interest did not manifest itself in either utilization of foreign technology nor international sales. The founder does have the ambition for his venture to eventually become a fully international enterprise. However, the primary focus is to aid Chinese industries to develop unique competencies in the domains of automation and industrial IT.

Venture C

The venture is characterized as an "Internet-plus company", meaning that it utilizes well-established internet platforms to merge different offline and online products and services. In the venture this is called "merging the vertical automobile industry". The venture relies exclusively on Chinese knowledge and competences in both the domain of IT/programming and the domain of the automobile industry. The interest in global markets is very low, both in terms of technology, business and markets. The offering of the venture is built upon the unique specificities of the automobile industry in China, and focuses exclusively on Chinese customers.

Venture D

The venture is in the very early stages of formation, and is trying to establish both technology, business and markets. The founder is driven by a clear ambition to become an entrepreneur, and is less concerned with the actual scope of the venture. He is convinced that for any opportunity he decides to pursue, there will be large business potential. The current focus is to develop an Android-based app for the Chinese market, which has a similar scope as the American-developed app Meet-up. The market estimate for the first year is 300,000 users. The technology is well-known globally, because the business idea is inspired by a global brand, but the market knowledge is exclusively Chinese. The founder does not actively think of his approach in connection to global markets, but considers it as part of the internet market, which transcends national boundaries.

Venture E

The venture is an online gaming company, which currently has seven products on the market. They pursue a market strategy defined by the technology platforms, Apple and Android. Currently they have 200,000 customers on Apple and 50,000 on Android. Both platforms are used by Chinese as well as international customers, and the entrepreneurs do not see any specific differences between the Chinese and the international markets. They see only one internet market. The technological knowledge behind the development of the gaming products is Chinese.

Venture F

This venture is one amongst many ventures started by the founder. The founder describes himself as a lifestyle entrepreneur, and part of a modern Chinese lifestyle. His venture develops and applies 3D visualization technology specifically to the area of antiques and art. The founder is intrigued by 3D visualization, and has identified that museums could enhance and expand their offerings significantly by applying this. The technological knowledge is partly well-known internationally, and partly further developed by the ventures. The business knowledge is inspired by an iTunes model, where museums are offered the system for free, and pay per use. The market knowledge is very specific to the Chinese context, where museums are funded through complex governmental programs and sales to these institutions are dependent on detailed knowledge and network in this domain. The international context is not explicitly influential in any parts of the business, though the technology and business models have international parallels.

Venture G

The venture is yet another example of a venture using the internet as the foundation of the business. The venture is an online gaming company, focusing specifically on games for mobile platforms. The founder previously worked at Xiaomi, but wanted to pursue a career as a self-employed entrepreneur. The venture is backed by significant capital investments from ZQGame, a public company investing specifically in online games. The venture has also entered into collaboration with Tencent (China's largest and most used internet service portal), and the game is featured in the QQ Zone. The venture has approximately one million registered users. The game itself is inspired by the American game DOTA, and uses a similar structure. The employees are all Chinese, and are highly educated from prestigious Chinese universities. When asked about the influence of global markets, the founder explains that the internet is one big market where technological knowledge and business opportunities flow freely across national boundaries. He considers the knowledge of the venture as much a part of the global knowledge in the domain as the other way around.

Venture H

The venture is one of the major distributors of ophthalmic equipment and the related ophthalmopathy computer assisted diagnosis system in China. The venture was founded while the founder did her PhD and spent one year in New York. The venture today has more than 960 Chinese hospitals as customers, and operates from 13 different sites in China. The original approach of the venture was based on sourcing and distributing American technologies and products to the Chinese market. The venture has subsequently invested heavily in its own R&D. Their R&D headquarters are located in New York. Several collaborations with American R&D partners have been established, and investments have also been made in a Canadian development company. Additionally, the venture has entered into R&D collaboration with a large Chinese R&D company. The authors consider this approach to the global markets as unusual in the sense that access to global knowledge and expertise is considered more important than access to global consumer markets or access to global investments. This is quite the opposite of the traditional thoughts of FDI driving the development of Chinese technologies.

Venture I

The venture develops and sells an information pattern recognition technology which enables, for example, online banks to improve their security, as well as military institutions to monitor communication. The technology development is based solely on Chinese competences in software as well as hardware. The venture operates from three different sites in the Beijing area, all located in close proximity to high-tech hubs and research institutions. The founder mentions this as a particular strategy to attract and gain access to human knowledge resources. The technology is in a domain (communication and security) which is highly controlled and monitored by the government, and therefore entirely dependent on certifications. The founder mentions that he at one point did consider launching his product on the American market, but he found the certification requirements to be too difficult to deal with. No further ambitions towards global markets have been made, not for technological knowledge, business knowledge, nor market knowledge.

Venture J

The venture is a bitcoin trading company, focusing on the Chinese and the US markets. Bitcoin is a virtual currency, created and held entirely electronically. The currency is global and decentralized (i.e. no one institution owns it, it is created through and by digital communities). The currency was first launched in 2008, and has since then established itself as a globally dominant currency. The venture was amongst the first to spot the opportunities connected to bitcoins, and it has rapidly developed into one of the largest digital currency trading companies in China. While the primary markets for this are the American and the Chinese markets, the founders did not talk specifically about the influence of global markets. Similarly to several of the other internet-based case companies, this venture also considers the internet to be one large market. The employees at the venture are all Chinese, and the founders favour employees with an entrepreneurial spirit and high self-motivation. Most employees are highly educated from top universities in the Beijing area.

The ten cases when analysed together provide a variety of insights about the influence of global markets on the knowledge and innovation of the companies. A summary of the results from the case studies can be found in Table 10.2.

4. DISCUSSION AND CONCLUSIONS

The descriptions of the ten case companies are presented above, in terms of an analysis of technological / scientific, market and business knowledge in relation to the KIE firm's in-house innovative capabilities and global influences. The understanding of the global influences provides grounds for learning about the influence of global markets of contemporary Chinese entrepreneurs working with indigenous Chinese innovation, and hence is closely aligned with empirical details underlying the arguments found in Chapters 5, 11 and 12.

Table 10.2 Summary of results from case studies

	Global influence on:		
Organization pseudonym	Technological/scientific knowledge	Market knowledge	Business knowledge
A	Low global influence – some awareness, but no direct relation	Low global influence – some awareness of price level of international providers of similar products	None
B	Low global influence – but some inspiration from global industrial initiatives	Low global influence	Low global influence
C	Low global influence – builds on well-known international technology	None	None
D	Medium global influence – builds on well-known international technology	None	Medium global influence – inspired by an American product
E	Low global influence – builds on well-known international technology	None	Low global influence – builds on well-known international platforms
F	Low global influence – builds on well-known international technology	None	Low global influence – inspired by an iTunes-like business model
G	Low global influence – builds on well-known international technology	None	Low global influence –builds on well-known international platforms
H	High global influence – sources international knowledge and technology	None	Medium global influence – exploits international technology in the Chinese market
I	Low global influence	None	None
J	Low global influence – builds on well-known international technology	Low global influence	Medium global influence – builds on well-known international platforms

In Figure 10.1 an overview is created of the results from the ten cases in relation to the global influence on their technological/scientific knowledge, market knowledge and business knowledge. The conclusions regarding global influence are summarized ranging from None, Low, Medium and High global influence.

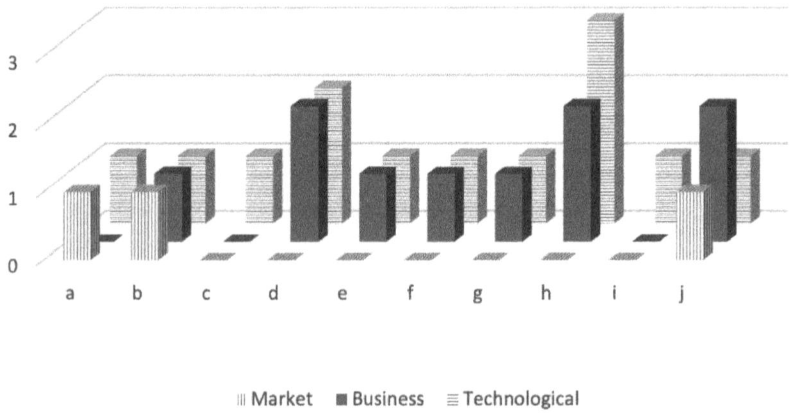

Figure 10.1 *Influence of global markets on indigenous innovation*

It is clear from Figure 10.1 that in general the influence of global markets is very low. Out of the 30 learning points, 10 equal None, 15 equal Low, 4 equal Medium, and only 1 equals High. This provides a picture which is very different from the traditional view of Chinese innovation being dependent on FDI or imitation of Western technologies.

When we take a closer look at each of the knowledge dimensions some differences are detected.

Regarding Market Knowledge, all of the ventures indicate that the global markets are of very little interest. They do not rely on investments or products from global markets, and the sales opportunities on the Chinese market are considered to be so significant that there is no need to cater especially to international customers. This provides a clear contrast to the traditional perspective on the role of Chinese companies in global innovation systems, where Asian countries in general have mainly been associated with cost-efficient exploitation of products and ideas developed in the Western world. While these findings are of course only based on a limited number of cases, they do raise interesting questions about the future geographical origin of new ideas and innovation, and where the benefit of such innovations will be. This has the potential to challenge the perceived competitive advantage of Western companies – in terms of innovation and development – relative to Chinese companies.

Regarding Business Knowledge, most of the ventures indicate that global markets are of low influence, and a few indicate that global markets are of medium influence. Also on this point distinct differences are observed, as compared to traditional approaches to global business knowledge. Traditional perspectives on the influence of global business knowledge emphasize that business knowledge spreads from more developed countries to lesser developed countries as a function of, for example, offshoring of specific competences (production and so on). However, this is not observed here. The type of global business knowledge which has some influence is of a much more conceptual nature, exemplified by business models utilized elsewhere (e.g. the iTunes model) and global trends (e.g. the Industry 4.0 initiative). These types of conceptual business knowledge are used as inspiration and idea development.

Regarding Technological Knowledge, all of the ventures showed some influence of global markets, and two ventures showed respectively medium and high influence. Not surprisingly, this is the knowledge category where global markets have the highest influence. The aspect of technology knowledge is traditionally strongly associated with inward FDI and adaptation/imitation of foreign technologies (e.g. Cheung, 2011). This, however, is not the type of global influence on technology knowledge identified in the Chinese ventures in this study.

The majority of the companies can be characterized as "internet plus" companies. They recognize that they work with communication technology which is globally well known and that the development of such technology often takes place in global open source forums. As such, they recognize that global technology knowledge has an influence, but they also demonstrate that they themselves also partake in the development of additional global knowledge. The pattern detected is hence a two-way learning process, as opposed to the unidirectional thinking behind the adaptation/imitation strategies.

The venture that is influenced to a high degree by global markets in terms of technology knowledge also demonstrates a significantly different approach to global knowledge. They have actively invested in Western R&D companies and formed alliances and partnership with Western knowledge institutions in order to be directly involved in the development of the newest knowledge in their domain. Outbound direct investment (ODI) is a rather new but rapidly growing phenomenon in China, and as such is not in itself an unusual strategy pursued by Chinese companies and investment funds. But, what is somewhat unusual is to see ODI as the very clear knowledge and innovation strategy of an entrepreneurial venture in China. Also, in terms of the geographical placement of ODI the venture stands out. The vast majority of Chinese ODI is, according to Casanova et al. (2015) placed in other Asian countries, while only 4 per cent is placed in North America. The venture in this study has invested in Canada, the USA, and Germany.

In conclusion, the analysis has illuminated that the contemporary Chinese entrepreneurs in the focus of the study in general are of the opinion that knowledge from global markets affects their knowledge base and innovation activities to a very limited degree. The opportunities pursued by these entrepreneurs are to a high extent affected by possibilities arising from the use of internet platforms and through this, the ease of access to the very large Chinese domestic market. Many of the entrepreneurs in this study think of the internet, the communication technologies behind internet possibilities, and the online customer base as one big market, making little distinction between national vs. global knowledge. Furthermore, they see themselves as much as contributors of knowledge as exploiters of knowledge.

Our results indicate two interesting patterns. 1) Contemporary Chinese entrepreneurs place much greater emphasis on their own abilities to develop and manage innovation than previously acknowledged in literature on innovation and globalization. 2) The significance of the internet for Chinese entrepreneurs is creating entirely new dimensions to consider in relation to understanding the dynamics of the Chinese innovation system and the interplay with global markets.

ACKNOWLEDGEMENTS

The Sino-Danish Center for Education and Research (SDC) has supported this research.

REFERENCES

Casanova, C., Garcia-Herrero, A. and Xia, L. (2015), 'Chinese outbound foreign direct investment: How much goes where after roundtripping and offshoring?', *BBVA Research Working Paper*, **15/17**.

Cheung, T.M. (2011), 'The Chinese defense economy's long march from imitation to innovation', *Journal of Strategic Studies*, **34** (3), 325–354.

Fagerberg, J. and Godinho, M.M. (2004), 'Innovation and catching-up', in Fagerberg, J., Mowery, D. and Nelson, R. (eds.), *The Oxford Handbook of Innovation*. Oxford: Oxford University Press, pp. 514–544.

Freeman, C. (1995), 'The "National System of Innovation" in historical perspective', *Cambridge Journal of Economics*, **19**, 5–24.

Gong, X.F.Y. (2011), 'Indigenous and foreign innovation efforts and drivers of technological upgrading: Evidence from China', *World Development*, **39** (7), 1213–1225.

Huang, Y. (2008), *Capitalism with Chinese Characteristics.* Cambridge: Cambridge University Press.

Lazonick, W. and Li, Y. (2012), 'China's path to indigenous innovation'. Conference proceedings to *Society for the Advancement of Socio-Economics*. Cambridge, MA: MIT.

Li, Y., Zhang, C., Liu, Y. and Li, M. (2010), 'Organizational learning, internal control mechanisms, and indigenous innovation: The evidence from China', *EEE Transactions on Engineering Management*, **57** (1), 63–77.

Liao, D. and Sohmen, P. (2001), 'The development of modern entrepreneurship in China', *Stanford Journal of East Asian Affairs*, **1**, 27–33.

Liu, F., Simon, D., Sun, Y. and Cong, C. (2011), 'China innovation policies: Evolution, institutional structure, and trajectory', *Research Policy*, **49**, 917–931.

Malerba, M. and McKelvey, M. (2016), 'Conceptualizing knowledge intensive entrepreneurship: Definition and model', in Malerba, M., Caloughirou, Y., McKelvey, M., and Radosevic, S. (eds.), *The Dynamics of Knowledge Intensive Entrepreneurship.* New York, NY, USA: Routledge.

Malerba, M. and McKelvey, M. (2018), 'Knowledge intensive entrepreneurship: Moving beyond the Schumpeterian entrepreneur', *Small Business Economics.*

Malerba, F. and McKelvey, M. (2020), 'Knowledge-intensive innovative entrepreneurship integrating Schumpeter, evolutionary economics, and innovation systems', *Small Business Economics*, **54**, 503–522.

McKelvey, M. and Lassen, A.H. (2013), *Managing Knowledge Intensive Entrepreneurship*. Cheltenham, UK and Northampton, MA, USA: Edward Elgar Publishing.

Tse, E. (2016), 'The rise of entrepreneurship in China', *Forbes online.* Accessed 18 July 2017 at https://www.forbes.com/sites/tseedward/2016/04/05/the-rise-of-entrepreneurship-in-china/#683150803efc

Xavier, S.R., Kelley, D. and Kew, J. (2013), *Global Entrepreneurship Monitor, Global Report*. London: Global Entrepreneurship Research Association.

Yin, R.K. (1994), *Case Study Research: Design and Methods*. London: Sage Publications.

11. A case study of the link between artificial intelligence and knowledge creation in an emerging technology in China

Peder Veng Søberg

1. INTRODUCTION

This chapter presents a case study of one Chinese knowledge-intensive innovative entrepreneurial (KIE) firm, Intellifusion, which develops artificial intelligence for visual information processing. The focus is primarily on the development of in-house capabilities in relation to technological and scientific knowledge as well as the importance of tacit market knowledge. Like Chapter 10, this chapter focuses upon the internal capabilities of KIE firms.

In the context of this book, the chapter focuses upon how internal firm capabilities and relationships have to be developed in order to access tacit knowledge from the market. In this broader sense, this chapter relates the entrepreneurial firm to users in the further development of technology. Companies are interested in identifying market and technological opportunities through interactions with users, to develop better products and services, and this can be particularly difficult in Asia (McKelvey and Bagchi-Sen, 2015). Users are an important element within innovation systems. Interactions around visual knowledge can help create knowledge that is useful for specifying that user demand into relevant characteristics for products and services.

The firm is active in visual intelligence, which is here defined as hardware and software solutions that can be used to analyse visual material, based on deep learning algorithms. This industry relies on artificial intelligence and big data, in order to process large sets of data to extract information for different purposes such as surveillance and security.

To develop our understanding of how this type of technical capability is developed, this chapter analyses the case study in relation to the knowledge management literature, and the distinction between knowledge as tacit or codified. Nonaka and Takeuchi (1995) proposed the SECI model, which is an abbreviation for socialisation, externalisation, combination, and internalisation. This chapter also brings in theories related to brain activities as well as operations management for visualisation of production processes (Amalric and Dehaene, 2016). This chapter analyses the challenges and responses by firms, when developing this type of technological capability, and proposes that the firms can benefit from field tests and prototypes to externalise knowledge, and to further develop advanced technical knowledge.

This is an interesting problem, also empirically. Especially in emerging industries, it is not always clear and explicit how technology can be further developed to meet user needs. Advanced technical knowledge can be difficult to externalise using linguistic verbalisation, and hence non-codified and non-verbal knowledge may be needed. There is also a strong entrepreneurial spirit in China, a focus on science and technology within education, and large investment into R&D by both the Chinese government and Chinese companies (see Chapter 2).

2. KNOWLEDGE CREATION THEORIES IN RELATION TO ADVANCED TECHNOLOGY

This chapter aims to contribute to research regarding knowledge creation in the context of advanced technical capabilities in entrepreneurial firms, and especially in relation to users in the innovation system in China. Many existing conceptual models about knowledge creation contain similar elements (Crossan and Berdrow, 2003; Crossan, Lane, and White, 1999; Hedlund, 1994; Nonaka and Konno, 1998), but we know little about how to operationalise them in different settings and particularly in advanced technology. The normative tenets of this type of knowledge creation theory recommend verbal interactions to externalise tacit knowledge. In contrast, this chapter explores how a Chinese start-up firm can work with other types of knowledge in articulating the unmet needs of users, and in situations where the user may not understand the technical knowledge and may also find it difficult to specify their expected solutions. In such situations, spoken words may fall short as means to enable interaction between technical expert developers and end-users, and therefore this case study explores other means of developing interactions.

2.1 Models Based on Tacit and Explicit Knowledge

Models about knowledge creation tend to emphasise the distinction between tacit and codified knowledge and are in that sense quite similar (Crossan and Berdrow, 2003; Crossan, Lane, and White, 1999; Hedlund, 1994; Nonaka and Konno, 1998). Of these models, existing literature suggests that the SECI model (Nonaka and Konno, 1998; Nonaka and Takeuchi, 1995) is particularly relevant for product innovation (Crossan, Lane, and White, 1999).

The SECI model has four key cycles, which can be studied independently or in moving between the cycles, as illustrated in Figure 11.1.

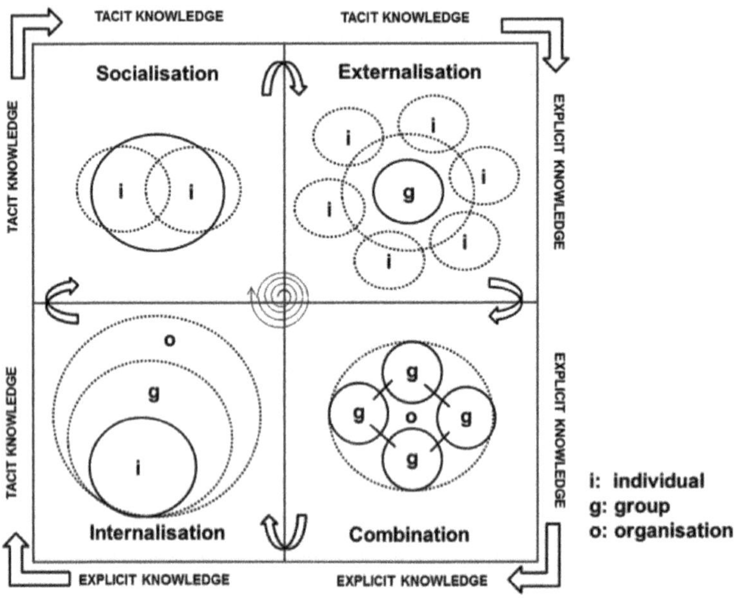

Figure 11.1 *Spiral evolution of knowledge conversion and self-transcending process*

Socialisation is the move from tacit knowledge to tacit knowledge; Externalisation is from tacit knowledge to explicit knowledge; Combination is from explicit knowledge to explicit knowledge, and Internalisation is from explicit knowledge to tacit knowledge. These cycles depend upon interactions among individuals, groups and organisations. The SECI model outlines how knowledge develops by iterative conversion back and forth in these two categories of tacit and explicit knowledge, in order to explain the relationships between knowledge at the individual, group and organisational levels.

In this model, knowledge is considered either tacit or explicit. This assumption has been criticised, and especially the assumption that tacit knowledge is convertible into explicit knowledge, by Tsoukas (2003). This chapter explores whether and how tacit and explicit knowledge complement each other, and beyond verbal language per se.

2.2 Untangling Tacit and Codified Knowledge in the Cycles of Socialisation and Externalisation

How does the SECI model embrace the transfer as well as the creation of tacit knowledge in the two cycles of socialisation and externalisation, in relation to advanced technology?

Explicit knowledge can be considered equivalent to codified knowledge. Codification is "the process of conversion of knowledge into messages that can then be processed as information" (Cowan and Foray, 1997, 596). Many technical advances such as big data and visual intelligence enable the codification of knowledge, and they make it cheaper to do so. The following analysis relates to the four cycles found in Figure 11.1 above.

In the socialisation phase, tacit–tacit knowledge transfers take place between different actors. To understand such transfers better, it is useful to distinguish between two types of tacit knowledge, namely the technical component such as know-how and the cognitive component such as mental models and beliefs as outlined by Nonaka and Konno (1998). An example of the transfer of the technical component in tacit–tacit knowledge transfers is a master–apprentice relationship, where the master teaches the apprentice skills, such as laying bricks to build a house. This type of technical know-how transfers from person to person. In relation to the interaction with users, the cognitive component likely works in parallel with the technical component. In this situation, the person with know-how is exposed to a new mental model or belief system, which enables them to develop new insights about how to apply the know-how (Søberg, 2011). An example of this is when an engineer with advanced technical skills interacts with potential customers who have different mental models than him/her. Here, the socialisation cycle can be used to indicate that these technical skills can be put to use to help the customer, where technical know-how is combined with a new mental model or belief system.

Moreover, and in line with how diversity can benefit creativity (Beeby and Booth, 2000), this chapter suggests that a mix of different types of tacit knowledge may also nurture creativity and knowledge creation. Interesting questions arise about what additional types of tacit knowledge exist, in order to enable potential customers to grasp possible future forms of know-how.

In the externalisation cycle, the model assumes that knowledge is converted from tacit to explicit knowledge. Based on previous work by the author on Chinese companies (Søberg, 2010), this chapter starts from the insight that one should consider the costs of converting tacit into explicit knowledge in relation to the speed of technical change in the future. If knowledge is useful and likely to be valuable for a long time in the future, then it will likely be worthwhile to invest into codification because more time is available to recoup the investment (see Ferdows, 2006). In the opposite case, the codification investments will likely not be worthwhile because of limited time to benefit from these investments. Therefore, to determine whether to codify knowledge or not, a firm should take into consideration how fast technology is evolving. Therefore, a firm may choose to allow tacit and explicit knowledge to complement each other, and will make decisions about which elements should be converted from tacit to explicit knowledge.

These insights are applied to the analysis of the case study below, by exploring and illustrating what happens when the firm converts only parts of tacit knowledge to explicit knowledge using prototypes, field tests, or other three-dimensional forms. These are considered a pre-linguistic embodiment of tacit knowledge.

2.3 The Importance of Non-verbal Aspects of Technical Knowledge

To explore further how to add visual knowledge into the model of Figure 11.1, this section draws upon a critique of an existing study of Apple as well as literature from other disciplines.

Even though Crossan, Lane, and White (1999) admitted that they did not develop a full Apple case, they still used the firm as a case study to demonstrate how language development is important to knowledge creation. They argue that if Steve Jobs had used other metaphors, then much of the development of the firm would have been different. Hence, language development within the firm is seen to influence greatly the technology. However, it is striking that their interpretation of Apple contradicts the view of Steve Wozniak, who also co-founded Apple. According to Wozniak and Smith (2006), in order to create something revolutionary, people should work alone, and not be part of teams or committees. Other indications of the importance of something more than language can be found in the words of Albert Einstein: "words seemed to play no role in his mechanism of thought, which instead relied on 'certain signs and more less clear images'" (Hadamard, 1945, IX).

This suggests that there are two opposing views on how a firm can develop technical capabilities using non-verbal interactions with users. One position is that language is vital for knowledge creation, as exemplified by Steve Jobs. The argument would be that knowledge creation necessitates verbal interaction between people, and for this to happen, they need language. Interacting with others can improve ideas and identify unmet demands. The other position is that language and communication are not needed, at least in early phases of technical development, as exemplified by Steve Wozniak. The argument would be that potential end-users have a hard time grasping the specific technical know-how, and hence they would find it difficult to specify needs, given they do not understand the technology or its potential applications.

Literature from other fields provides some insights which are useful to explore how visualisation and other non-verbal forms of communication may be very useful in product development.

One field is operations management, which suggests that for some types of interactions, using fewer words may be more efficient than a process based on extensive verbal interaction. Hence, we can take literally the statement that "learning processes can be compared to production processes" (Crossan, Lane, and White, 1999, 535). In operations management, the line layout has the benefits that it reduces the need for verbal communication, and it shortens the gap between different partners. Lean manufacturing promotes visual management and at-a-glance transparency, which should enable the sharing of key information without lengthy verbal elaboration. Another element in lean manufacturing is to locate adjacent processes as well as the early and late steps close to each other. Locating process steps closer together (Bicheno and Holweg, 2009) enables more tacit–tacit knowledge transfers across different process steps. In the case of a breakdown, the idea is that operators in this process step can ask nearby operators to have a look at what is wrong, as opposed to calling other operators and trying to explain the problem. The co-location of process steps enables the use of the collective experience of different operators to diagnose and solve problems faster.

Amalric and Dehaene (2016) have questioned the conceptual notion that language development and verbal interaction is important for knowledge creation. Through the use of functional magnetic resonance imaging (fMRI), it is possible to determine which parts of the brain are active during different activities. When the brain carries out activities such as math or spatial thinking that are often essential for technical knowledge creation, different parts of the brain are more active than those related to language (Amalric and Dehaene, 2016).

3. METHODOLOGY

This case study aims to develop insights and understanding in a particular phenomenon, which is a relevant research strategy when exploring complex real-life phenomena (Yin, 2009) and studying "how things work" (Stake, 2010). The criteria for selection included: well-performing entreprenuerial firms in an emerging technological field in China; involvement in hardware development as well as software development; and access to persons for interviews. A leading well-performing firm was chosen in order to increase the likelihood of best practice identification to explore this issue. The emphasis on an emerging technological field focuses attention on start-up companies in industries which may grow in the future. Choosing a Chinese firm relates to understanding a context where, increasingly, a relatively large effort is focused on R&D and technical development.

The data collection entailed semi-structured manager interviews alongside observations and informal talks with lower-level employees. The empirical data were analysed primarily using the pattern-matching logic (Yin, 2009). The interviews were digitally recorded and transcribed, and key findings and chapter draft received informant feedback.

4. INTELLIFUSION: THE CASE STUDY FIRM

Intellifusion, founded in 2014, provides artificial intelligence solutions for visual material, that is, solutions that analyse video material through the use of deep learning algorithms. The two co-founders have complementary overseas education and also previously worked together at the Center for Signal and Image Processing at the Georgia Institute of Technology (Hua, 2016). Each also has industrial experience in hardware and software development, respectively, from ZTE Corporation and Cisco. The two Chinese founders are both members of the Recruitment Program of Global Experts (also known as the Thousand Talents Program) that attracts special and top overseas technological and scientific talents back to China.

The firm invests heavily in R&D, and delivers big data services with a focus on surveillance systems. The number of employees has been growing quickly, and 30 of the 45 employees worked with R&D in 2016. This firm generates a good cash flow from different applications, including surveillance systems with face recognition for crime reduction as well as loans. Intellifusion won the Peacock Award in 2015 that included 20 million RMB in funding for the industrialisation of visual intelligence technologies, plus a 20 million RMB, five-year, low-interest loan. There are many potential applications for visual intelligence systems, but it can be challenging to understand customer needs.

The specific software and hardware technologies developed by the firm can be used in different applications. One example of a successful application is that the firm won a bid to help the border police identify sick people at the arrival hall. With globalisation, it is becoming increasingly important to identify people spreading diseases such as SARS. For this purpose, efforts are made to identify sick individuals going through immigration, for instance between Hong Kong and China. In an existing technology, infrared cameras that trigger temperature alarms can help detect people with fever. However, this solution also generates false alarms because objects like tea bottles and cell phones are usually warmer than human foreheads, and the system is unable to distinguish between objects and humans. Therefore, the existing solution would be particularly suitable for use at an airport, where people are not allowed to bring tea, and where cell phones are just turned on after landing and not yet warm. However, for crossing of land borders, the firm provides an alternative solution, which only generates an alarm when the high-temperature object from the video is confirmed (simultaneously) to be above a human forehead or neck. To understand this need, the developers had to spend time with customers to understand their problems.

The following quote indicates that it is a challenge when customers are unable to specify what they want: "I think this is a very high skill, to read the customers and deliver something that is good enough for your business to continue. That is a piece of art" (Interview with Manager). This illustration can also be used to explore how the firm worked with the interdependencies of software and hardware. So far, the firm has sold solutions involving cameras as well as algorithms. However, it is expensive for the customer to buy new cameras, and many cameras are useful in that the benefits of using this technology often increase with the number of cameras. Moreover, it is inefficient to transfer all video material from every camera to a back office for analysis or up to the cloud. An option they are developing involves cameras with embedded algorithms on a chip, which can pre-analyse the video material and only send back key information. However, a problem with existing chips is that they cannot be updated. Over time, as you learn, it is important to update different algorithms. It would be beneficial to have a chip that is flexible enough to allow for new updates to the algorithm. Therefore, the firm is developing a chip that can be integrated into existing cameras and allows continuous updates while reducing energy consumption to 2–5 percent of that of existing solutions. Their goal is to become the Intel of the visual intelligence industry by providing the advanced chips that enable wider application of this technology.

However, developing the chip also represents a new approach for the firm, with implications for field testing. For software, it is faster to fine-tune algorithms in the field than to test everything beforehand. However, chip development (as hardware) is different from software development in that iterations are much more costly and take longer time. The firm needs to consider every possibility and design everything correctly before starting the manufacture of a new chip. A malfunctioning chip prototype is almost useless. Hence, the firm has a need to solve the software and hardware together, in relation to different modes of testing.

5. LINKING VISUAL INTELLIGENCE AND KNOWLEDGE CREATION IN THE ANALYSIS

Based on an analysis of the empirical material in the case study using the above concepts, Table 11.1 proposes four key challenges of developing this type of advanced technology as well as firm responses.

The first challenge is to understand customer needs when the customer cannot specify what they want.

When viewing the empirical data through the lens of the SECI model, our analysis is that the firm performs well regarding the advanced skill of socialisation with customers; it is able to understand what customers want even though the customers are not able to explain this well. Therefore, their solution is spending time socialising with customers. When socialising with customers, for example by visiting the border control, engineers in the firm identify the unmet needs of these customers. It is considered an advanced skill to be able to read the customers and continuously deliver something that satisfies customer demands.

Table 11.1 Key challenges and how the case company responds

Challenges	Company responses
Understanding customer needs, when the customer can't specify what they want	Socialising and spending time with customers Showing field tests and getting feedback Convincing customers that the solutions can work Field testing
Engaging in too much group discussion	Delegating tasks for people to solve
Financing much R&D	Good contracts with local police force delivering surveillance systems regarding cameras and algorithms that provide a good cash flow Prize award and low-interest loan Investors buy stocks in the company
Avoiding too many costly prototypes of the chip development	Consider every possibility and design everything right before starting the manufacture of a new chip

Source: Nonaka and Konno (1998), adapted to UK English.

The second challenge is engaging in too much group discussion. We suggest that the firm has a problem concerning too much reliance on verbal externalisation in internal processes. The interviews suggested that many would prefer the delegation of tasks to people rather than discussing them at length. Group discussion is verbal externalisation following the SECI model, and it may be unproductive in the situation because the verbal discussion is unlikely to trigger parts of the brain related to math and spatial thinking relevant to solving advanced technical problems (Amalric and Dehaene, 2016). Group discussion can provide new perspectives on the problems and help coordination, but they may not be sufficient to create the solutions.

The third challenge is how to finance a high level of R&D. The firm has low-interest loans from the government and also benefits from policies for recruiting talents. Moreover, it delivers its solutions continuously and on time, whereby they ensure a good cash flow from customers. Part of the success may be due to field tests implemented far in advance of the project deadline. Rather than documenting every piece of their solution before launching it, they test it in the field and allow time for changes, in advance of the project deadlines.

The fourth challenge is avoiding working with too many costly prototypes of the chip. In hardware, they need to consider every possibility and design everything right before starting the manufacture of a new chip. This requires a different way of working from software.

Hence, analysis of the case study illustrates the need for non-verbal tools to facilitate knowledge generation, and in particular, to enable the firm to further develop its technical know-how in relation to applications, including unmet but unarticulated needs of the users.

One addition is the context of emerging technology in China. As mentioned in the theory section, explicit knowledge is more likely available in a codified form in mature industries based on existing technology than it is in fast-changing emerging technological fields. The excessive focus on "the old" industries may have biased the resulting frameworks and assumptions (Boisot and Child, 1999; Crossan and Berdrow, 2003; Crossan, Lane, and White, 1999; Hedlund, 1994; Nonaka and Konno, 1998), and normative tenets in this literature to fit those companies in particular. Emerging technological fields often experience a high speed of technological change and customers are unable to grasp the technology and unable to specify what they want. In this case, it is relevant to allow some tacit elements to stay tacit longer. If feasible, these situations call for an embodiment of tacit knowledge in artefacts such as prototypes and field tests that leave some elements in a tacit form.

In contrast, the case study illustrates how the firm uses prototypes and field testing to use non-verbal knowledge, thus suggesting ways of expanding the SECI model. The engineers socialise internally in the firm when they exchange experience by building field tests together and by showing each other how they do what they do. Field tests are a non-verbal way to externalise tacit knowledge. For customers, the field test reduces risks and shows that something works, even if they may not always know how it works. The field test constitutes a bridge between the customers and engineers. An example of internalisation concerns when the engineers implement their hunches for improving ongoing field tests. Note that although field tests are adequate concerning the software algorithms, the development of the new chip necessitates another approach, which takes a longer time and more money.

The SECI model is overly incremental in its focus on existing explicit knowledge while somewhat neglecting its embodiment. Nonaka and Konno (1998) only mention embodying explicit knowledge as part of the internalisation step where existing explicit knowledge is part of simulations presumably used as stepping stones to gain experiences based on existing explicit knowledge. However, Nonaka and Konno (1998) disregard embodying tacit knowledge in three-dimensional artefacts such as prototypes that can aid in the externalisation of tacit knowledge, while keeping certain aspects of the knowledge in a tacit form.

In contrast, the analysis of this case study suggests that these types of tools are non-verbal alternatives. They take on a hybrid form of both tacit and explicit elements, and using them in this context makes it easier for the firm to bridge the different phases needed for knowledge creation. Hence, this chapter adds the notion of a pre-linguistic embodiment of tacit knowledge as a necessary but currently missing element in the SECI model.

Our recommendation is that managers should critically reflect upon the knowledge management requirements for their particular situations. They should consider the relative usefulness of verbal and visual communication. Language focuses energy in different areas of the brain than those needed for technology, such as math, spatial thinking, and so on. Hence, it is relevant to consider how best that engineers can externalise their know-how. Moreover, the manager needs to consider the time to return on investment in making tacit knowledge more codified, because that likely depends on the speed of technological change.

ACKNOWLEDGEMENTS

The Sino-Danish Center for Education and Research (SDC) has kindly supported this work. I am grateful for the generous help and hospitality particularly from Han Yang from Intellifusion.

REFERENCES

Amalric, M. and Dehaene, S. (2016), 'Origins of the brain networks for advanced mathematics in expert mathematicians', *Proceedings of the National Academy of Sciences*, 113 (18), 4909–17.

Beeby, M. and Booth, C. (2000), 'Networks and inter-organizational learning: a critical review', *The Learning Organization*, 7 (2), 75–88.

Bicheno, J. and Holweg, M. (2009), *The Lean Toolbox: The Essential Guide to Lean Transformation*, Buckingham: Picsie Books.

Boisot, M. H. and Child, J. (1999), 'Organizations as adaptive systems in complex environments: the case of China', *Organization Science*, 10 (3), 237–52.

Crossan, M. M. and Berdrow, I. (2003), 'Organizational learning and strategic renewal', *Strategic Management Journal*, 24 (11), 1087–105.

Crossan, M. M., Lane, H. W., and White, R. E. (1999), 'An organizational learning framework: from intuition to institution', *Academy of Management Review*, 24 (3), 522–37.

Cowan, R., and Foray, D. (1997), 'The economics of codification and the diffusion of knowledge', *Industrial and Corporate Change*, **6**(3), 595–622.

Ferdows, K. (2006), 'POM forum: transfer of changing production know how', *Production and Operations Management*, 15 (1), 1–9.

Hadamard, J. (1945), *The Mathematician's Mind: The Psychology of Invention in the Mathematical Field*, Princeton, NJ: Princeton University Press.
Hedlund, G. (1994), 'A model of knowledge management and the N-form corporation', *Strategic Management Journal*, 15 (Special summer issue), 73–90.
Hua, C. (2016), 'Chipping in the future on artificial intelligence', *China Daily*. Updated 22 December 2016, accessed 14 April 2017 at www.chinadaily.com.cn/hkedition/2016-12/22/content_27742122.htm
McKelvey, M. and Bagchi-Sen, S. (2015), *Innovation Spaces in Asia: Entrepreneurs, Multinational Enterprises and Policy*, Cheltenham, UK and Northampton, MA, USA: Edward Elgar Publishing.
Nonaka, I. and Konno, N. (1998), 'The concept of "ba": building a foundation for knowledge creation', *California Management Review*, 40 (3), 40–54.
Nonaka, I. and Takeuchi, H. (1995), *The Knowledge-Creating Company: How Japanese Companies Create the Dynamics of Innovation*, Oxford: Oxford University Press.
Stake, R. E. (2010), *Qualitative Research: Studying How Things Work*, New York: Guilford Press.
Søberg, P. V. (2010), 'Industrial influences on R&D transfer to China', *Chinese Management Studies*, 4 (4), 322–38.
Søberg, P. V. (2011), 'The transfer and creation of knowledge within foreign invested R&D in emerging markets', *Journal of Technology Management in China*, 6 (3), 203–15.
Tsoukas, H. (2003), 'Do we really understand tacit knowledge?', in Easterby-Smith, Mark and Marjorie A. Lyles (eds), *The Blackwell Handbook of Organizational Learning and Knowledge Management*, Oxford: Blackwell Publishing, pp. 410–28.
Wozniak, S. and Smith, G. (2006), *iWoz. Computer Geek to Cult Icon. How I Invented the Personal Computer, Co-Founded Apple, and Had Fun Doing It*, New York: W.W. Norton & Co.
Yin, R. K. (2009), *Case Study Research: Design and Methods*, Thousand Oaks: Sage Publications.

12. CEVT of Geely: a broker and global facilitator between Geely and Volvo Cars

Jun Jin and Maureen McKelvey

1. INTRODUCTION

Globalization offers new innovative opportunities for companies, and this chapter focuses upon a global development of accessing science and technology in Chinese firms, through acquisitions and global ventures. The increasingly global research and development (R&D) and global development of Chinese firms has attracted the interest of a considerable number of scholars, and knowledge about this issue is growing substantially. Scholars explore the motives, challenges, impediments, strategies, and policy initiatives that compel firms from emerging countries, such as Chinese firms to go abroad for knowledge sourcing (von Zedtwitz, 2005). With the growth of Huawei, Alibaba, Tencent, and Haier, much attention on globalization and global R&D is keeping an eye on Chinese multinational enterprises (MNEs) in ICT industries and electronic industries (Duysters et al., 2009). The global R&D of other Chinese industries has not been as extensively studied, although one of the major acquisitions was by Geely Group (Geely in Short) of Volvo Cars (VCC in short). Geely purchased VCC from Ford in 2010 because of the financial crisis impact on Ford. Our focus is on the most recent developments after the merger and acquisition (M&A) of Geely and VCC. Therefore, this chapter develops a case study of how the bridge cooperation between Geely and VCC through CEVT (Chinese European Vehicle Technology) occurs and allows the firm/companies to develop new forms of innovation.

So what do we know about the global R&D in Chinese manufacturing industries beyond the information and communication industry and electronic industry, like the auto industry? The automotive industry has traditionally been classified as a traditional and scale-intensive industry. As such, the industry focus on innovation has been on the improvement of existing products such as safety or fuel mileage, and production processes such as lean manufacturing.

Globalization of production through supply chains has been visible for many decades, and most recently in global value chains. However, recent characteristics of globalization offer innovative opportunities for companies to rethink what the global automotive industry is, and how to compete in the global market. This chapter focuses on the role of CEVT, an overseas R&D center of Geely Auto, and its impact on the global strategy of Geely and Geely Auto.

This is an interesting case, where the Chinese firm Geely aims not only to shake up the global automobile industry, but also to develop and closely link domestic and global networks in related companies. In order to access advanced technology in the auto industry, to ascend to the high end of the global auto market and to be a global firm, M&A has become the preferred global approach of Chinese auto firms (Deloitte China, 2016). But what the global R&D of Chinese auto companies is, is still a question under research.

With the increasing M&A activities of Chinese firms in Europe and the USA, the fate of the merged firm after M&A has diverted attention from industries, researchers, and officers. This is the same for the M&A between Geely and VCC and their operation and performance after the M&A. However, the new R&D center in Gothenburg, Sweden, which is called CEVT, operated by Geely Auto and VCC, has not been attracting attention. What is the development of this R&D center? The vision of CEVT is "Bring Geely to be Global". How does CEVT work for this vision? In other words, what kind of role does CEVT play in the global development and innovation of Geely? Chapter 8 in this book focuses on the knowledge transfer and technological upgrading among Geely Auto, VVC, and CEVT. This chapter is going to pursue the following research question "what kind of role does CEVT play in the global development process of Geely to be global" based on analyses of the development, the strategic position and roles of CEVT in Geely. The illustration of the strategic roles of CEVT in Geely will contribute to theories and practices of global R&D in manufacturing industries from emerging countries.

2. LITERATURE REVIEW ON R&D GLOBALIZATION

Globalization – also called internationalization – describes cross-national flows of products, services, and some important production factors, such as labor and capital (Dunning and Lundan, 2009). In the context of innovation and R&D activities, the globalization of innovation is used to describe the phenomenon of "globalization" experienced by the world of invention and innovation (Archibugi and Michie, 1995). They are activities by multinational enterprises across different countries, resulting in cross-border flows of R&D-related resources such as knowledge, R&D personnel, R&D investments, and new technologies (Cantwell, 1999).

The research on R&D globalization has mainly focused on several specific aspects of: locational factor (Howells, 1990; Le Bas and Sierra, 2002; Demirbag and Glaister, 2010), driving factors for going abroad (Khurana, 2006; Faeth, 2009), types of foreign R&D labs (Casson, 1991; Florida, 1997), offshore R&D in emerging countries, such as China (Zhou et al., 2002; Chen, 2004; Gassmann and Han, 2004), and so on.

Moreover, from the firm perspective, the globalization of innovation is driven in large measure by the technology factor because the "globalization of R&D is one of the key strategic decisions that almost every firm has to make" (Khurana, 2006: 49). In addition, companies conduct R&D overseas in order to access (1) technology and know-how through partnership with local universities, private labs, and so on, and (2) customers and markets (Khurana, 2006).

In recent years, the explosion in domestic market growth rates, and a burgeoning pool of well-educated but low-cost labor in some leading developing countries, such as Brazil, Russia, India, and China (BRIC), have increasingly attracted new R&D sites of MNEs from advanced economies (UNCTAD, 2005; Karabag et al., 2011). Additionally, an increasing number of MNEs from emerging countries are quickly expanding their innovation activities into advanced countries by means of technology-oriented M&As, greenfield R&D investments, offshore R&D, and cross-border innovation cooperation in an effort to undertake global exploitation of technology, global technological collaboration and global sourcing of technology (von Zedtwitz, 2005; Jin et al., 2014). The USA and countries in Europe, like the UK and Germany, are the main locations for the overseas R&D activities of MNEs from emerging countries (Economist Intelligence Unit, 2004).

The emerging industries and high-technology industry seem to be the key industries in adopting the strategy of global innovation because it is simultaneously globalized and knowledge-based, and because the globalization of innovation is driven in large measure by technology factors (Florida, 1997). For instance, technology transfer, foreign direct investment (FDI), capability transfer (Sutton, 2007; Dunning and Lundan, 2009) and other forms of cross-border value-adding activity have already influenced some Chinese industries, such as software (Plechero and Chaminade, 2010), ICT (Bruche, 2009; Wei et al., 2011), pharmaceuticals (Wadhwa et al., 2008). However, the global R&D of auto industries is under research, especially the global innovation of auto companies from emerging countries in advanced countries and the catch-up of auto industries from emerging industries. Encouraged by policies of going abroad, more and more outward investment is being conducted by Chinese auto companies, such as M&As, greenfield investment, and so on (Deloitte China, 2016). However, only a few of the automobiles produced by companies from emerging countries are exported to advanced countries, although the auto companies from emerging countries, such as Tata from India, Geely from China, Cherry from China, export their cars to other countries.

With the accumulation of local technology capability and reverse engineering (Cheung and Lin, 2004), the globalization of the auto industry has gradually focused on innovation globalization, which has helped China go out of the domestic market by providing opportunities for Chinese enterprises to get into international markets (Gan, 2003; Richet and Ruet, 2008; Balcet and Ruet, 2011; Balcet et al., 2012) and to realize the goal of catch-up or leapfrogging through innovation (Balcet et al., 2012; Wang and Kimble, 2013). The acquisition of world-leading transmission producer DSI in 2009 to reach the goal of internalization of the entire series of AT technology, and the acquisition of world-famous car brand Volvo by Geely in 2010 are good examples (Balcet et al., 2012; Gifford et al., 2015). However, research on the globalization of innovation in the auto industry, especially the management and strategies after the merger, and overseas R&D centers is limited compared with other sectors. With the increasing M&As and outward investment of companies in the Chinese auto industry, it is necessary to explore the manifestation of global innovation of Chinese auto companies.

Moreover, it appears that innovation may be changing in this industry. The automotive industry has traditionally been classified as a traditional and scale-intensive industry. The globalization of production through supply chains has been visible for many decades, and most recently in global value chains. However, recent characteristics of globalization offer innovative opportunities for companies to rethink what the global automotive industry is, and how to compete.

3. RESEARCH METHODOLOGY

Case study is widely recognized as a method for explorative research (Yin, 2009). The methodology can help answer the research questions of our study, based on the principles of engagement with practice (Voss, 2009; Yin, 2009). Through case studies, we can enlighten and explain real-life phenomena that are too complex for tightly structured designs or pre-specified data sets (Voss et al., 2002; Yin, 2009). In addition, the case studies are suitable for unraveling concepts (Yin, 2009) and building theories (Eisenhardt, 1989). This chapter adopts the case study method to analyse the globalization strategies and strategic role of an overseas R&D center of a Chinese auto manufacturer, Geely, which is an area that is ignored in the Chinese auto industry and an area in R&D globalization in mature industries that lacks enough study.

The case description presented below is based on in-depth interviews as well as a series of written material in English, Swedish and Chinese. Two informal interviews and five formal interviews at CEVT were undertaken with senior managers of CEVT in 2016. Each interview lasted 1–1.5 hours. In addition, one of the authors visited the Geely headquarters in Hangzhou in 2014 to listen to a presentation about R&D strategy and the overseas R&D center. Public information from websites and the companies' introduction documents were also used as background information and to triangulate the data. Additional data has been collected.

4. DEVELOPMENT OF THE CHINESE AUTO INDUSTRY AND CEVT

4.1 Development of the Chinese Auto Industry

Since its establishment in the 1950s, and with the initial technological support from the former Soviet Union and heavy investment from the Chinese government, the Chinese auto industry covered 58 automakers, 192 assembly companies, and about 2,000 spare parts suppliers in different region in China by 1980 (Gan, 2003). With the enforcement of the open-door economic policy from 1978, attracted by the large potential passenger car market in China, the Chinese auto industry has increased fast since the 1980s. For instance, Volkswagen (Germany) established a joint venture in Shanghai (Shanghai VW) in 1985. Many other leading automakers in the world, like General Motors, Hyundai, Honda, Toyota, BMW, etc., established joint ventures in China too. It helps the development of Chinese auto industry (Li et al., 2016).

The strategy of the auto industry in China at that time was called "trading market access for technology" (Qiu, 2013), in order to improve the product development capability and R&D capability of Chinese automakers through the technology transfer in the joint ventures which were invested in by leading foreign automakers in the world.

After joining the WTO in 2000, in ten years, the Chinese auto industry has kept an average annual growth rate of nearly 24 percent (MOFCOM, 2011). Since 2009, China has become the world's largest auto market (Tang, 2009), the sale volume in 2016 was over 28 million (Auto-Stat, 2017), and China has become the largest auto producer in the world too. With the growth of the Chinese auto market, Chinese domestic automakers are developing fast too. Their market share in the Chinese passenger car market increased to 43.2 percent in 2016 (Auto-Stat, 2017). However, the Chinese domestic automakers suffered a lot from insufficient improvement in management techniques and technology (Tang, 2012; Qiu, 2013). Volkswagen (including FAW VW and Shanghai VW), General Motors, and so on, continue to be the leading automakers in China as a result of the failure of Chinese policy on the auto industry "trading market access for technology". Nevertheless, Chinese auto companies are growing in the competition. Geely has become one of the most valuable 500 brands in the world in 2017 (Brandirectory, 2017).

Chinese auto companies need technology and patents in order to ascend to the high end of the global auto market, although they invested increasingly in R&D to nearly 3 percent. With the strong support of the Chinese government, domestic automakers have gradually attempted M&As with foreign auto companies (Zheng and Sheng, 2015). More and more M&A deals have been completed by Chinese auto firms in the last three years, according to the Report on Outward Foreign Investment of Chinese Auto Firms issued by Deloitte China in 2016 (Deloitte China, 2016). For example, Beijing Auto purchased Saab Automobile's intellectual property rights, Zhejiang Geely acquired 100 percent shares of VCC and property from Ford to the value of 1.8 billion USD (Chandera and Widjojo, 2015; Wan, 2015). But most of the investment is on auto components. In addition, most of the international investments of Chinese auto companies are conducted by state-owned companies. How and what do Chinese private auto companies in this outward investment waive? There are lots of open and challenging questions here.

4.2 Background of CEVT

As discussed in Chapter 8 in this book written by Alvstam and Ivarsson, Geely acquired VCC in 2010 and CEVT was set up in 2013. Since 2010, Geely has produced passenger cars with two groups of brands, Geely Auto, and VCC, and taxis with a brand of London Taxi.[1] Since September of 2013, CEVT has started its operation jointly by the Geely Auto and VCC. It is the first overseas subsidiary completely set up by Geely itself. Although it is an R&D center of Geely Auto in law and wholly invested by Geely, CEVT is jointly operated by Geely Auto and VCC.

Guiding with its vision "Bring Geely to the world", CEVT is working to achieve its missions in four aspects: (1) build the most cost-efficient, customer-focused and technology-oriented engineering center in the automotive industry; (2) define and develop world-class products with outstanding quality and performance at competitive price levels; (3) be a fully integrated part of Geely and form an outstanding team for the success of Geely; and (4) lay the foundation for Geely Auto in Europe.

Focusing on architecture development, shared component development, and complete vehicle design, CEVT covers all aspects of passenger car development – from the total architecture, powertrain and drive line components, to top hat engineering as well as the vehicles' exterior design. Following a modular technology approach, CEVT is developing a new, modular architecture for world-class cars – CMA platforms, and then developing different new models of cars based on CMA platforms. After three years, several new models of car have been introduced into markets as models of a new brand, Lynk & Co, for the global market.

In three years, from ten persons in 2013, CEVT has grown to be an R&D firm with around 2,000 persons from 22 countries and regions located in Gothenburg (Sweden). Most of the employees work at Gothenburg. The employees working at CEVT include CEVT employees, and contracted employees from VCC and other companies. In addition, CEVT has established a clear decision process following modern corporate management. Although CEVT is an R&D firm invested in by a Chinese firm, a large percentage of middle and high level managers in CEVT are not Chinese. Only one Chinese is a member of the top management team as a deputy vice president. Two of five board members of CEVT are Chinese. The board of CEVT includes the CEO of Geely Auto, CEO of VCC, CEO of CEVT, CFO of Geely Group, and an Advisor of Chairman Li Shufu[2] of Geely.

5. DISCUSSION: ROLE OF CEVT AT GEELY AND VCC

Compared to most Chinese auto companies, as a private firm Geely goes further in the globalization, which it uses to develop technical and market capabilities. As in the globalization methods reported by Deloitte China (2016), Geely goes abroad through the method of M&As, such as their deals with DSI, London Taxi and VCC, greenfield R&D investment like the establishment and operation of CEVT, and exports to Asian and other markets. The companies that Geely merged with consist of the providers of key components, such as Drivetrain Systems International Pty Ltd., and makers of vehicles, such as MB Holding (London Taxi) and VCC.

However, although since the merger of DSI, MB Holding, and VCC, Geely Group has overseas automobile subsidiaries and a global brand (Volvo), Geely Group, especially Geely Auto, is not widely recognized as a really global firm and brand in the world. We assume there are three reasons. First, it is because after the M&As, the expanding manufacturing plants and markets are still concentrated in China, not outside of China. For instance, the new Chinese factories of VCC were built in Chengdu and other cities after 2010, while the factory of DSI in China provides products to Geely and other Chinese auto companies. Second, it is also because the operations of DSI, MB Holding, VCC, and Geely Auto are independent with respective autonomy and individual brands after the merger. With the exception of VCC, the deals with DSI and MB Holding are not well known widely. Third, the companies and factories of DSI, MB Holding and VCC outside of mainland China have not been set up by Geely himself. They help Geely to be global. But the brand and operation of Geely Auto and Geely is not global without its own overseas subsidiaries from the Chinese mind-sets. As the first overseas subsidiary of Geely Auto, CEVT is thought of as a chance for Geely Auto and Geely Group to be a really global firm, like Volkswagen.

In this section, the roles of CEVT among Geely Auto, VCC are analysed to illustrate the strategy of how CEVT enables Geely to be global.

5.1 CEVT as the Promoter of Global Strategy

The vision of CEVT and interviews indicate that CEVT plays a critical role in the process of Geely being a global firm. As the Vice President of CEVT, Mr. Wei said, to be a global firm, Geely needs global employees, global technology, and a global market. Several interviewers emphasized that employees are from many countries and a large percentage of middle and senior managers at CEVT are not Chinese. CEVT works as a platform to make contributions to Geely to formulate and improve the globalization of products, talents, and the R&D system. For instance, 50 percent of employees at the department of Product Planning and Vehicle Line Management work in China, and 50 percent of employees work in Sweden. In this department, 90 percent of engineers in the group of product definition work in China, while most of the engineers in the team of vehicle lines work in Sweden.

Since product development for the global market based on the CMA platform is a priority at CEVT, the global strategy could be seen as a product-oriented global strategy. In this CEVT platform, Geely Group can develop products with the advantages of Volvo quality and Geely low cost. The CMA platform at CEVT is not only used for the new models of car developed for Geely Auto, but also for the new models of car development by VCC. It is a platform open to CEVT, Geely Auto and VCC. In order to develop new products in three years, CEVT recruits technical experts and other positions from around the world. As mentioned above, currently the employees at CEVT Gothenburg and CEVT Hangzhou are from 22 countries and regions. Even at CEVT Hangzhou, there are non-Chinese nationality employees. In the eye of foreign employees, CEVT is a global firm. Perhaps it is because of the high percentage of non-Chinese at CEVT that makes CEVT a Chinese-established firm without the deep influence of Chinese culture.

From the nationality of board members of CEVT as shown on their public website and information collected from interviewers, the main team leaders in CEVT, such as in the business project team, the quality management team, R&D team, and so on, are European, like the Swedish. For example, only one of the senior managers we interviewed is from China, but with intensive work experience outside of China. This influences the management process of CEVT. In addition, since CEVT was founded in Sweden, CEVT follows Swedish regulation. Through the mobility and frequently communication of employees between CEVT Gothenburg and CEVT China, as well as those between CEVT and Geely Auto, the management system and thoughts of the global firm diffuse in CEVT and potentially influence the management system in Geely Auto.

As mentioned above, a new brand, Lynk & Co, the new models of cars developed by CEVT was introduced into the global market, as a new brand bridging the brand gap between the Volvo brand and Geely brand. Lynk & Co models of cars were launched in the Chinese market at the end of 2017 and the European and American market in 2018. In order to ensure the product quality of the new brand and distinguish it from VCC and Geely cars, new plants at Zhejiakou and Luqiao in China were built. These plants only produce new brands of cars developed by CEVT. In these new plants, new governance systems are implemented, such as the centralized purchasing system of components, which is different from the original purchasing system at Geely's plants. With the running of new plants, the new governance system in new plants will be gradually infiltrated into the management system of Geely.

In sum, as an overseas R&D center, CEVT not only takes the responsibility for accessing the latest technology, providing technical support to the foreign markets, and developing new technology and new products (Khurana, 2006), but also takes the role of accessing markets in advanced countries, attracting global talents, and driving the diffusion of a new governance system. Finally CEVT will put forward Geely's globalization to be a leading global automobile manufacturer. In short, CEVT is working not only for the new global technology, but also for the new global market, new governance system, and new global brand. It provides evidence to enrich theories of global innovation (UNCTAD, 2005), that the purpose of an overseas R&D center can be expanded from a technology or R&D place to a carrier and promoter of the global strategy of a firm in aspects of global technology, global market, and global persons.

Thus, we assume that with the growth of the overseas R&D center and its astrategic position, the overseas R&D center could be played as a mediator or the catalyzer of globalization for a firm from emerging countries with global talents, a global market, global technology and its own global brand.

5.2 CEVT as the Broker Between Geely Auto and VCC

CEVT works as a global knowledge flow and lubricant among Geely Auto, VCC and other parts of the Geely Group. For instance, although CEVT is a firm for product development, the quality team is in charge of the quality, the governance system, and the centralized purchasing of new plants at Gent (Belgium, for VCC), Zhangjiakou (China, for Lynk & Co cars) and Luqiao (China, for Lynk & Co cars) to produce new models developed based on CMA platform technology. In addition, as mentioned above, CMA platform technology at CEVT is open to the new product development of VCC and Geely Auto. The mobility of employees between CEVT Gothenburg and CEVT Hangzhou forms a knowledge transfer between these two facilities. Because CEVT Hangzhou shares offices with Geely Research Institute in Hangzhou, sometimes there is knowledge diffusion between Geely Research Institute and CEVT Hangzhou too. For example, CEVT provides technical support to KC product development of Geely Auto in Hangzhou. Therefore, CEVT is a node to connect the technology and production between VCC and Geely Auto. According to the future strategic plan, CEVT will provide technical support to London Taxi too. Thus, we propose that CEVT is a broker in Geely Group (as shown in Figure 12.1) to link Geely, Geely Auto, and VCC. The technology transfer among Geely Auto, VCC, and CEVT will be analysed in detail in future.

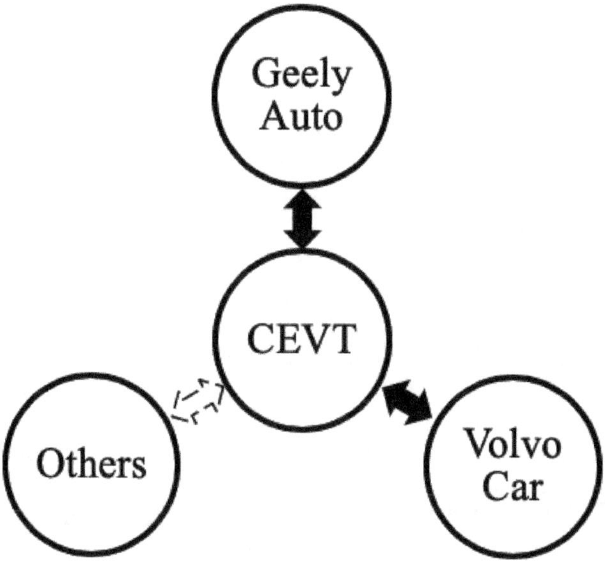

Figure 12.1 Broker role of CEVT in Geely Holding Group

One reason for the need for an intermediary organization is the need to develop certain types of technologies, for a car more like a smart phone than a large physical investment. Another reason may be found in agreements between Ford – the previous owner of VCC – and Geely, to keep certain intellectual property rights and related automobile platform systems separate between VCC and Geely for a number of years.

6. CONCLUSIONS

This chapter illustrates how CEVT plays a role in bringing Geely to be global in the era of globalization. The case of CEVT of Geely provides a profusion of information on the global strategy and the role of an R&D center in the globalization of a firm. The overseas R&D center can be a promoter to support the mother firm from emerging countries to be a really global firm from the aspects of global persons, global market, global technology, and global management system. It enriches the theories on global innovation, especially the global innovation of companies from emerging countries.

Implicit in this case of globalization is an understanding that a firm from emerging countries can elevate its globalization through its global R&D strategies. In addition, the broker role of CEVT between Geely Auto and VCC perhaps can be recognized as a method to reduce the influence of conflicts between two companies after M&A. It provides a new aspect for us to consider strategies after M&A.

From the aspect of organization management, we assume that there are some characteristics of ambidextrousness in CEVT. Perhaps we could adopt theories of an ambidextrous organization to review the relationship among CEVT, Geely Auto, and VCC and to analyse the strategic roles of CEVT in Geely Holding Group in future research.

With the development of CEVT, CEVT as well as Geely Auto undergo changes in their management and strategies. It is possible a co-evolutionary process. Thus, the co-evolutionary development of CEVT, Geely Auto and VCC could be studied in the future. In December 2016, some Swedish organizations invested money in VCC, in apparent anticipation of a stock market offering in the future, and subsequently Geely purchased shares in the Volvo Group (e.g. trucks and heavy machinery). These cross-national ownership patterns raise new questions about what is Chinese and what is Swedish about this story. Additionally, with the continuous and sustainable growth of CEVT, will the strategic position of CEVT in Geely be raised and changed? Will CEVT become the European headquarters of Geely, not just a technology center? Much future research can continue on the interrelationships between Geely, Geely Auto, VCC, and CEVT.

ACKNOWLEDGMENTS

This research is sponsored by project grants from the National Natural Science Foundation of China (NSFC: 71172111, 71232013 and 71672172) and Zhejiang Natural Science Foundation (ZJNSF: LY16G020010).

NOTES

1. In 2006, Geely and MB Holding (UK) established a joint venture to produce the iconic London Taxi in Shanghai. In 2013, Geely acquired all the core business and assets of MB Holding (UK) and 48 percent of the shares of the joint venture with MB Holding. Since 2013, London Taxi Firm became one part of Geely Holding.
2. Chairman Li Shufu is the founder of Geely Group.

REFERENCES

Archibugi, D. and J. Michie (1995), 'The globalisation of technology: a new taxonomy', *Cambridge Journal of Economics*, **19**, 121–140.

Auto-Stat (2017), *The Development of Chinese Auto Industry in 2016*, accessed on 8 February 2017 at http://www.auto-stats.org.cn/ReadArticle.asp?NewsID=9619

Balcet, G. and J. Ruet (2011), 'From joint ventures to national champions or global players? Alliances and technological catching-up in Chinese and Indian automotive industries', *European Review of Industrial Economics and Policy*, **3**, 1–24.

Balcet, G., H. Wang and X. Richet (2012), 'Geely: a trajectory of catching up and asset-seeking multinational growth', *International Journal of Automotive Technology and Management*, **12**(4), 360–375.

Brandirectory (2017), *Global 500 2017: The Most Valuable Brands in 2017*, accessed on 10 February 2017 at http://brandirectory.com/league_tables/table/global-500-2017

Bruche, G. (2009), 'The emergence of China and India as new Competitors in MNCs' innovation networks', *Competition and Change*, **13**(3), 267–288.

Cantwell, J. (1999), 'From the early internationalization of corporate technology to global technology sourcing', *Transnational Corporations*, **8**(2), 81–92.

Casson, M. (1991), *Global Research Strategy and International Competitiveness*, Cambridge, MA: Basil Blackwell.

Chandera, Y. and H. Widjojo (2015), 'Value creation through acquisition strategy: a study of Volvo's acquisition by Geely', *International Research Journal of Business Studies*, **5**(2), 129–143.

Chen, S. (2004), 'Taiwanese IT firms' offshore R&D in China and the connection with the global innovation network', *Research Policy*, **33**(2), 337–349.

Cheung, K. and P. Lin (2004), 'Spillover effects of FDI on innovation in China: evidence from the provincial data', *China Economic Review*, **15**, 25–44.

Deloitte China (2016), *The Report on Outward Foreign Investment of Chinese Auto Firms in 2016* (in Chinese), accessed on 10 August 2016 at https://www2.deloitte.com/content/dam/Deloitte/cn/Documents/manufacturing/deloitte-cn-mfg-china-automotive-industry-outbound-investment-report-2016-zh-160606.pdf.

Demirbag, M. and K. Glaister (2010), 'Factors determining offshore location choice for R&D projects: a comparative study of developed and emerging regions', *Journal of Management Studies*, **47**(8), 1534–1560.
Dunning, J.H. and S. Lundan (2009), 'The internationalization of corporate R&D: a review of the evidence and some policy implications for home countries', *Review of Policy Research*, **26**(1/2), 13–33.
Duysters, G., J. Jacob, C. Lemmens and J. Yu (2009), 'Internationalization and technological catching up of emerging multinationals: a comparative case study of China's Haier group', *Industrial and Corporate Change*, **18**(2), 325–349.
Economist Intelligence Unit (2004), *Scattering the Seeds of Invention: The Globalization of Research and Development*, accessed on 10 August 2016 at http://graphics.eiu.com/files/ad_pdfs/RnD_GLOBILISATION_WHITEPAPER.pdf
Eisenhardt, K. (1989), 'Building theories from case study research', *Academy of Management Review*, **14**(4), 532–550.
Faeth, I. (2009), 'Determinants of foreign direct investment: a tale of nine theoretical models', *Journal of Economic Surveys*, **23**(1), 165–196.
Florida, R. (1997), 'The globalization of R&D: results of a survey of foreign-affiliated R&D laboratories in the USA', *Research Policy*, **26**, 85–103.
Gan, L. (2003), 'Globalization of the automobile industry in China: dynamics and barriers in the greening of road transportation', *Energy Policy*, **31**(6), 537–551.
Gassmann, O. and Z. Han (2004), 'Motivations and barriers of foreign R&D activities in China', *R&D Management*, **34**(4), 423–437.
Gifford, E., M. Holgersson, M. McKelvey and S. Bagchi-Sen (2015), 'Tapping into Western technologies by Chinese multinationals: Geely's purchase of Volvo Cars and Huawei's hiring of Ericsson employees in Sweden', in M. McKelvey and S. Bagchi-Sen (eds.), *Innovation Spaces in Asia: Entrepreneurs, Multinational Enterprises and Policy*, Cheltenham, UK and Northampton, MA, USA: Edward Elgar Publishing, pp. 231–267.
Howells, J. (1990), 'The location and organisation of research and development: new horizons', *Research Policy*, **19**(2), 133–146.
Jin, J., Y. Wang and W. Vanhaverbeke (2014), 'Patterns of R&D internationalization in developing countries: China as a case', *International Journal of Technology Management*, **64**(2–4), 276–302.
Karabag, S., A. Tuncay-Celikel and C. Berggren (2011), 'The limits of R&D internationalization and the importance of local initiatives: Turkey as a critical case', *World Development*, **39**(8), 1347–1357.
Khurana, A. (2006), 'Strategies for global R&D', *Research-Technology Management*, **49**(2), 48–57.
Le Bas, C. and C. Sierra (2002), 'Location versus home country advantages in R&D activities: some further results on multinationals' locational strategies', *Research Policy*, **31**(4), 589–609.
Li, Y., X. Kong and M. Zhang (2016), 'Industrial upgrading in global production networks: the case of the Chinese automotive industry', *Asia Pacific Business Review*, **22**(1), 21–37.
MOFCOM (2011), *Golden Ten Years: Explosive Growth of the Chinese Auto Industry*, accessed on 8 February 2017 at http://cwto.mofcom.gov.cn/article/n/201112/20111207872938.shtml
Plechero, M. and C. Chaminade (2010), 'Different competences, different modes in the globalization of innovation? A comparative study of the Pune and Beijing regions', *Circle Working Paper*, Paper no. 2010/03.

Qiu, X. (2013), *Technology Transfer in Chinese Automobile Industry*, Master of Science Thesis INDEK 2013:108, KTH Industrial Engineering and Management Industrial Management.

Richet, X. and J. Ruet (2008), 'The Chinese and Indian automobile industry in perspective: technology appropriation, catching-up and development', *Transition Studies Review*, **15**(3), 447–465.

Sutton, J. (2007), 'Quality, trade and the moving window: the globalization process', *The Economic Journal*, **117**, 469–498.

Tang, R. (2009), 'The rise of China's auto industry and its impact on the U.S. motor vehicle industry', Washington, DC: Congressional Research Service, accessed on 9 February 2017 at http://digitalcommons.ilr.cornell.edu/key_workplace/688

Tang, R. (2012), *China's Auto Sector Development and Policies: Issues and Implications*, Congressional Research Service.

UNCTAD (2005), *Globalization of R&D and Developing Countries*, Geneva and New York: United Nations.

von Zedtwitz, M. (2005), 'International R&D strategies in companies from developing countries – the case of China', in UNCTAD (ed.), *Globalization of R&D and Developing Countries*, Geneva and New York: United Nations, pp. 117–140.

Voss, C. (2009), 'Case research in operations management', in C. Karlsson (ed.), *Researching Operations Management*, New York: Routledge, pp. 162–196.

Voss, C., N. Tsikriktsis and M. Frohlich (2002), 'Case research in operations management', *International Journal of Operations and Production Management*, **22**(2), 195–219.

Wadhwa, V., B. Rissing, G. Gereffi, J. Trumpbour and P. Engardio (2008), *The Globalization of Innovation: Pharmaceuticals: Can India and China Cure the Global Pharmaceutical Market*. Available at SSRN 1143472.

Wan, R. (2015), *Cultural Integration of Cross-Border M&A Activities in the Chinese Auto Industry: Case Study: The Acquisition of Geely and Volvo*, University of Applied Sciences Bachelor Thesis, Helsinki, accessed on 10 February 2017 at https://theseus32-kk.lib.helsinki.fi/bitstream/handle/10024/89853/Wan_Ruoling .pdf?sequence=1

Wang, H. and C. Kimble (2013), 'Innovation and leapfrogging in the Chinese automobile industry: examples from Geely, BYD, and Shifeng', *Global Business and Organization Excellence*, **32**(6), 6–17.

Wei, Y., I. Liefner and C. Miao (2011), 'Network configurations and R&D activities of the ICT industry in Suzhou municipality, China', *Geoforum*, **42**, 484–495.

Yin, R. (2009), *Case Study Research: Design and Methods*, Thousand Oaks: Sage.

Zheng, W. and Z. Sheng (2015), 'Research on the problems and countermeasures of Chinese automobile enterprises transnational merger and acquisition', *Business and Management Research*, **4**(2), 13–17.

Zhou, C., A. Delios and J. Yang (2002), 'Locational determinants of Japanese foreign direct investment in China', *Asia Pacific Journal of Management*, **19**(1), 63–86.

13. Fitting into innovation ecosystems: case studies of Huawei and Xiaomi

Xingkun Liang, Xianwei Shi and Yongjiang Shi

1. INTRODUCTION

This chapter applies an innovation ecosystem perspective to understand how and why certain latecomer Chinese firms developed strategies and aimed to become global innovative firms. These large multinational Chinese firms – and particularly those that have become innovative and globally competitive – have changed their strategy from the previous stereotypical "copycat" or labor-intensive assembling methods. Over time, as their presence in the global market grew, they competed not only by providing products at reasonable prices, but also by adding technological and innovative features. Like Chapters 5, 8, and 12, this chapter focuses on large multinational firms that innovate. This chapter also draws out implications about the ways in which these Chinese firms became more innovative, which can be useful for both the academic community and practitioners in the field.

Several studies (e.g., Mu and Lee, 2005; Wu et al., 2010; Wu et al., 2012) examined how these newly established Chinese firms were able to grow up to be industrial leaders in either domestic or international markets. These studies focus on technology management and latecomer strategy (e.g., Cho et al., 1998; Mathews, 2002), since most latecomer multinational companies (MNCs) have succeeded through technological learning and development with heavy investment in research and development (R&D) (Lee and Lim, 2001). Most scholars also explain these firms' stories from an individual firm's perspective, such as by considering the strategic advantages of firms (e.g., Mathews and Cho, 1999) or using the resource-based view (e.g., Mathews, 2002). Innovation management is a large field, concerned with market and technology in relation to firm capabilities (Cetindamar et al., 2009; Dyer and Singh, 1998; Gregory, 1995).

These traditional theories capture the main features of technological catch-up. However, it may be difficult to explain how Chinese latecomers can become industrial leaders merely from such a perspective, because advantages in technology may not be sources of competitive advantage (Barney, 1991). Firms may also work within institutional settings (Lee and Hung, 2014). Meanwhile, a recent trend aims to understand firms' innovations from the innovation ecosystem perspective (e.g., Adner and Kapoor, 2010; Iansiti and Levien, 2004), which emphasizes wide technological interdependence between focal firms and other organizations. This theoretical perspective enables researchers to understand key factors in a firm's context and business environment, which are critical to enable the focal firm's innovation and business success. We therefore apply this perspective, because it provides a new opportunity to understand Chinese latecomer firms.

2. LITERATURE REVIEW

2.1 Latecomer Firms and Latecomer Strategy

Latecomer firms are existing or potential manufacturing companies that face two sets of competitive disadvantages in attempting to compete in export markets (Hobday, 1995): technological isolation and dislocation from leading-edge markets and demanding users.

Mathews and Cho (1999) suggested three dimensions to understand latecomer firms: strategic goal, mode of operation, and organizational learning. The strategic role of latecomer firms is to catch up with industrial incumbents, who are industry leaders. Mathews (2002) further elaborated that a latecomer firm is a late entrant to an industry, not by choice but by historical necessity. In general, latecomer firms refer to those that are initially resource-poor and at a disadvantage in terms of technology and the market, compared with industrial incumbents. In addition, latecomer firms have some initial competitive advantages, such as low costs, which they can utilize to leverage a position in their industry of choice. From this perspective, many Chinese companies can be regarded as latecomer firms, since they fit well with these criteria.

Latecomer firms have adopted a variety of strategies to acquire and leverage the resources and capabilities they need in order to compete with industry leaders. These strategies are referred to as "latecomer strategies." Studies on latecomer strategies are very abundant, and generally focus on case studies of East Asian firms in various industries, spanning from the semiconductor to automobile industries.

In the 1990s, most researchers focused on the latecomer strategies of the Korean and Japanese semiconductor industries, where they found inter-company innovations, organizational learning, and technological leapfrogging to be the key strategies (Cho et al., 1998; Hobday, 1995; Mathews, 2002; Mathews and Cho, 1999). Other researchers revealed that technology trajectory and catch-up processes, such as path-following and stage-skipping, are important latecomer strategies (Lee and Lim, 2001; Mu and Lee, 2005). More recently, researchers have turned to focus on Chinese latecomers. They have found that secondary innovation, strategic networking with external resources, and innovation with external alliances are the key latecomer strategies in China (Mu and Lee, 2005; Wu et al., 2009; Wu et al., 2010).

In summary, these latecomer strategies align with Cho et al.'s (1998) claim that appropriate latecomer strategies aim to overcome latecomer disadvantages while exploiting latecomer advantages, in order to catch up with industry leaders. However, most of these latecomer strategies are focused on enhancing technology and innovation capability, according to the resource-based view (Barney, 1991; Mathews, 2002).

2.2 The Innovation Ecosystem

Recently, the resource-based view has been extended by considering inter-organizational linkages that can potentially increase a firm's accessibility to resources (Dyer and Singh, 1998; Lavie, 2006); an ecosystem view has been established accordingly (Adner and Kapoor, 2010; Ansari et al., 2016). Moore first defined a business ecosystem as "an economic community supported by a foundation of interacting organizations and individuals – the organisms of the business world. The economic community produces goods and services of value to customers, who are themselves members of the ecosystem" (1996: p. 26). Moore also identified four evolutionary stages of business ecosystems: birth, expansion, leadership, and self-renewal or death. Iansiti and Levien (2004), however, insisted that a business ecosystem mainly consists of loosely interconnected companies that create and share value together. Borrowing from the biology concept, they also state that business ecosystems are "formed by a large, loosely-connected network" (p. 2) of companies that "interact with each other in complex ways" (p. 20). Although Iansiti and Levien's definition is narrower than Moore's, it has been adopted as a commonly used definition in this area. Shang (2015) summarized that the players within a business ecosystem are diverse, and include focal firms, players from the supply side, players from the demand side, and intermediary players that facilitate value creation across the supply chain but are not directly involved in the process, such as government and universities.

Adner (2006) proposed the concept of the innovation ecosystem and argued that firms needed to consider innovation capability at an ecosystem level. His work showed that diverse players in an innovation ecosystem could potentially affect individual firms' innovations and the value creation of innovative products and services. Adner and Kapoor (2010) further explored how innovation ecosystems affect the innovation capabilities of focal firms, with a particular focus on external innovators such as downstream suppliers, upstream complementors, and customers, as well as their relationships with focal firms. Most of these studies focus on understanding how an innovation ecosystem can affect the innovation of first-movers. However, Ansari et al. (2016) showed that disruptive innovators can also deliberately take advantage of an ecosystem in order to compete with well-established firms.

It should be noted that an innovation ecosystem is not as simple as a traditional network; as Iansiti puts it, "by connecting even simple components in the right way, complex and difficult problems beyond the abilities of the individual components are solvable, and new capabilities are acquired" (Iansiti and Levien, 2004). Hence, a business ecosystem could potentially assist an individual company to acquire resources and capabilities to solve problems that it cannot handle alone, as an innovation ecosystem involves many different players. As mentioned earlier, these players include focal firms, suppliers, complementors, customers (Adner and Kapoor, 2010), and other intermediators that are not directly involved in the focal firm's value creation but can facilitate the value creation (Shang, 2015).

2.3 Research Gap

Based on the literature review above, we identified a tendency to understand a firm's innovation from an ecosystem perspective, which could potentially provide a wider and more holistic perspective to understand innovation. In contrast, most existing studies on latecomer strategy simply focus on an individual firm's perspective in order to understand how latecomer firms undertake technology management; they neglect organizational and contextual issues. Most existing studies on the innovation ecosystem focus on first-movers. Therefore, there is a research gap in the current understanding of the innovations and catch-up of Chinese latecomer firms from the ecosystem perspective.

Based on the identified research gaps, the research question addressed in this chapter is: How can Chinese latecomer companies develop to become industrial leaders from the innovation ecosystem perspective?

3. CASE STUDY DESIGN

As shown in the literature review, there have been a few studies relevant to the research question. The development of Chinese firms is embedded with rich contextual factors, including the Chinese and international business environment, policies, industrial conditions, and interactions with different organizations. All of these factors require full consideration, indicating the necessity of an inductive and explorative study (Yin, 2009). Meanwhile, the nature of development is also a process, and thus requires a longitudinal design. Considering both options, a longitudinal case study is the most suitable for this research, as that method permits intensive and interactive contact with the case companies to get more information on and understand how firms fit into the innovation ecosystem and their development over time (Miles and Huberman, 1994; Yin, 2009).

The cases were selected from a consideration of the theoretical basis (Siggelkow, 2007). Chinese firms that have established their innovation ecosystems were initially chosen. We decided to focus on a pair of polar cases within the information and communication technology (ICT) industry for comparison (Eisenhardt, 1989). The ICT industry was chosen because firms in this industry require the integration of software, hardware, and service, and thus require more complicated innovation ecosystems. We conducted background research with secondary data and identified two cases from firms in the ICT industry: namely, Huawei and Xiaomi. The reasons for this choice are threefold. First, both companies recently entered the Chinese smartphone industry, which facilitates the capture and comparison of the evolutions of establishing a position, and thereby fitting into, innovation ecosystems, considering the similar temporality. Second, while both companies have developed to become innovative and market leaders in the industry, they used different approaches, which indicates potential to explore a greater variety of ways to fit into ecosystems. Lastly, both firms are MNCs that have explicitly mentioned the innovation ecosystem as their strategy. These features allow us to systematically understand how firms can fit into their innovation ecosystem within a long and turbulent period. The aim is to develop typologies in relation to issues of innovation management in an ecosystem (Doty and Glick, 1994; Phaal et al., 2004; Robson, 2011).

The unit of analysis of this research is set as the focal firm and its interactions with all of the players in its innovation ecosystem. Based on the background research and literature review, we developed a data collection protocol, which included two main sections: (1) the focal firm's innovation capability and its development; and (2) the innovation ecosystem of the focal firm and its dynamics. With this protocol, primary data were collected from onsite visits with semi-structured interviews in each company. Interviews were conducted through several rounds to allow clarification and explorations. In addition to interviews, during the site visit, we participated in group meetings and training, and observed the companies' daily working routines. In total, we conducted over 40 in-depth semi-structured interviews with a wide range of people related to these companies. Of these, 28 interviews are valid for this study and have been transcribed accordingly.

We have attempted to validate the constructs identified in our case analysis with multiple sources of evidence (Yin, 2009) through triangulation. For example, we collected data from each side of an interaction between these two sides in order to understand the interaction comprehensively. Furthermore, when striving to understand the importance of an innovation of the case companies, we considered not only the interviewee's statements and arguments, but also relevant news, patent data, and industrial reports. Our intent was to reach theoretical saturation of the data in our collection, by comparing both cases (Eisenhardt, 1989). In accord with grounded theory, we conducted three-level coding to analyze all of the data collected (Miles and Huberman, 1994).

4. CASE STUDIES

4.1 Huawei: Fitting into its Innovation Ecosystem

4.1.1 Huawei's incentives

Huawei was founded in Shenzhen, China, as a dealer of private branch exchange switches imported from Hong Kong. Today, Huawei has become a world-leading multinational company headquartered in Shenzhen and specialized in networking and telecommunications equipment and services. This 28-year-old firm achieved revenues of over $60 billion USD in 2015. Huawei has been very successful thanks to its innovation and internationalization, with over 70 per cent of its total revenue coming from the overseas market with its innovative products.

Huawei has emphasized R&D and innovation activities. Its profits in 2015 were over $7 billion USD, while over $9 billion USD (15 per cent of revenue) was invested into its R&D activities. There are nearly 80 000 R&D staff members, accounting for 45 per cent of the total employees of this company around the world. Huawei's heavy and continuous investment in R&D has resulted in outstanding innovation performance; as an R&D manager said:

> Huawei has set a rule for continuous investment in R&D – a minimum of 10 per cent of the annual revenue is invested into R&D, 10 per cent of which is used to conduct basic research that advances new technologies ... Huawei's innovation resulted from such continuous input, to the most degree.

Huawei's incentives in innovation are rooted in its customer-centric innovation strategy. When Huawei was first established in the 1980s, the telecommunication industry was in fierce competition with foreign multinational giants such as Ericsson and Cisco, which took over the market with both technological and financial advantages, and with Chinese state-owned-enterprises (SOEs) such as ZTE and Datang, which had enjoyed preferential policies from the government. This created a competing environment for Huawei. As a manager noted:

> We always considered survival when we established and entered the hi-tech industry. Hi-technology means both high risk and high return. We faced competition with Cisco and domestic competitors ... [we] tried to differentiate [from them].

Innovation and technology became the key to differentiation; as one of the R&D managers further stated:

> ... to survive in a high-tech industry, firms must have their own technological advantages ... [In particular,] our competitors had advantages over us in production activities, and owning the technology became the only way for survival.

At the beginning, Huawei's R&D activities focused on reverse engineering so that the R&D team could understand the architecture of the switches and modify the products to the Chinese market accordingly. In 1994, Huawei achieved its first breakthrough, delivering the most advanced switch in China at that time. This huge success significantly improved Huawei's revenue; according to a sales manager:

> The first breakthrough in product enabled [us to] earn a lot ... The manager teams decided to make strategic use of the profits ... We further invested them into R&D that potentially led to building up our own technology.

Now, sustained R&D funding, internationalizing R&D facilities, and expanding R&D teams have enabled Huawei to become innovative and profitable.

4.1.2 Huawei's approach

Huawei interacted with many players in its innovation ecosystem, including customers, universities, competitors, innovation clusters, consulting firms, suppliers, industrial associations, and international standardization organizations. Internationalization triggered Huawei to develop a customer-centric innovation strategy in order to maintain its position. Around 2000, the company moved its focus to overseas markets development, after Huawei won its first bid in Germany. The managers realized the importance to have the competence to develop its own technology; as an R&D manager commented:

> When we were able to make extra profit from overseas markets, we further realized the importance of our own technology ... Not only in a sense that we could have better margin when we develop a new technology. Rather, we realized that we could fully meet more requirements of overseas customers, who usually have more specific and demanding needs.

In this sense, Huawei's mode of fitting into its innovation ecosystem stemmed from customer needs and interacting with customers.

Since then, Huawei has scaled up its R&D team by recruiting more talent, which involved many activities to interact with research institutes and competitors in order to attract talent to join Huawei's R&D team. Huawei reinforced its development capabilities in China by establishing new development centers in large Chinese cities where the best universities in telecommunication technology are located. Diversified development centers enabled Huawei to attract many local engineers; as a manager said:

> I was quite willing to stay in the city [where my university is located] and [was] not interested in moving to Shenzhen, but still, I chose Huawei because its development center was quite near my university in order to recruit us.

In 1999, Huawei established a development center in Bangalore, where Huawei could employ cheap yet qualified software engineers and access key resources for software development. This later became critical for nurturing Huawei's lasting customer service. Advanced telecommunication technologies were mainly developed overseas, which pushed Huawei to internationalize its R&D in order to develop its competence in research. Huawei gradually built up new research centers in Sweden, the United States, and other developed countries with expertise in telecommunication technology. As the manager also added:

> We have established a portfolio of research centers around the world. A global vision is important. The [technological] sources are globally distributed.

These centers, when established, were actually used to scan and learn new technologies from competitors, universities, or industrial clusters that had excelled in technologies. This revealed Huawei's interactions with innovation clusters related to its core R&D priorities. Huawei also took advantage of industrial associations, international standardization organizations, and conferences to share knowledge and to learn from other firms; as one of its supply-chain managers said:

> We also participated in many international organizations, enabling us to communicate with suppliers and other firms in the industry ... They [these organizations] are similar to a platform [to] enable mutual learning, seeking partnership and knowing the latest progress of the industry ... We also contribute to these associations now, taking up leading positions, sharing our experiences, and promoting our standards and patents.

Since 1998, Huawei had initiated a series of organizational supports aimed at changing the ways of management and creating an innovative and efficient organization, with help from consulting firms such as IBM on integrated product development and Hay Group and Mercer on human resources management. Meanwhile, Huawei had to cope with the growing size of the company and with new requirements for internationalization; as its senior manager commented:

> Innovation is rooted in Huawei and our employees. We have changed a lot to cultivate a better structure that can facilitate our innovations ... In particular, Huawei has to move [forward] and change [accordingly] as Huawei grows and the industry upgrades.

With foreign consulting firms, Huawei has established organization interfaces for innovations.

Now, Huawei is working well with 45 top operators worldwide and serving over one-third of the world population, as its development of technological capabilities realizes the importance of leading the industry by proactively applying for technological patents and standards. Since the 3G era, Huawei has owned over 7 per cent of WCDMA essential patents and 5 per cent of UMTS patents, and is ranked in the top five telecommunications firms globally. For the CDMA area, Huawei owns over 1000 patents. Its strong technological capabilities have enabled Huawei to become a core member of the 3GPP2, an industrial standard associated with the 3G technologies. Huawei has shown an even stronger leadership in the industry in the 4G era, as the company occupies over 25 per cent of core LTE/SAE standards as well as 20 per cent of essential patents, and is ranked number one in the industry. Furthermore, according to the World Intellectual Property Organization (WIPO), since 2007, the number of patents applied for by Huawei has ranked in the world's top five under the Patent Cooperation Treaty among all industries, and ranked top in the telecommunication industry. In 2008 and 2014, Huawei also topped the WIPO's patent filing. Huawei's proactivity in applying for new patents and industrial standards shows the impact of its independent innovation. In total, Huawei has received numerous awards for various reasons, including its technology breakthroughs, innovative products, first solution launched in the industry, and best services.

4.2 Xiaomi: Fitting into its Innovation Ecosystem

4.2.1 Xiaomi's incentives

As a latecomer in the Chinese smartphone market, Xiaomi needed to leverage its ecosystem resources in order to integrate with the innovations already existing on the market and deliver high-caliber products. The reason for this situation is twofold. First, Xiaomi did not have the necessary resources and capabilities to innovate independently in order to compete with international brands. As a latecomer, Xiaomi started with poor resources and few experiences in terms of smartphone production; therefore it was nearly impossible for them to independently obtain a technological leading edge in a short amount of time. Second, previous failed cases of Chinese domestic mobile phone companies have shown that, in order for Xiaomi to compete with these multinational corporations, adopting the conventional "low price (and poor quality)" approach was no longer feasible. At the time when Xiaomi entered the smartphone market, Apple's iPhone 4 had just ignited the market. However, with a price of nearly $800 in China, many consumers were simply unable to afford it. Xiaomi targeted these consumers and adopted a consumer-centric approach in order to capture the market. Indeed, by deeply interacting with these consumers, Xiaomi was able to deliver exactly what they wanted: cheap yet good products and similar user experiences compared with Apple. Such a consumer-centric approach required Xiaomi to interact and coordinate with different players in the innovation ecosystem in order to successfully launch the right products.

Hence, Xiaomi did not try to innovate in terms of core technologies such as mobile device chips. Instead, it chose to innovate incrementally – integrating existing innovations by interacting with different players in the innovation ecosystem.

Xiaomi has put in a great deal of effort to fit into its innovation ecosystem. As a brand new company, Xiaomi started to cultivate its presence in the market while simultaneously seeking opportunities for integration. Xiaomi started by launching its operating system MIUI based on an in-depth customization of Android. With such a system, Xiaomi was able to communicate, attract, and understand consumers. Xiaomi accessed potential consumers using the social media that they preferred, and actively interacted with them online. With these interactions, Xiaomi was able to build up its presence among consumers, fully understand the needs of its target consumers, and better differentiate itself from other competitors by offering lower costs than traditional methods. As one of the marketing managers in Xiaomi suggested:

> [We adopt] a user-oriented strategy in marketing ... We do not waste money in traditional advertisement. Instead, we focus on users, stand with them, interact with them, and develop products for them. They are satisfied and even speak for us.

Xiaomi has also designed a flat organizational structure with only three levels from partners, to department leaders, to employees. This structure helps Xiaomi get closer to its customers and react to market demands very quickly, due to efficient information transmission between its frontlines and executives. Xiaomi's other key method involves forming cross-functional teams very frequently in critical projects. This has made Xiaomi flexible enough to deal with the sheer uncertainty that comes with the rapid changing needs of smartphone customers.

Informally, Xiaomi relies on its cofounders' social networks to access tacit resources such as top-tier suppliers. As a start-up, it is extremely difficult to persuade top-tier suppliers to supply key components. However, some of Xiaomi's cofounders, including senior managers, are from the China offices of Google, Microsoft, Motorola, and so on, and thus have abundant experience in dealing with nearly every aspect of developing a smartphone. For example, the former hardware director of Motorola China was initially in charge of Xiaomi's supply chain, and helped Xiaomi to succeed in ordering key components such as chips and panels from top-tier suppliers. In fact, all of the cofounders have particular backgrounds that are necessary for developing Xiaomi smartphones. One of Xiaomi's supply-chain managers told us:

> He [Lei Jun] kept a good relationship with Dr. Zhou [the former hardware manager of Motorola in China], who later became a key member in the initial founder team of Xiaomi. His joining helped us to source components from top suppliers.

The availability and accessibility of key technologies could not ensure Xiaomi's success in the market. Xiaomi also needed to control the cost, considering that Xiaomi's components are from top-tier suppliers just like those of Apple and Samsung, but Xiaomi's smartphones are much cheaper. Xiaomi took various actions to reduce the cost, including direct sales from an official website, which eliminated the cost of dealers and channels between Xiaomi and consumers; pre-orders to control inventory and ensure cash flows; and launching only one model each year to achieve economies of scale and to profit from the fall in the costs of components over time.

4.2.2 Xiaomi's approaches

Xiaomi's approach to fit into its innovation ecosystem is to coordinate and embed relationships with multiple sides through formal and informal means. The ecosystem of a firm is visualized in Figure 13.1.

Once Xiaomi understood its potential consumers, it was possible to make an informed decision on market positioning. Just before Xiaomi entered the industry, the iPhone was very popular among Chinese young people due to its superior user experience and fashionable design. However, the price was too high for many young people. Xiaomi entered the market while iPhone 4 was being launched and positioned its smartphone as providing a similar experience to an Apple iPhone yet at a much more affordable price.

With clear positioning, Xiaomi had to consider accessing technologies that could realize the production of its products in order to meet consumer needs.

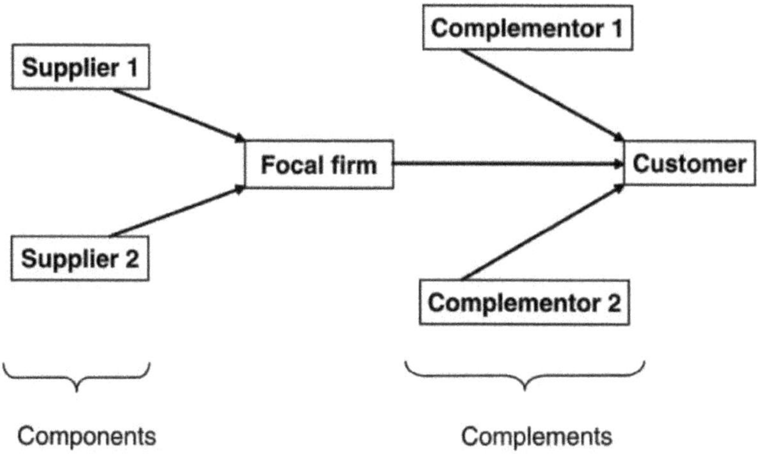

Source: Adner and Kapoor (2010, p. 309).

Figure 13.1 Innovation ecosystem schema of a firm

Coordination became the only possible way to access these technologies when in-house development was not available. Thus, Xiaomi developed strong coordination capability in order to achieve these goals. Leveraging external technological resources relies on coordinating suppliers and complementors in the innovation ecosystem, through either informal or formal linkages.

As mentioned earlier, personal relationships that came from hiring senior managers from other established firms enabled Xiaomi to access top-tier technologies of chips and smartphone screens. Meanwhile, Xiaomi also collaborated with complementors to access certain technologies. For example, Xiaomi and China Telecom cooperated in launching 4G smartphones at affordable prices, in which Xiaomi accessed 4G technology via China Telecom. In other words, Xiaomi acted well as an integrator to coordinate and leverage external resources. Most of such resources were technological. It is notable that accessing technology does not mean absorbing or understanding the technology. The use of the word "accessing" only indicates a situation in which a firm can make use of the technology, rather than knowing and understanding it. However, "accessing" does not necessarily indicate that the firm *cannot* know or understand the technology. Accessing these key technological resources from suppliers enabled Xiaomi to deliver qualified and competitive products that could better satisfy the market. In fact, access to key technologies is not very difficult or expensive. In particular, this finding indicates that the development of coordination competence needs a relatively mature industry and an established innovation ecosystem, where the value chain has been fully or highly specialized. Key components suppliers should be in fierce competition or accessible, while adequate assembling firms are also present in the industry.

Having coordination competence does not mean that these firms, such as Xiaomi, are not innovative because they may not take advantage of these technologies to create new technologies. These firms can still produce innovative products through creative integration, as illustrated by the high-performance but very low-cost mobile phones of Xiaomi. However, competitors may easily imitate coordination capabilities. Thus, gradually, Xiaomi has embedded its value creation strategy with those players it coordinated with, and has reinforced these relationships so that other competitors cannot easily follow its strategy. For example, Xiaomi's engagement with customers has not been limited to online interactions. Xiaomi extended these interactions to offline clubs that were officially organized by Mi fans, with some sponsorship from Xiaomi. The official data show that there are over 90 city-based fan clubs and over 200 college-based fan clubs, serving over 10 million users. Many of these clubs have already been in active operation for more than five years. The role of these clubs is to promote communication among users, assemble people with shared interests in Xiaomi's products, and create a mutual learning environment for users to better use the MIUI. When consumers are actively involved in offline clubs, it becomes much more difficult to convince them to choose a competitor's offering. This is because the offline interactions allow these customers to embed their needs with Xiaomi and accumulatively develop an emotional preference for Xiaomi. The establishment of these clubs requires passion, funding, and interests – and, more importantly, the accumulative efforts of both the company and consumers. Although it is much easier to interact with customers online, the real-life impacts of these clubs can create a solid barrier against competitors who are trying or have tried to imitate Xiaomi's strategy, especially other new entrants to the industry. As one of the Mi fans we interviewed said:

> Xiaomi not only makes use of online platforms, forums, and social media [for instance, Sina Weibo] to interact with us, but also engages users to be offline participants through MIUI clubs that are established by fans at city and university levels. For instance, I am a member of the Xiaomi club in my university as well as the Beijing Xiaomi club. The club is a lovely community for users of Xiaomi smartphones to learn and better use the system … I know a lot of friends who share the same interests in exploring their products through multiple activities [in the club].

Similarly, Xiaomi tried to embed its relationship with other players in the innovation ecosystem, creating a tightly coupled feature for value creation. The relationship-embedding process is time-consuming and requires accumulation over transactions, which is quite socially complex and implicit, and not easy to recognize. Embedded relationships also reinforce Xiaomi's innovation, as they can reduce the transitional cost to understand consumers and to coordinate suppliers and complementors in producing and delivering the required products to consumers. As a supplier manager noted,

> ...it took us a lot of effort to persuade our collaborators, especially those top-tier suppliers at first, but when our products performed very well, they were happy to continue the contracts and even provide opportunities to conduct R&D together ... it is a win–win situation.

Embedded relationships have also helped Xiaomi to diversify its product lines by repeating similar approaches. After the success of the Xiaomi smartphone, Xiaomi entered another industry, television manufacturing, because it knew customers well, had gained experience with the coordination process, and had embedded its relationships with core players in the innovation ecosystem. That transfer, when Xiaomi launched its innovative TV in 2013, proved to be much easier and more successful than expected. Now, Xiaomi's product lines cross various industries and it continues to build up its ecosystem by coordinating and embedding with many players.

5. DISCUSSION AND CONCLUSION

Both cases show that Chinese latecomer firms are interacting with different players in their innovation ecosystems, including customers, suppliers, complementors, and other intermediators. Although both firms show variances in their specific approaches to interacting with these players, it is undeniable that the interactions with these players play key roles in these companies' catch-up and innovation. From such a perspective, we argue for an alternative view to understand the innovations of latecomer firms. To overcome latecomer disadvantages and utilize latecomer advantages, latecomer firms need to fit into their innovation ecosystems by interacting with various players in the ecosystems. As shown in these two cases, the innovations of both Chinese firms were outcomes from intensive interactions with all of these players.

Huawei is a more technology-oriented firm, while Xiaomi is a more market-oriented firm. Given these different orientations, both latecomer firms have different incentives and resources to fit into their innovation ecosystems. However, both showed similar strategic goals and processes to catch up and innovate by fitting into their innovation ecosystems. In the beginning, latecomer firms are poor in resources. Hence, they need to understand customer needs precisely in order to optimize the utilization of their limited resources to make products. Therefore, both companies first interacted with customers to identify niche market opportunities. Also, because of this shortage in resources, latecomer firms need to interact with other firms in related industries, including complementors and suppliers, to leverage the resources that are required for value creation by offering products for the niche market they have identified. In contrast to traditional studies (e.g., Cho et al., 1998), we found that manufacturing capability is not necessarily required. When the latecomers grow up from their initial success, these firms accumulate experiences and resources. The initial success enables these firms to interact with other partners and organizations across different industries, such as complementors, consulting firms, and universities, in order to achieve further expansions and development. In these ways, latecomer firms can both fit into their innovation ecosystem and catch up with industrial leaders.

The incentives and inputs of a latecomer firm that is fitting into its innovation ecosystem have an impact on the focus and implementation of its latecomer strategies. For example, Huawei's incentive and input pushed the company to focus on in-house R&D and achieve innovation through technological catch-up strategies, similar to the cases in the previous literature. However, Xiaomi's incentive and input made that company focus on networking with other players in its innovation ecosystem and achieve innovations through integrating, in an approach that differed from technological catch-up. However, both approaches fit well with the companies' innovation ecosystems.

Our cases further suggest that fitting into innovation ecosystems involves more than interacting with players within the innovation ecosystems. They also suggest it is necessary to coordinate these players in order to co-create value. Interacting with these players enables latecomer firms to learn relevant knowledge needed in the industry. However, these learning processes cannot guarantee the success of these firms in these industries unless the newly learned knowledge is applied to value creation. As suggested from these two cases, after interacting with ecosystem players, latecomer firms can understand how their own value creations can be incorporated into other players' value creations so that the latecomer firms can achieve innovation through shared value creation with other ecosystem players. In this sense, fitting into an innovation ecosystem extends the boundary of value creation from the level of the individual company and the industry level to an ecosystem level, so that more players can benefit from the focal firm's value creation process, regardless of whether these players are involved in this value creation process or not. Because of this extension, latecomer firms can deploy more resources – either owned or from other ecosystem players – in their innovation and catch-up process. This indicates a value-sharing mechanism that explains why latecomers need to fit into their innovation ecosystem in order to formulate and implement a latecomer strategy.

To conclude, our case study makes two contributions to the theory in this field. First, our cases complement previous studies on technological catch-up (e.g., Cho et al., 1998; Mathews, 2002) by offering a new perspective to understand the innovations of latecomer firms. Most previous literature (e.g., Lee and Lim, 2001; Mu and Lee, 2005) tends to explain the innovation of latecomer firms from the perspective of an individual firm's technological capability. Our cases suggest that the innovations and catch-up of latecomer firms should be understood from an ecosystem perspective, as many ecosystem players are critical in these innovations and catch-ups. This perspective is different from traditional studies on leveraging external resources (e.g., Mathews, 2002). Consistently, latecomer firms need external resources from other ecosystem players. However, more specifically, the ecosystem perspective enables latecomer firms to understand which players they need to seek out in order to gain external resources, rather than looking for resources in the environment in general (Adner and Kapoor, 2010).

Second, our studies reveal different approaches for latecomer firms to fit into innovation ecosystems. These approaches make it possible to understand the incentives and processes of how Chinese latecomer firms can fit into innovation ecosystems; they also help to reveal the relationships between these incentives and processes. Thus, we have provided detailed processes of these approaches. By revealing the processes of the implementation of latecomer strategies, we complement current studies on latecomer firms and latecomer strategies that focus on the strategizing, outcomes, and strategic reasons of latecomer strategies. These processes can also provide detailed linkages between theories on strategizing and the outcomes of latecomer strategy research, which are not easily identified from quantitative studies.

Our work complements studies on the innovation ecosystem that focus on analyzing the impacts of an innovation ecosystem on first-movers, as we have suggested how latecomer firms can catch up by integrating and benefitting from their surroundings. Like Ansari et al.'s (2016) study on disruptive innovators, our study suggests that latecomer firms access resources by fitting into their ecosystem. However, our study focused more on the catch-up process than on the process of disrupting the market.

Our case study only considers catch-up strategy from an innovation ecosystem perspective, which complements prior studies on understanding the innovation ecosystems of first-mover firms. However, due to the explorative nature of our case studies, we did not incorporate comparisons with the innovation ecosystems from previous studies. Therefore, future studies can be conducted either to consolidate how firms in general (either latecomers or first-movers) can strategize from an innovation ecosystem perspective, or to validate our constructs with surveys or archival data.

REFERENCES

Adner, R. (2006), 'Match your innovation strategy to your innovation ecosystem', *Harvard Business Review*, **84**(4), 98–107.

Adner, R. and R. Kapoor (2010), 'Value creation in innovation ecosystems: How the structure of technological interdependence affects firm performance in new technology generations', *Strategic Management Journal*, **33**(3), 306–33.

Ansari, S. S., G. Raghu, and A. Kumaraswamy (2016), 'The disruptor's dilemma: TiVo and the US television ecosystem', *Strategic Management Journal*, **37**(9), 1829–53.

Barney, J. B. (1991), 'Firm resources and sustained competitive advantage', *Journal of Management*, **17**(1), 99–120.

Cetindamar, D., R. Phaal, and D. Probert (2009), 'Understanding technology management as a dynamic capability: A framework for technology management activities', *Technovation*, **29**(4), 237–46.

Cho, D.-S., D. J. Kim, and D. K. Rhee (1998), 'Latecomer strategies: Evidence from the semiconductor industry in Japan and Korea', *Organization Science*, **9**(4), 489–505.

Doty, D. H. and W. H. Glick (1994), 'Typologies as a unique form of theory building: Toward improved understanding and modelling', *Academy of Management Review*, **19**, 230–51.

Dyer, J. H. and H. Singh (1998), 'The relational view: Cooperative strategy and sources of interorganizational competitive advantage', *Academy of Management Review*, **23**(4), 660–79.

Eisenhardt, K. (1989), 'Building theories from case study research', *Academy of Management Review*, **14**(4), 532–50.

Gregory, M. (1995), 'Technology management: A process approach', *Proceedings of the Institution of Mechanical Engineers Part B: Journal of Engineering Manufacture*, **209**(5), 347–56.

Hobday, M. (1995), 'East Asian latecomer firms: Learning the technology of electronics', *World Development*, **23**(7), 1171–93.

Iansiti, M. and R. Levien (2004), 'Keystones and dominators: Framing operating and technology strategy in an innovation ecosystem', Working Paper, Harvard Business School, 3-61.

Lavie, D. (2006), 'The competitive advantage of interconnected firms: An extension of the resource-based view', *Academy of Management Review*, **31**(3), 638–58.

Lee, C. and S. Hung (2014), 'Institutional entrepreneurship in the informal economy: China's shan-zhai mobile phones', *Strategic Entrepreneurship Journal*, **36**, 16–36.

Lee, K. and C. Lim (2001), 'Technological regimes, catching-up and leapfrogging: Findings from the Korean industries', *Research Policy*, **30**(3), 459–83.

Mathews, J. (2002), 'Competitive advantages of the latecomer firm: A resource-based account of industrial catch-up strategies', *Asia Pacific Journal of Management*, **19**(4), 467–88.

Mathews, J. A. and D. Cho (1999), 'Combinative capabilities and organizational learning in latecomer firms: The case of the Korean semiconductor industry', *Journal of World Business*, **34**(2), 139–56.

Miles, M. B. and A. M. Huberman (1994), *Qualitative Data Analysis: An Expanded Sourcebook* (2nd ed.), Thousand Oaks: Sage Publications.

Moore, J. F. (1993), 'Predators and prey: A new ecology of competition', *Harvard Business Review*, **71**(3), 75–86.
Moore, J. F. (1996), *The Death of Competition: Leadership and Strategy in the Age of Business Ecosystems*. New York: HarperCollins.
Mu, Q. and K. Lee (2005), 'Knowledge diffusion, market segmentation and technological catch-up: The case of the telecommunication industry in China', *Research Policy*, **34**(6), 759–83.
Phaal, R., C. J. Farrukh, and D. R. Probert (2004), 'A framework for supporting the management of technological knowledge', *International Journal of Technology Management*, **27**(1), 1–15.
Robson, C. (2011), *Real World Research: A Resource for Users of Social Research Methods in Applied Settings* (3rd ed.), Oxford, UK: John Wiley & Son.
Shang, T. (2015), 'Business ecosystem capabilities: Explorations of the emerging electric vehicle industry', unpublished doctoral dissertation, Cambridge University Engineering Department.
Siggelkow, N. (2007), 'Persuasion with case studies', *Academy of Management Journal*, **50**(1), 20–24.
Wu, W., B. Yu, and C. Wu (2012), 'How China's equipment manufacturing firms achieve successful independent innovation', *Chinese Management Studies*, **6**(1), 160–83.
Wu, X., R. Ma, Y. Shi, and K. Rong (2009), 'Secondary innovation: The path of catch-up with "Made in China"', *China Economic Journal*, **2**(1), 93–104.
Wu, X., R. Ma, and Y. Shi (2010), 'How do latecomer firms capture value from disruptive technologies? A secondary business-model innovation perspective', *IEEE Transactions on Engineering Management*, **57**(1), 51–62.
Yin, R. K. (2009), *Case Study Research: Design and Methods* (4th ed.), London: Sage.

14. Conclusions

Maureen McKelvey and Jun Jin

1. INTRODUCTION

How do Chinese companies learn to innovate and compete on global markets? This book has provided a rich range of chapters, which explore how Chinese firms are developing capabilities for innovation and globalization, in relation to their economic environment.

The broader theoretical framework for the chapters in this book was introduced in Chapter 1. Taken together, the key processes related to technology, innovation and internationalization are constituted by the key interactions between the firms and knowledge-intensive innovative ecosystem. Figure 1.1 visualizes that the micro-level of the firms – set at the center – is highly affected by the macro-level in terms of industrial dynamics and innovation systems. Three core concepts in our analytical framework are: firm search and capabilities for technology and innovation, industrial dynamics, and innovation systems. These three concepts have been related, in explaining how Chinese companies can learn to innovate and compete on the global market, by interacting with knowledge-intensive innovation ecosystems.

Chapters in this book have been organized around these themes:

- Theme: Specifying where innovation systems can affect the ability of Chinese firms to identify and act upon innovative opportunities.
- Theme: Analyzing why Chinese firms' acquisitions and collaboration can affect their capabilities for technology, innovation and globalization.
- Theme: Exploring how Chinese firms develop new capabilities.

Below, covering each theme, the sub-sections include an overview of the results of each chapter in this book, followed by our propositions and topics for future research.

Table 14.1 Results on theme: specifying why innovation systems can affect the ability of Chinese firms to identify and act upon innovative opportunities

Chapter	Contribution
Chapter 2	Provides synthesized empirical details about the development of China and Chinese firms Uses a conceptualization of innovative opportunities as consisting of technological, entrepreneurial and productive opportunities Explains how these seven empirical phenomena are impacting technology, innovation and globalization
Chapter 3	Evaluates the role of Chinese National High-Tech Industrial Development Zones (NHTZs) in the development of KIE ventures in high-tech industries Analyzes the role of science parks, in the development of high-tech industries Concludes that the variety of innovation output in firms can be explained partially by diversified geographical concentration of universities and research institutes and partially by local entrepreneurial willingness. These correspond to source of talent, and to being located in area with supportive environment, risk-taking business culture, and active market economies
Chapter 4	Analyzes patent and firm performance data on Chinese technology-based SMEs in the pharmaceutical industry Explores their embeddedness in both explorative and exploitative patent collaborative networks, and analyzes them in relation to their innovation performance Concludes that especially explorative patent collaborative networks provide breakthrough paths and opportunities. This helps these firms to acquire innovation resources and enhance their innovation capabilities
Chapter 5	Provides comparative case studies of Chinese multinational firms in telecom equipment, concrete machinery and vehicle diesel engine industries Defines and argues that the concept of technological self-reliance, enables firms and industries to catch-up Reveals that the evolution of embedded demand and the accumulation of national technological capability in an industry helps determine success in technology and innovative capabilities

2. THEME: SPECIFYING WHERE INNOVATION SYSTEMS CAN AFFECT THE ABILITY OF CHINESE FIRMS TO IDENTIFY AND ACT UPON INNOVATIVE OPPORTUNITIES

By promoting independent and global innovation, Chinese companies depend upon the development of a company's innovative capabilities to access and respond to opportunities, technologies, and markets (see Table 14.1).

The chapters of the book reveal that the Chinese innovation ecosystems and the competitiveness of Chinese firms have been increasing in the past decades, which contribute to the innovation and globalization of Chinese firms (e.g. Chapter 2). In addition, the high- and new-tech industrial development zones in different regions in China play key roles in the development of knowledge-intensive entrepreneurship (KIE) industries and technology transfer in industries, especially in university–industry collaboration, which can be found in Chapters 3 and 4. Moreover, the high- and new-tech industrial development zones benefit the growth of the regional and sectoral innovation systems, as shown in Chapter 3. Furthermore, the alliances on patents provide opportunities and innovation resources to emerging KIEs to conduct exploitative and explorative innovation, as indicated in the pharmaceutical industries in Chapter 4. The growing capabilities of sectoral innovation are the result of the balance between technological self-reliance and cooperation, including international technological cooperation, which contributes to the catching-up in the Chinese sectors, revealed in Chapter 5.

Our first proposition is that we must understand firms in relation to the knowledge-intensive innovative ecosystem, because their ability to access resources and ideas, manage and develop the firm and also evaluate performance depends upon their network relationships.

The chapters on the Chinese entrepreneurial ecosystem analyzed key features related to the national and regional innovation systems, as well as special initiatives such as science parks and collaborative networks, in order to study the impact upon large companies and entrepreneurial ones. They have shown that by developing specific elements of public policy and technological collaboration in the Chinese entrepreneurial ecosystem, this in turn helps promote innovations in private leading companies. Studies of specific firms in relation to their ecosystems have also shown the importance of interactions.

Thus future research should tackle these questions: How can the processes of innovation, globalization and technological capabilities be further integrated conceptually together? Does the Chinese entrepreneurial ecosystem work differently than in other countries, and if so, why and how? What is unique about Chinese companies and their interaction with the entrepreneurial ecosystem? Are innovations developed in relation to firm capabilities and opportunities in the ecosystem the key ones, because developing such processes enables the companies to compete on the global market?

Moreover, the diffusion of digital technology and the implementation of "internet +" policies in business in China indicate that the knowledge-intensive innovation ecosystem will influence the strategies and processes of the digital transformation of firms. However, more research is needed in order to reveal the influence mechanism in this process and how SMEs can benefit from different aspects of the business ecosystem, in order to reach such digital transformation.

3. THEME: ANALYZING WHY CHINESE FIRMS' ACQUISITIONS AND COLLABORATION CAN AFFECT THEIR CAPABILITIES FOR TECHNOLOGY, INNOVATION AND GLOBALIZATION

The growing innovative capability within Chinese knowledge-intensive entrepreneurial ventures and Chinese MNEs relies on increasing their technical and market capabilities. Chapters in the book show that acquisition and collaboration are the main internationalization methods of Chinese SMEs and MNEs and the way to build the technological capabilities of Chinese firms (see Table 14.2).

Different methods of international technology transfer are adopted by Chinese firms, from greenfield to the joint ventures, as in the case of Geely in Chapter 8. In addition, the international technological collaboration, international technological learning and the international technology transfer are determined by the knowledge bases and patent portfolios of firms, such as the research in Chapter 6, as well as the international experiences of firms, such as the research in Chapter 7. Finally, the increasing capabilities enable Chinese firms to transfer their technologies to firms from advanced countries, which are reverse innovations of Chinese firms, studied in Chapter 8. This contributes to the internationalization of Chinese firms.

Our second proposition is that Chinese firms are leading globally, because they are also able to translate knowledge and technology into innovative opportunities, through the organization of a large firm or entrepreneurial venture. The firms studied here are able to learn and develop longer-standing capabilities in relation to technology, innovation and internationalization.

The chapters in this book do have a particular focus on the forefront of industry, and have specifically chosen KIE firms and multinational firms which are becoming leading globally. In doing so, we acknowledge that we have a particular focus on especially the coastal provinces of China, which have good infrastructure and investment in education.

Future research questions include: How do Chinese companies improve their innovative capabilities to achieve catch-up and leapfrog in the global value chain? How much depends upon technological capabilities as opposed to market capabilities? What influences the building process of the technological capability of Chinese companies? What is the role of KIE ventures in China, and in relation to both public policy and MNEs? Should we define new types of dynamic capabilities in the digital era? If we should, what are the network capabilities and digital capabilities of firms and new dimensions of dynamic capabilities?

Table 14.2 Results on theme: analyzing why Chinese firms' acquisitions and collaboration can affect their capabilities for technology, innovation and globalization

Chapter	Contribution
Chapter 6	Explores the technological characteristics of firms in high-tech industries, to examine different degrees of technological distance, in relation to acquisitions Analyzes 95 acquisitions involving Chinese medium- and medium–high-tech multinational enterprises, which undertake cross-border acquisitions in the EU, USA and Japan Concludes that investor firms with stronger internal knowledge bases (that is with more diversified and larger patent portfolios) are more likely to invest in more technologically distant regions
Chapter 7	Provides an in-depth case study of Goldwind Technology, a wind energy firm Investigates the building of technological capability within this firm, in relation to their process of internationalization Illustrates the importance of cross-border technological learning and cross-border relationship building for globalization
Chapter 8	Focuses on the acquisition of an advanced firm in a Western country, by an emerging market multinational enterprise Describes a case study of the knowledge transfer processes in the automobile industry, after acquisition, between Volvo Car Corporation and Geely Group Explores the processes of transfer of technology and knowledge to new owner, after acquisition
Chapter 9	Addresses reverse technological innovation in relation to globalization, from the perspective of emerging market multinational enterprises Provides three case studies, namely: a firm in the high-speed train industry; a firm in the nano-tech industry; and a firm in the renewable energy industry Proposes a matrix framework to understand reverse innovation, in order to take into account the firm's innovation strategy and the location of commercialization

4. THEME: EXPLORING HOW CHINESE FIRMS DEVELOP NEW CAPABILITIES

Chinese firms develop new capabilities by developing specific elements of public policy and technological collaboration in the Chinese entrepreneurial ecosystem which in turn helps promote innovations in private leading companies (see Table 14.3).

Table 14.3 Results on theme: exploring how Chinese firms develop new capabilities

Chapter	Contribution
Chapter 10	Analyzes ten case studies of KIE ventures in the health care, ICT and finance industries Addresses how these firms can pursue Chinese independent innovation as well as the influence of global markets on them Demonstrates that the most important sources of innovation are the internal skills and knowledge of the KIE ventures
Chapter 11	Describes a case study of a Chinese KIE venture in artificial intelligence, for visual recognition and surveillance systems Explores the process of internally developing new knowledge in the firm, in relation to their overall technical capabilities Defines the challenges and relevant firm responses, when this knowledge creation also includes tacit knowledge embedded in experiences
Chapter 12	Analyzes the rapid development of CEVT (Chinese European Vehicle Technology), an international technology center of Geely Group in automobiles Reveals that the overseas R&D center can be operated as a facilitator of innovative capabilities and globalization by being a broker between organizations in the foreign and home countries
Chapter 13	Describes two case studies in the IT and telecommunication industries, namely Huawei and Xiaomi Analyzes the development of innovative capabilities of these firms, in relation to the Chinese innovation ecosystem, in terms of two complementary approaches Argues that for both approaches, the latecomer firm to an industry needs to interact and co-create value with its innovation ecosystem

The chapters of the book discuss the development of innovation capabilities in the KIEs, particularly those in the emerging industries like AI (Chapter 11), the influence of indigenous innovation on globalization, such as global market exploitation (Chapter 10), and the building of global R&D centers (Chapter 12) and the innovation ecosystem of Chinese MNEs (Chapter 13). All of these are seen as the new innovation strategies of Chinese firms. Moreover, the co-value creation to partners is critical to the success of the innovation strategies of Chinese firms, as is shown in the CEVT case in Chapter 12 and the Huawei and Xiaomi cases in Chapter 13.

Our third proposition is that independent innovation within Chinese companies is possible, but the internal development of capabilities should go hand-in-hand with stimulation within a rich knowledge-intensive ecosystem.

The chapters have found that the increasing innovative capability within Chinese knowledge-intensive ventures and MNEs heavily relies upon their ability to improve internal technical and market capabilities. Hence, promoting the independent and global innovation of Chinese companies depends upon the development of companyies' innovative capabilities to access and respond to technologies and markets.

Important questions for future research include: What are the sources of knowledge and innovative ideas of Chinese companies? Which factors will affect the innovation of Chinese companies in the future? How do Chinese MNEs promote and work with technical innovation after mergers and acquisitions? Do innovation processes in leading large companies differ from those in knowledge-intensive ventures and, if so, how?

5. FUTURE RESEARCH ON DIGITALIZATION AND GLOBALIZATION AFTER THE COVID-19 PANDEMIC

With the development and diffusion of digital technology in business and society, the digital transformation has moved very rapidly into many fields in China. More and more business model innovations and disruptive innovations are being spurred. New trends of the innovation activities and innovation system are emerging in China. For example, crisis in Chinese means the co-existence of challenges and opportunities. The crisis from combating the COVID-19 virus in 2020 has pushed many Chinese organizations to accelerate investment in the internet of things, cloud platforms and smart factories. For example, the emerging cloud online trade fairs in Zhejiang will disrupt the traditional international trade fair, which could reduce the cost for participants and limitations arising from the geography and time. The increasing use of the remote education mode brings innovation to the whole education system. For instance, Zhejiang University launched its online education platform and remote teaching system in February of 2020 and its online research platform at the end of March 2020.

Considering the embeddedness of digital technology in business and society, important questions for future research in this field include: What are the new types of innovation and innovation strategies of different organizations in China? How do firms conduct the intra-entrepreneurship based on the digital technologies? How do firms improve their capabilities to deal with challenges from the digital transformation? What changes will happen in the organization behaviors and organizational learning in the digital transformation? What are routines and trajectories of firms in the digital era? What is the digital readiness of Chinese firms?

Furthermore, because of the pandemic of the COVID-19 virus in the world, many countries have imposed restrictions on work and life in order to curb the spread of the virus. Therefore, international business and transportation have been influenced. Governments and businesses have to consider the possibility of building the local supply chain in order to meet basic local living demands and the continuation of production in the period of time with limited cross-boundary transportation. The debate on globalization and deglobalization is increasing. Some questions are emerging. For instance, how could and should we balance the resources allocation in the local value chain network and the global value chain network? How can we define the international cooperation enabled by the digital technology? How could we enhance the international cooperation to create and increase the co-value of partners in the cooperation? What resilience capabilities should firms have?

Thus, future research should continue to tackle themes related to technology, innovation and internationalization as Chinese companies become leaders in their fields, but in new ways, under new institutional regimes.

Index